Rupert Goldsworthy

CONSUMING//TERROR

Rupert Goldsworthy

CONSUMING//TERROR

Images of the Baader-Meinhof

CFP Publishers, NY

Published by **CFP Publishers, NY**

ISBN: 9781070791746
Second Edition, 2019

Cover design by **Jan Wandrag**
Cover painting by **Rupert Goldsworthy**,
drawn from an anonymous RAF sympathizer
poster from late 1977.

www.rupertgoldsworthy.com

ACKNOWLEDGEMENTS

Many thanks to the following for their advice, feedback, and support over this project: Graham Bader, Erik Bakke, Nancy Barton, Bob Brandhorst, Christopher Clark, Steven Evans, Gretchen Faust, Elspeth Goldsworthy, Vesna Goldsworthy, Barbara Rose Haum, Juliet Jacobson, Steven Johnson, Elisabeth Kley, Alexis Knowlton, Wolfgang Kohl, Charles Krewson, Elliott Levine, Cindy Maguire, Rob McCallum, Cynthia Miller-Idriss, Judy Nylon, Dana Polan, Gerald Pryor, Avital Ronell, Robert Rosenblum, Priya Shankar, J. David Slocum, Mark Stewart, Robert Storr, Alyson Taub, Jeremy Varon, and Edmund White.

TABLE OF CONTENTS

iii

vi

LIST OF FIGURES

1

All that we see or seem is but a dream within a dream.
-Poe

Chapter I

THE WAR OF IMAGES BEGINS

In a time when acts of political violence such as bombings and hijackings have changed many people's lives worldwide, images termed "terrorist" pervade a variety of cultural contexts. This study concerns the 1970s—the era when Left-wing political violence first exploded onto our screens through spectacular acts such as bombings, hijackings, and assassinations. I focus on one Leftist terror group active in West Germany during this period, the Red Army Faction (RAF) also known as Baader-Meinhof.[i]

Located in the shadows of the Cold War, the story of RAF is an interesting example of the role of the visual in 1970s terrorism, how particular understandings of the RAF have changed, and what produces such perceptual shifts.

An analysis of IMAGERY relating to the RAF is an aspect of this group's history that has not been greatly discussed.[ii]

Although the RAF officially disbanded in 1998, their story is not entirely over. The group's ghostly presence still haunts the German psyche in 2008. Group members continue to be released from prison thirty years later. [iii] What can a consideration of imagery tell us that other types of research have not? What role does the visual play both during the terror phenomenon and in its later assimilation? Such a study allows a discussion of these issues, and of the importance of imagery in the construction of a "rhetoric of terror" by terrorists, media and state.

Exploring the migration of RAF-related imagery provides the opportunity to track perceptual shifts concerning one body of controversial media images. After a confluence of cultural forces, public associations with this imagery have changed (in significant ways). This imagery defined in the 1970s as "terrorist" has now developed additional resonance in a variety of contexts—cinema, museums and popular culture.

This research explores the way that the RAF has seeped into mass culture. Terror imagery moves through society, providing: insights into the role of culture? in the construct[ion] /and or re-assembly/of public identity? Specific works have re-contextualized the group.

The study continues from my earlier projects relating to the visuals of violent left-wing terrorists in the 1970s like the RAF, the U.S's Weather Underground[iv] and Symbionese Liberation Army[v]—groups around which the Western news media first established their conceptions of a terrorist archetype. A consideration of these images defined in the 1970s as "terrorist" can provide insights into the construction of this terror phenomenon. This study assesses the role of imagery in "media terror" and the new contexts and conditions in which terror imagery emerges. The study takes in consideration the continued use, operation, and regulation of these images, and discusses patterns in their continuing development.

The History of the RAF

The RAF formed in 1970 as an urban guerrilla cadre, a violent offshoot of the West German S.D.S (Students for a Democratic Society) and A.P.O. (Ausserparlimentarische Opposition), two largely non-violent New Left organizations.

Art historian Robert Storr states that the RAF's violent aims were based on the Maoist notion that "the triumph of the revolutionary Third World over the reactionary First World depended on bringing the battle from the margins to the center of the empire." [vi] [vii] Some would say that despite such an intent, the RAF's aim to bring the war home,[viii] to return the anti-imperial struggle to its Western origins, instead produced a media circus around the fear of a younger generation turned in Oedipal revolt.

April 1968, prior to the RAF's founding, Andreas Baader, his girlfriend Gudrun Ensslin, and two others plant fire-bombs in two department stores in Frankfurt to protest against the war in Vietnam. All four are soon apprehended and jailed.

May 1970, with the direct assistance of a prominent Left-wing journalist Ulrike Meinhof, Baader escapes from jail. A guard is shot during the escape. A nationwide hunt begins. The media name the gang the "Baader-Meinhof Bande." At this juncture, the Rote Armee Fraktion (RAF) form and release their first communiqué. They escape to Jordan for clandestine training with Palestinian guerrillas.

May 1972, the RAF bomb American army bases in Frankfurt, Heidelberg, and Augsburg to protest U.S. involvement in Vietnam. After weeks on the run, by the end of June 1972 the group's leaders, Baader, Ensslin, Meinhof, Horst Mahler, Jan Carl Raspe, Holger Meins, and several other RAF members are all arrested.

During this period, the media portray the RAF in hyperbolic terms. Mugshots of alleged bombing perpetrators are branded as the "faces of terror." Through such media rhetoric, the RAF are presented as larger-than-life figures. The climate of fear and panic generated around the group reaches melodramatic proportions.

In jail, the arrested RAF members protest against being kept in isolation wards for long periods and being subjected to extreme levels of deprivation. They appeal unsuccessfully to the European Court of Human Rights, claiming status as political prisoners.

Summer 1974, they begin hunger strikes to protest their conditions. Later the same year, a RAF member, Holger Meins, dies after fifty-seven days of refusing food. Gruesome images of his emaciated corpse appear in the headlines.

This was the first time since World War Two that West Germany witnessed this kind of shocking imagery in the Federal Republic.

From this point on, the RAF's strategy shifts from bombing Vietnam-related sites to attacks on individuals—assassinations and the kidnapping of prominent politicians in the hope of bartering them for the release of their imprisoned comrades. It was suspected the leadership were masterminding these attacks from with jail.

February 1975, a RAF-associated terror group Bewegung 2.Juni kidnap Berlin mayor CDU candidate Peter Lorenz. He is quickly traded for several West German terrorists, including some RAF members, who are put on a plane bound for the Middle East.

April 1975, the RAF attempt a similar coup by taking over the West German Embassy in Stockholm. This action fails. A large RAF bomb self-detonates, killing many, including two of the five terrorists involved.

May 1976, Ulrike Meinhof, the most well-known RAF member is found dead in her prison cell, an apparent suicide.

April 1977, the RAF assassinate a high-ranging state judge Siegfried Buback who has presided over many RAF court cases. Later the same month, imprisoned RAF leaders Baader, Ensslin and Raspe are all sentenced to life imprisonment charged with four murders and fifty-four attempted murders.

July 1977, RAF members murdered Dresdner Bank head Jürgen Ponto during a kidnap attempt. The kidnappers included Ponto's god-daughter, Susanne Albrecht. The terrorists escaped. The press had a field day discussing the crypto-Oedipal aspects to this attack.

September 1977, the RAF kidnap a high-ranking state official Hans-Martin Schleyer and display him in home-made hostage video tapes. They are devoured by the media. Schleyer is kidnapped on 5 September 1977 and held for one and a half months. The German government do not give in to the RAF's demands. The hostage-takers demand the release of Baader, Ensslin, Raspe and others. The government refuses to negotiate. In response, four Palestinian RAF sympathizers hijack a plane full of German tourists leaving Majorca and fly them to Yemen and then on to Mogadishu in Somalia. On October 18th, the plane is stormed by German special forces. The same night, Baader, Ensslin and Raspe are all mysteriously found dead in their prison cells from knife and gunshot wounds. Another RAF member in a nearby cell survives knife wounds. Two days later the corpse of Hans-Martin Schleyer is discovered in a car trunk on the French border.

This period, October 1977, is commonly seen as the climax of the RAF insurgency in Germany.

From 1972 until today, the specter of domestic terror is repeatedly invoked in West Germany. Issues of social justice and civil liberties become derailed amid a hysterical media terror circus. Under the guise of combating left-wing extremism, the West German state was able to circumscribe the political field to such an extent that voices in any way critical of the government's policy around the RAF were eliminated from political and social spheres (through legislation such as the *Radikalenerlass*).[ix] Equally during this period, the relationship between the state's and the media's portrayal of events appeared to grow in proportion to the demise of moderate oppositional analysis.[x]

Despite the deaths of five of the RAF leaders in jail during the 1970s (Meins, Meinhof, Baader, Ensslin and Raspe), and of many other RAF members in police shoot-outs, the group's second and third generation continued sporadic campaigns of anti-state bombings and assassinations until 1993. A communiqué released by the RAF in 1998 stated that the group had now finally disbanded.

A final, ironic twist to this tale is that thirty-five years after targeting West Germany as a "fascist state," the last surviving founding member of the RAF, Horst Mahler, is now known as an outspoken right wing public figure.[xi]

The RAF as Subjects of Countercultural Production

Beyond RAF coverage in the mainstream media, since the 1970s there has been a broad wave of cultural production concerning the group. This in turn has also significantly affected public conceptions of the RAF.

Writer Heinrich Böll stated that during the 1970s era, due to the politically sensitive nature of the RAF topic, the government closely monitored all media coverage of the group.[xii] [xiii] Any public figures that expressed a sympathetic perspective on the RAF were subject to state harassment. In response to this shutdown on the RAF, more open discussion on the subject could only occur in marginal settings such as literature, arthouse cinema, and fine art.

In the late 1970s, all the leading figures of the emerging

West German New Wave cinema produced celebrated works related to the RAF story. These films presented a much more insightful picture of the debacle than the state or mass media provided. Such works included Fassbinder's contribution to *Deutschland im Herbst* (1978), Schlöndorff and Böll's *Die verlorene Ehre von Katharina Blum* (1980), and von Trotta's *Marianna und Juliana* (1981).[xiv] The more sympathetic presentation of the RAF topic in these works encouraged a broader wave of cultural engagement.

An example of this trope in fine art is Gerhard Richter's celebrated painting series, *October 18th 1977*. Richter's works, produced in 1988, re-produced famous media images of the RAF's leaders. The current public stature of this work illustrates the level of ocular acculturation around the subject. In 1996, New York's Museum of Modern Art (MOMA) spent three million dollars to acquire these paintings—works that (to some degree at least) appear to valorize dead terrorists.[xv] Due to patterns such as these, the RAF subject and imagery related with the group have fractured from their tabloid associations, and are fetishized/re-framed as outlaw.

Richter is not the only high-visibility fine artist who has worked with difficult political themes. Over the past forty years many museum-level American and European artists have appropriated public images relating to violent political struggle.[xvi] They have done so with a range of strategies and intentions. But in one sense the reproduction of imagery using the connotative charge of Leftist terrorism in a Western art museum context creates a strange dichotomy: Images associated with violent anti-capitalism are re-contextualized in bleeding-edge artworks that then develop currency in a high-end capitalist cultural marketplace, traded and collected by the same demographic—industrialists—who had been earlier targets of left-wing terrorism.[xvii] What do these dynamics ask us about the relationship between ownership and the need to assimilate the oppositional?

What role does this "difficult" imagery play as it enters the contexts of art museums and popular commerce? The public recognition of Richter's work brings up further questions: What does the museum acquisition of paintings of terrorists tacitly acknowledge and what further permissions does it create? Richter's use of the RAF subject appears to have created a precedent for a later wave of contemporary artists and curators using the RAF subject where public perception and the aestheticization of terror are explored. But what happens to this subject as a result of these perceptual shifts?

The debate around museum involvement with RAF-related imagery provides a nodal point around which to consider the broader re-use of RAF imagery across a variety of contexts. Despite the U.S. art museum canonization of the RAF through its acquisition and exhibition of Richter's paintings, in Germany any public discussion on the RAF subject still marks this topic as difficult and unresolved territory. Notably no German museum acquired Richter's works. In Berlin in 2005, an exhibition *Zur Vorstellung des Terrors: Die RAF* at the Kunst-Werke Kunstverein was mired in controversy when its curators attempted to use the museum's state funding for a show that gathered works on the RAF made by a range of well-known artists and filmmakers. Funding was withdrawn and the exhibition became the subject of scandal and much public hostility from both conservatives and the Left.[xviii]

As the Kunst-Werke furore illustrated, the RAF subject remains problematic for many Germans even thirty years after the group's first leaders' deaths and nine years after the RAF officially disbanded. The strength of this particular controversy indicates that visuality still remains a powerful element in this terror group's public identity.

The Kunst-Werke exhibition exemplifies a broader recent trend of cultural engagement with the social history of the 1960s and 1970s across a range of commercial, academic and institutional settings. Within such settings in the last ten years the framing of this subject becomes increasingly defined and foreclosed by academic pundits and curators—often under a rubric related to a big-name cultural producer such as Richter. In such a setting, the RAF is seen as a piece of cultural "real estate," a location around which the discursive territory is increasingly monopolized and defined by the academic establishment and state-funded institutions. How can one unpack the complex cultural operations that occur around this subject? What makes this troublesome and oppositional topic so intriguing to such cultural producers? And further, what impact might the current study have to this foreclosing tendency around the RAF?

The continuing controversy around the control and re-use of RAF imagery thirty years after its era illustrates how the phenomenon of 1970s West German terror has left a very visible imprint on the broader society. These patterns of cultural requisitioning of the RAF have not gone unnoticed to some formerly involved in terrorism. In an article for *Jungewelt* in 2007, one-time RAF member Inge Viett writes:

> Unsere Begriffe und Symbole, für uns leidenschaftliche Antizipation eines anderen Lebensentwurfs, angefüllt mit geschichtlicher Inspiration, bezogen auf die historische Unbeugsamkeit der Klassenkämpfe auf der ganzen Welt, waren unsere verbalen Waffen, die den Gegner kennzeichneten und den Verbündeten Solidarität und Gemeinsamkeit signalisierten. Sie stehen heute im Dienst der Herrschenden. Ihre Hüllen baumeln am ideologischen Kanthaken der imperialen Räuber und ihrer Medienhorden, ihrer Hofhistoriker und Systemexperten. Unsere Begriffe und Symbole werden mit

Assoziationsketten gefüllt, die aus der
Waren- und Kriegswelt stammen - aus dem
Reich der Zombies. [xix]

Viett provides a terse but not inaccurate assessment of
contemporary cultural spores. She pinpoints the tendency of the
post-Cold-War capitalist marketplace to appropriate many
evocative symbols previously associated with 1960s and 1970s
Left. Che's image is now best known as a mass-produced T-
shirt and the ideological charge of this icon has been almost
erased due to its continual deconnotated usage as "polit-kitsch."
(Cliché Guevara). Such ideologically-laden imagery—explicitly
anti-capitalist in its original setting—has become subject in the
post-Postmodern period to ironic/-re-contextualization in neo-
commercial con-textes—due entirely to its earlier political
valence.

Now these icons have developed further associations due
to our changed political and cultural circumstance. RAF images
re-appear for a number of reasons. To some analysts the RAF
logo has become an extended cultural signifier because it is a
"hot sign" from one cultural moment that gets picked up in a
next life.[xx] Alternately, in a Gramscian interpretation, the
presence of such a symbol in later mainstream cultural
production is conceived of as a deliberate, politically-expedient
reassignment made by elements who attempt to neutralize this
powerful, politically-provocative Leftist identity through its
repeated deconnotated usage as "radical chic."

Viett's argument concerning the re-use of Cold War
Leftist imagery also highlights another important cultural
intersect. Viett claims these symbols as the creation and
property of her own demographic, the Radical Left 1968
generation. Writing in German, she refers to these symbols as
"Unsere Begriffe und Symbole" (Our concepts and symbols).[xxi]

These issues of authenticity, originality and piracy around
Left signs are key to grasping the fuller history of RAF-related

imagery.

       This study traces 1970s RAF-related images in order to understand the ways that shifting contexts and framing change the perception of a terror group. The study considers contexts where the public comes across terror imagery after its news usage, and with what kinds of understandings. It explores the reasons why visuals associated with a terror group remain in play across a range of milieus after the fact. The nature of the reframing of RAF imagery reveals much about the importance of context in shaping conceptions of history. Is there a tendency within culture to re-address difficult subjects as a way of making peace with the past? Are these images used to fill a particular "historicizing" role in post-war German national history? This discussion considers the relation of RAF images to those from the Fascist era. It also suggests why modern cultural producers are interested in re-engaging with these images. In a laissez-faire, free-market economy, where so much iconic historic signage is already packaged, marketed, and consumed—"formerly-outlawed," uncopyrighted, eye-catching, imagery like that related to the RAF is sourced across a huge semantic field.

       Issues concerning the re-contextualization of terror images and ethics surrounding their use are explored over the following chapters. The presence of 1970s West German Leftist terror imagery in these locii questions possible patterns concerning the future use of similar, more contemporary images of public trauma, such as those relating to 9/11 and Abu Ghraib.

Chapter Outline

       The next chapter "Outlaw Images" considers the history of the RAF logo and its relation to signs associated with earlier global left-wing movements. I trace sources the RAF appeared to draw from to establish the group's public identity and to construct a mythos around the group, and to promote the conception that they were part of a broader Leftist movement. I consider the relation of this Leftist signage to the emerging visual regimes and legal systems of the Modern era and to technological developments during the Cold War.

Chapter Three "Cloning Che" considers Leftist icons of the 1960s and 1970s such as Che Guevara, Angela Davis, and Jane Fonda. I trace the history of the famous 1960 Che photograph by Alessandro Korda, and discuss how patterns in the migrations of this image relate to similar shifts that have occurred with specific RAF images.

Chapter Four ""Das ist Terror": The Post-War West German Press Villain" considers the socio-cultural climate that the RAF subject entered, and to what other German imagery RAF images have a relation, such as those associated with National Socialism.

Chapter Five "The RAF in the Media: The Crime Location, the Woman Terrorist, and the Hostage" considers the RAF's media-oriented strategies and the relation of their acts to concurrent technological developments. It discusses what public conceptions initially emerged around the RAF, and what happens to the group's public identity as it shapes, is shaped by, and interacts with broader networks of communication.

Chapter Six "Punk Rock Terror Style" considers the re-use of RAF imagery in the rock music industry during the late 1970s. It looks at the way in which the adoption of RAF signs in a removed setting appears to expand conceptions of the group's identity.

Chapter Seven "Consuming Terror" looks at the broader significance of cultural production around the RAF. It traces the use of the RAF subject in cultural, academic and commercial contexts, and discusses the ability of academic study and fine art to shift, legitimize and re-formulate public conceptions of the group's identity. It considers the history of Richter's paintings of the RAF and the impact of the introduction of these images into a museum setting.

Chapter Eight "German History and the Undead Body"

concludes this study by considering the uses of the RAF subject in relation to other traditions in German culture concerning the historic dead. This chapter also looks at the connections between this book and ongoing discussions in Cold War and terror studies. I end by considering what further aspects in this field of study still remain to be addressed.

It is noticeable while discussing the visual history of 1970s West German terror, that although an existing web of meanings surround these images, they remain semantically in play. The following chapters attempt to map these shifting histories.

[i] In popular parlance the RAF have also been referred to as the "Baader-Meinhof." This name combines the names of two RAF group leaders Andreas Baader and Ulrike Meinhof. The name "Baader-Meinhof Bande" was first adopted in 1970 by the police and mainstream German press to suggest that the group's violent acts were not politically-motivated, but those of a band of Bonnie-and-Clyde-style criminal gangsters.

[ii] Among an array of RAF literature, informative to this study's are the works cited in the bibliography by Aust, Storr, Varon, and Peters.

[iii] This is contrary to what many RAF historians presume. Peters among others ends his book with this conception, using the official disbanding of the group to frame such a supposition (p.715-26).

[iv] The Weather Underground was a terror group who emerged from the American New Left movement Students for a Democratic Society (SDS). During the early 1970s the Weather Underground bombed various government buildings to protest against the Vietnam War. Unlike the RAF, they did not intentionally target either civilians or government employees. They attacked only unoccupied state buildings.

[v] The Symbionese Liberation Army (SLA) were a violent California-based "urban guerrilla" group most renowned for kidnapping newspaper heiress Patricia Hearst in 1974. After a short period as a hostage, Hearst publicly announced that she had joined the SLA. The whole debacle created huge sensational press coverage. The SLA were all apprehended or killed by the police by 1977.

[vi] Robert Storr, *Gerhard Richter: October 18th 1977,* p.54

[vii] Such an intent can be witnessed in the RAF's written communiqués. Examples of this rhetoric in RAF communiqués include the Rote Armee Fraktion, *Das Konzept Stadtguerilla*. Communique, 1971. Available at http://www.baader-meinhof.com/students/resources/communique/deuconcept.html.

[viii] The rhetoric of U.S. anti-Vietnam protest spoke likewise of "bringing the war home."

[ix] As von Dirke cites, p.71, the *Radikalenerlass*, passed in 1972, also known as the *Berufsverbote* required a thorough background check for all government and state employees, including their political beliefs and history of activism. Membership in a communist or other left-wing student group could lead to exclusion from employment in the public sector. This law was threatening for those young people whose professional skills were in demand almost exclusively in the public sector, for instance, the entire education sector, where the government had a monopoly on job distribution. Another example is the expansion of the Federal Agency for the Protection of the Constitution (*Verfassungsschutz*) As von Dirke writes "In a desperate attempt to put an end to terrorist violence, the government authorities tried to control the entire public discourse. This meant the aesthetic culture was as affected by new legislation as the criminal justice system itself. Terrorism achieved that which the student movement had been striving for: the breakdown of the boundaries between art and politics." In 1976 amendments were passed in parliament to the already existing

legislation on the distribution of written or visual products glorifying and promoting violence. This newly drafted legislation referred specifically to politically motivated violence (*Gewaltparagraphen* 88a, 130a). But as von Dirke also notes, the television and film industries did not have to fear liability for their portrayal of acts of everyday violence.

[x] This argument also made by Peifer, p.56.

[xi] R.A.F. co-founder Horst Mahler joins NPD. Cited in Varon, p.120.

[xii] Böll, Introduction to Baumann, p.i-ii.

[xiii] Böll, Introduction to Baumann, p.i-ii.

[xiv] Other such works include Fassbinder's *Die dritte Generation* (1979), *Mutter Kuster* (1979) and a number of further films by von Trotta and Schlöndorff from the 1980s till the present.

[xv] Storr, *Gerhard Richter: October 18th 1977,* p.55.

[xvi] Examples of artists using edgy Leftist subject matter include Andy Warhol, Cady Noland, and Johan Grimonprez. This subject is discussed at further length in Chapter Eight.

[xvii] As Aust and Storr note, Schleyer and many other RAF assassination victims were high-ranking leaders of West German industry. Ironically, many of the New York MOMA board members, involved for the $3 million acquisition of the Richter work also come from the field of industry. Citation of Richter sale price from Storr, p.55.

[xviii] Biesenbach, p.i-iv.

[xix] Viett writes in German: "Our linguistic terms and symbols—for us a passionate anticipation of a different way of life, were filled with historic inspiration drawn from the historic unbreakability of a worldwide class struggle. These terms and symbols were for us verbal and visual weapons that labelled our enemy and signalled our solidarity and unity to our allies. They stand today in the service of the ruling forces. Their empty shells now hang from the ideological boarding hooks of the imperialistic robbers and their media hordes, their court historians and system experts. Our linguistic terms and symbols have become filled with chains of association from the world of the consumer and from the world of war, from the Empire of Zombies." From May 12th 2007 *Tageszeitung* article by Inge Viett "Lust auf Freiheit. Unsere Geschichte als Klassenkampf von unten verteidigen." http://www.jungewelt.de/2007/02-24/017.php?print=1

[xx] To borrow McLuhan's term. p.33.

[xxi] But arguably, Viett is engaged here in a form of colonial Eurocentric thinking concerning 1960s radical Leftist imagery—a style and gestalt that itself was drawn from the political contexts of Latin America and South East Asia. As we shall see, the RAF's own graphics borrowed heavily from a visual language originally associated with the Third World geographies. A presumption of RAF ideology was to imagine that by adopting visuals and strategies from Third World anti-colonial struggles and the black U.S. civil rights movement, that they the RAF—despite being white, middle-class and European—were then entitled to identify themselves as the oppressed, as subjects of world historical agency.

Chapter II

THE RED STAR AND OUTLAW IDENTITY

As noted in Chapter One, Robert Storr states that the RAF aimed "to bring the struggle of the revolutionary Third World to the reactionary First World."[1] His assessment provides an interesting counterpoint in a consideration of RAF imagery. How did the graphic/tactics of the RAF relate to that of earlier movements?

The RAF adopted strategies from earlier radical and terror groups which had developed and created high-visibility identities and strategies that intentionally aimed to provoke public outrage. The RAF's tactics owe a clear debt to the avant-garde shock tactics of particular art groups of the post-War period. Some RAF members had been involved in the Munich theatrical circle around Fassbinder in the late 1960s before joining the group. Some members were clearly influenced by French provocational art groups the Lettrists and Situationist International (SI). The RAF adopted the Situationist tactic of *détournement* (see Chapter Six), an example of both this tactic, and the S.I.'s influence on the RAF is the *détournement* of the very name RAF, parodying the acronym of World War Two victors the British Royal Air Force responsible for the devastation of many German cities. Dieter Kunzelman, a Kommune 1 founder and RAF associate, had been involved in the Situationist International during the early 1960s.

Beyond these influences, the media-savvy antics of Berlin's late 1960s hippie commune scene helped to shape RAF thinking. The antics and theatrics of Kommune 1 during this period had similarities to those of their contemporaries, U.S political pranksters the Yippies. Baader had lived briefly in Kommune-1 in the late 1960s.

Given the familiarity of some RAF members with the world of avant-garde theater, another likely inspiration appears to have been Antonin Artaud. His "Theater of Cruelty" deliberately intended—through transgressive and horrific theatrics—to shock an audience out of their cultural desensitization.

Informed by the earlier proximity to these milieus, RAF terror strategy adopted shocking theatrical modes of engagement—to produce a type of violent political theatre. These methods were adopted along with more clearly terroristic strategies, such as bombings, bank robbery, kidnapping and assassination of high-level government figures. Similar terror acts by the I.R.A, the Brigate Rosse and the Tupamaros received global media coverage in the late 1960s. Thus the zeitgeist of the 1960s informed the RAF's terror tactics.

To discuss a history of RAF imagery, one also needs to begin before the group's formation and consider Leftist visuals of the 1960s. This West German group began to engage in terror tactics in response to Vietnam, and along with adopting a broader anti-imperialist struggle, the RAF also adopted a visual lingua franca of radicalism that had been generated by a range of earlier left-wing militant groups.

Outlaw Imagery

The RAF terror phenomenon in West Germany involved a complex series of events where a strong visual identity was a key element. As well as acting as a signature in a range of communiqués, a terror group's logo is a crucial authorial stamp, brand, and meaning-maker—a sign that is used by a phantom presence, the terror group, which creates a spectacular and horrific display and then disappears. In such a context, the visual resonance of a terror group's logo is of central importance.

The history of the group's most recognizable identifying symbol—their logo and its relation to earlier Leftist movements—is crucial. Studying the genealogy that precedes the RAF can explain something about the visual impact of this German group. In this chapter I argue not only that the RAF logo drew from specific international reference points, but that all these Leftist signs were....unstable in meaning, a quality that affects the later public understanding of the RAF's identity.

The design of the RAF logo is often attributed to group leader Andreas Baader and graphic designer Holm von Czettritz.[2] It first appeared in 1970 in the group's communiqués and in locations like underground political magazine *883*.

The logo clearly draws its graphic style from three particular logos used by high-profile terror and radical groups active during the late 1960s in other parts of the world.

The RAF logo design takes graphic elements from the logos of Italian terror group, the Brigate Rosse (the red star and militaristic name); from that of Uruguay's Marxist guerilla group the Tupamaros (the central three initials on the star); and from the logo of the newspaper of the American "armed community activists" the Black Panthers (a star with a soldier holding a gun). A further reference in the RAF's name is to the acronym of the British Royal Air Force. Another reference here is to the Japanese Red Army (JRA), a contemporaneous Leftist terror group, from whom some claim the RAF adopted their name. The JRA were best known for their involvement in the airport massacre at Lodz, Israel in 1972.

By adopting these signs, the RAF logo suggested from the outset that the group's strategies—like the other groups—would include hijacking, bombing and the use of guns. The sign itself explicitly indicated the type of war in which the RAF aimed to engage. This logo exemplifies both the RAF's ideological intent at their inception, and also their visual plundering. It also reveals a degree of identity confusion and mystification.

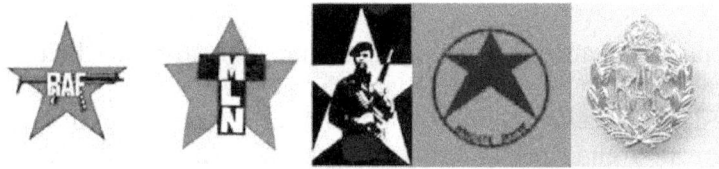

Fig. 1: The RAF logo and some of its precursors: Red Army Faction logo, 1970; Tupamaros logo, 1960s: Black Panther newspaper logo, 1967; Brigate Rosse logo, 1960s; British Royal Air Force insignia, c.1930s.

What does this graphic borrowing also reveal? Does the RAF attempt to develop as a sub-brand spinning off from a global brand of left-wing terrorism, and what does this pattern imply about the loose currency of this type of imagery during this period? What was the RAF's role in the broader dissemination of a free-floating transnational graphic style denoting the Leftist guerrilla? These questions concerning authenticity and branding are important terrains to map.

The graphic punch of the RAF's logo was key to the notoriety that this particular group achieved in a short time on a national scale. One reason for the RAF's logo's visual resonance was their synchronicity with the cultural zeitgeist of the era. The RAF logo was understood to suggest a world-historical engagement. This founding imagery of the RAF makes this particular group's identity stand out from the many other self-styled urban guerilla groups active in West Germany during the same period, such as the "Hasch Rebellen," "Bewegung 2.Juni," "Sozialistisches Patienten Kollektiv," or "Rote Zellen."[3]

The RAF's visually commanding logo closely resembled the style of already globally-recognized Leftist groups, and this made the group's identity stand out. But what also made the RAF's visual identity resonant was their ability (consciously and unconsciously) to tap into further mythologies and signifying streams. As we shall see in Chapter Four and Five, parallel to the RAF's own intent to mythologize their identity, the West German media increasingly portrayed this particular group in mythic terms—*as the embodiment of outrageous terror*.

In relation to the idea of a terror group attempting to adopt signs signaling the mythic, powerful and world historic, it is important to consider the RAF's deliberate invocation of a global rhetoric of terror in the construction of their public image. As noted, some within the RAF leadership had worked in the media. These included RAF leader Ulrike Meinhof, who was former editor of *konkret,* the leading West German left-wing magazine, Andreas Baader, at one point an aspiring journalist,[4] and Holger Meins, a filmmaker.[5] As figures familiar with the patterns of news construction, all were aware of the importance of arresting visuals in the success of news-grabbing public actions.[6]

The RAF logo was clearly inspired by the group logos already cited. But it is also important to track what other signifying systems their logo appears to tap into. Other kinds of associations with different types of symbolism are also apparent. Some of these signs may initially appear unrelated, but on closer consideration it is easier to see a connection.[7]

While the RAF logo clearly inherits the visual grammar of other violent Leftist groups, it also directly and indirectly draws from a language related to other social organizations, such as trade unions and worker movements which rely on the presence of a logo as a group identifier. The RAF graphics also have stylistic affinities with a visual language associated with the contemporaneous hippie subculture of the 1960s, the American Civil Rights movement, and also the Chinese Cultural Revolution.

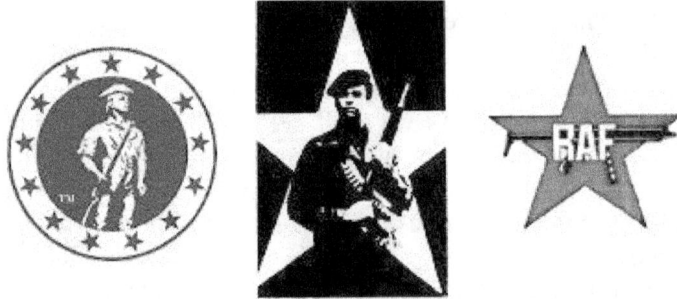

Fig. 2. Three logos featuring a star and a gun: Minutemen logo, 1800s; Black Panther newspaper logo, c.1967; Red Army Faction logo, 1970.

The RAF logo also indirectly draws from right-wing signage. An example of this connection is that the RAF logo draws from the Black Panthers' newspaper logo—a sign that with its image of a soldier at arms deliberately hijacks the visual rhetoric of the logo adopted by the Minutemen, known in the 1960s as a US racist militia group.[8]

Like many other Western countercultural groups of the era, the RAF logo is related to markings of alterity, such as Islamic stars and pagan symbols, mythic, pre-Christian and Classical narratives.

Other contemporary examples from the 1970s include the U.S. urban guerrilla group, the Symbionese Liberation Army (SLA), formed in 1972, kidnappers of heiress Patty Hearst. The SLA logo adopted the mythological several-headed Hydra snake. The Black Panthers' logo featured a running

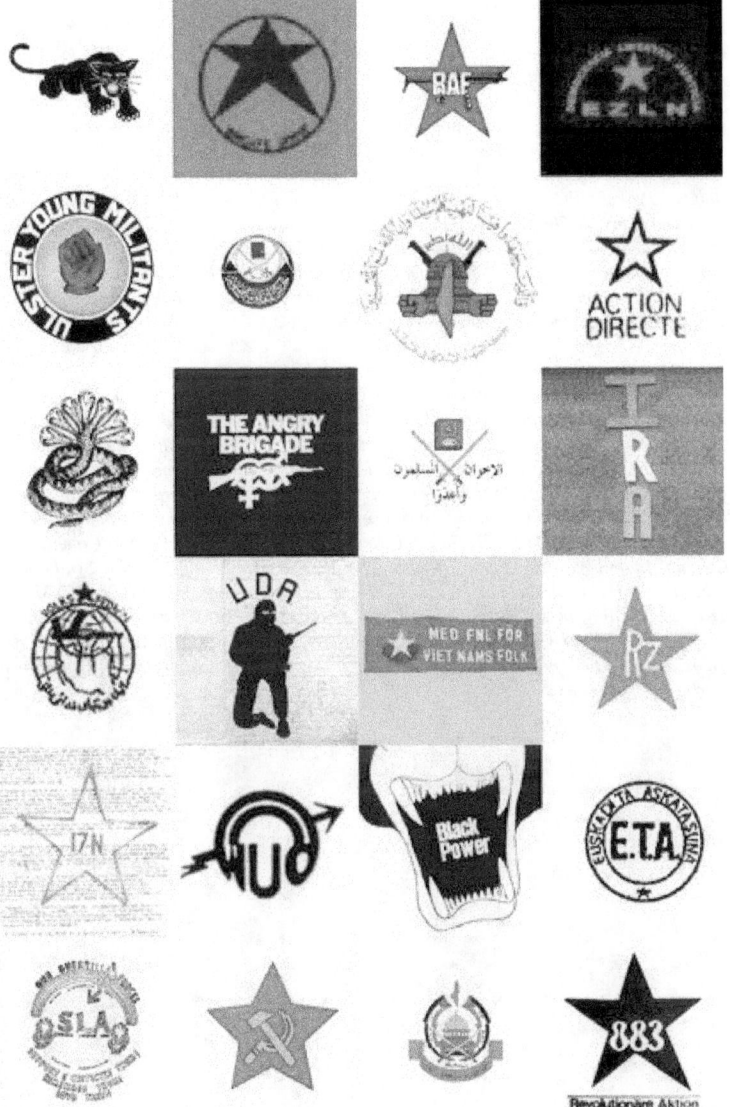

Fig. 3. Radical and Terror Group Signs from the 1920s to the Present: Left-right, top to bottom: The Black Panthers logo, c.1967; Brigate Rosse logo, Italy, 1960s; Red Army Faction logo, West Germany, 1970; Zapatista group logo, Mexico, 1990s; Ulster Young Militants logo, Belfast, Northern Ireland, 1970s; Hamas logo, 1960s, Palestine; Palestinian terror group logo, 1980s; Action Directe logo, France, 1970s; Symbionese Liberation Army logo, San Francisco, 1971?; The Angry Brigade, London, 1970s; Islamical terror group, Middle East, 1970s; IRA street sign, Belfast, 1980s; West German-Iranian Leftist militant group, Iran/Germany, 1970s; Ulster Defense Army, Belfast, 1960s?; Viet Cong solidarity flag, Western Europe, 1970s; Rote Zellen logo, West Germany, 1970s; 17th November group, Greece, c.1960s; Weather Underground logo, U.S, c.1970; OSPAAAL Black Power solidarity poster, Cuba, c.1970; Basque separatist movement ETA, 1950s? logo; SLA/Weathermen solidarity poster, U.S, 1974; Russian Communist logo, early 1920s; Japanese Red Army logo, Japan/Palestine, c.1970; 883 magazine logo, West Germany, late 1960s.

Fig. 4.Further Leftist, Radical and Terror Group Signs from the 1960s to the Present. Left-right, top to bottom: Brigate Rosse, Italy, 1960s; Bewegung 2.Juni, West Germany, 1970s; Cellules Communistes Combattantes, France, 1970s; ERP, Latin America, 1960s; MIR, Latin America, 1960s; Animal Liberation Front, Britain, 1980s; Wobblies, U.S, 1900s; Israeli group logo, 1980s; Red flags; ELN, Latin America, 1960s; Kommunistische Partei Deutschlands/Marxisten-Leninisten, West Germany, 1970s, MLN, Latin America, 1960s, Hasch Rebellen, West Berlin, 1960s; Partido Communista Circolo Antonio Gramsci, Italy, 1970s; U.S.S.R. Red Army badge, 1920s; Symbionese Liberation Army communiqué, U.S, 1975; Hezbollah logo, Palestine, 1980s; 26th March group, Latin America, 1980s; FSLN, Latin America, 1960s; Mozambique Communist group, 1970s; West German graphic from 1970s, with a range of radical and terror logos; Radical Feminist log, U.S?, 160s; Iranian Communist group, 1970s; Communist Party, South East Asia, 1970s

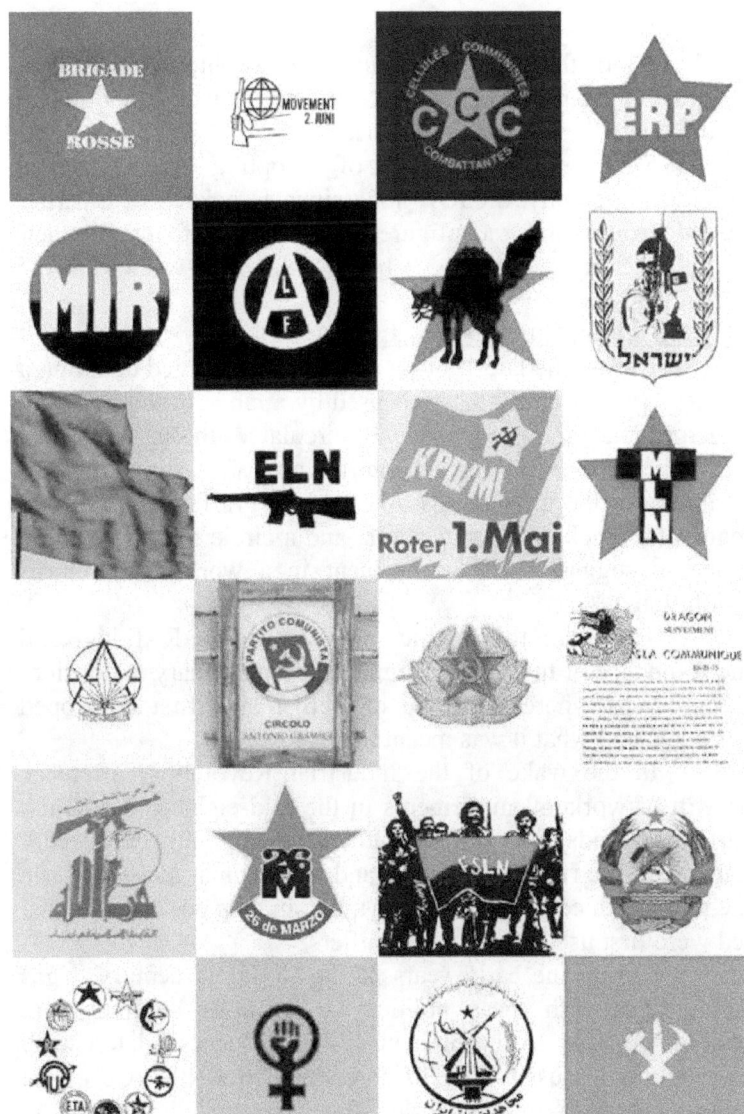

panther. Both these logos use anthropomorphic symbolism to suggest the untameable power of the animal kingdom to mythologize their groups' identities.[9]

Similar to this pattern of co-opting older powerful public iconography, the RAF took signs associated with earlier Leftist groups and reconfigured this signage to create their group's identity.

The Red Star in Guerrilla Signage

During the late 1960s a visual style emerged denoting a Leftist radical identity that was used by a range of international underground groups. This style circulated through political magazines, banners, pins, T-shirts, and in settings on the periphery of the urban landscape, such as graffiti. These group logos often included a star, a gun, and a circle representing the globe to suggest their involvement in a worldwide Marxist revolution.

To explain this mythic component of the RAF logo and the resonance of this kind of signage, it is necessary to consider the contexts where this type of Leftist sign first developed currency, and what it was meant to suggest.

In the wake of the Industrial Revolution, after the growth of workers' movements in the mid-eighteenth century, particular kinds of worker-identified iconography emerged.[10] Later with the rise of Anarchist and Communist movements in the nineteenth century, the star symbol and the colors black and red were first used as Leftist signifiers.

During the early years of the twentieth century, signs and images with these political associations became more widespread. Due to the high visibility of successful left-wing revolutions in Russia in 1917 and China in 1949—two of the largest countries in the world—this genre of signs grew in public visibility internationally.

Such signs were often used as graphics in textual tracts, printed broadsheets, posters, and newspapers. Crucial to the dissemination of these symbols was their mass-reproducibility and their uncopyrighted status.[11] These signs developed as a discrete category denoting Leftism among a wider catalog of politically–identified public signage. But this particular identity was understood to loosely refer to a somewhat-amorphous collection of political identities: insurrectionary groups, official Communist parties, anti-imperialists, the "politically-radical"— and later, Leftist terrorists.

A central formal element used in the design of the RAF logo is the red star of Communism. The history of the red star as a Communist signifier can be traced back to its association with the Red Guard in the immediate post-World War-One period. The history of this sign reveals much about the particular resonance of much Leftist iconography. There are a number of competing claims as to the origins and exact meaning of this symbol. What seems clear is that the red star emerged as a Communist sign at the end of the First World War, in the context of the Russian Revolution.

Russian troops fleeing from the Austrian and German fronts found themselves in Moscow in 1917 and mixed up with the local Moscow garrison. To distinguish the Moscow troops from the influx of retreating Russians, the officers gave out tin stars to the Moscow garrison soldiers to wear on their hats. When those troops joined together with the Red Army and the Bolsheviks, they painted their tin stars red to symbolize Communism—thus creating the first official Communist red star. Another claim of origin for the red star comes from an alleged encounter between Trotsky and the Bolshevik revolutionary Nikolai Krylenko during this period. Krylenko, an Esperantist, was wearing a green star lapel badge; Trotsky enquired as to its meaning and received an explanation that each arm of the star represented one of the five traditional continents. On hearing this, he specified that a red star should be worn by soldiers of the Red Army.[12]

The five-pointed red star is also said to represent the five fingers of the worker's hand. A further suggestion is that

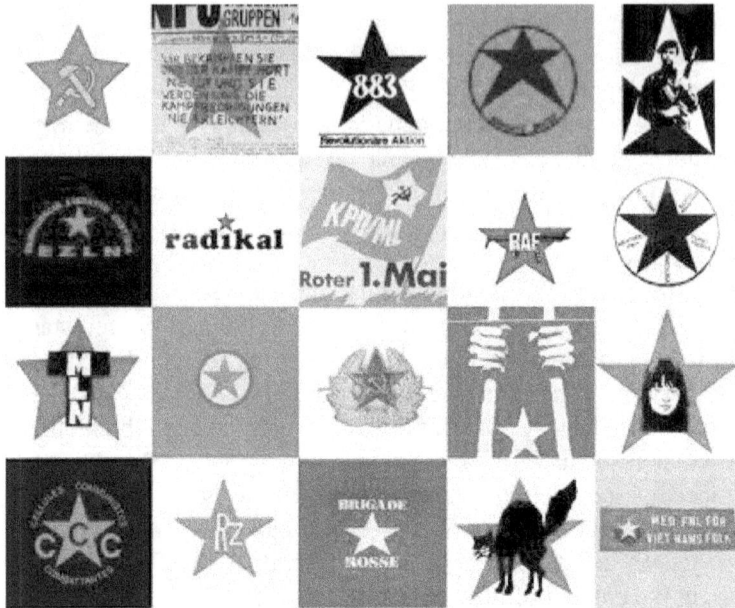

Fig. 5. Leftist, Radical and Terror Signs Featuring the Red Star from the 1920s to the Present, left to right, top to bottom: USSR Communist Party Logo, 1920s; Info magazine, West Germany, 1970s; 883 magazine, West Germany, 1960s; Brigate Rosse, Italy, 1960s, Black Panthers newspaper, U.S, 1960s; Zapatistas, México, 1990s; Radical magazine, West Germany, 1960s; Kommunistische Partei Deutschlands/Marxisten-Leninisten, West Germany, 1970s, Red Army Faction group logo, 1970; Graphic from 883 magazine, West Germany, 1970s; Tupamaros, Uruguay, 1960s; Vietnam flag, 1970s; U.S.S.R Red Army insignia, 1920s; Latin American poster in solidarity with Leftist prisoners, 1970s; Ulrike Meinhof on a red star, from RAF solidarity poster, West Germany, 1970s; Cellules Communistes Combattantes, France, 1970s, Rote Zellen, West Germany, 1970s; Brigate Rosse solidarity T-shirt, Italy, 1980s; Wobblies, U.S, 1900s; West European Viet Cong Solidarity flag, 1970s.

the five points on the star were intended to represent the five social groups that would lead the nation to Communism: Youth, the military, industrial workers, agricultural workers and the intelligentsia.[13]

All these competing historical narratives develop around the red star as it emerges as a sign identified with Communism. The sign appeared resonant because it lent itself to many projections and associative narrative threads. A range of differing legends, myths and associations around the sign's meaning appear to solidify its wider symbolic stature in society. The use of the color red in Communist imagery can be traced back to the memorializing of the red flag flown by the Paris Commune of 1871. Red symbolizes the blood spilt by workers the world over in the fight for their emancipation. The red flag in Paris symbolized blood to indicate no surrender (as opposed to the white flag of surrender). Added to this, red has traditionally always had very positive connotations in Russian language and culture. The word "red" ("красный") is etymologically related with the words "прекрасный" ("very good", "the best") and "красивий" ("beautiful"). Red is also a color prominently featured in Russian Orthodox Christian Easter festivals.[14] Until communist Russia's adoption of the hammer and sickle in 1924, the red flag was one of the key founding symbol associated with a worker's government.[15]

This set of explanations for the originations and meanings of the red star seem logical and coherent in the Russian setting, but it is important not to disclude other histories around the five-pointed star, particularly as a sign related to non-Christian religions, powers, and ideologies. It would simplify things to claim the red star sign emerged with Leftism. But it is also important to look at star symbolism in other contexts—to consider its resonance across a wider range of historical settings. This can explain more about the mythical aspect to this type of sign.

We can begin by noting that, regardless of color, the eye-catching formal qualities of the star already suggest a particular set of associations. Its geometric form intrinsically installs a semantic connection with the heavenly and exceptional, making it an apt symbol of a rupturous or avant-gardist movement.

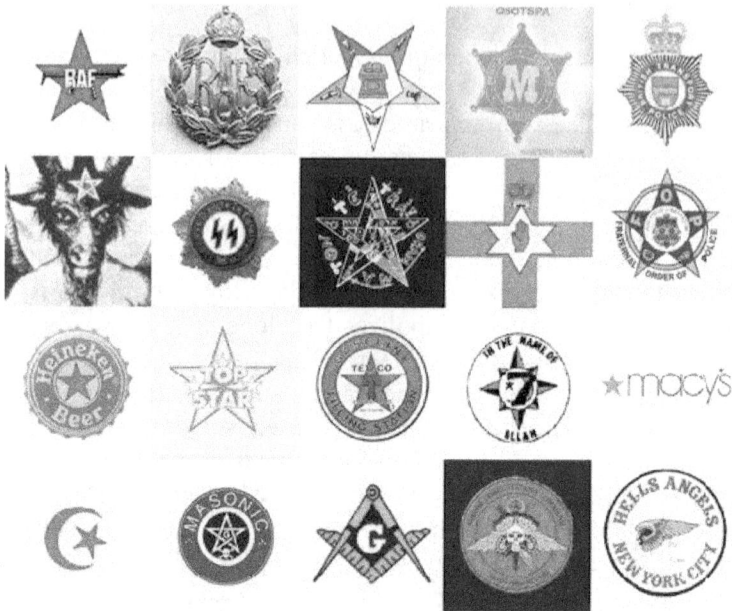

Fig. 6. Non-Leftist group logos featuring the five-pointed star, from the 1920s to the present, left to right, top to bottom: RAF logo, 1970; Royal Air Force insignia, Britain, 1920s?; Masonic Temple sign, U.S, 1800s; Osotspa drink featuring U.S. sheriff's insignia, Britain, 2005; British Transport Police crest, 1900s?; Satanic goat with pentagram sign, Victorian graphic, Britain, 1800s; Nazi SS insignia, Germany, 1930s;Occult pentagram graphic, Western Europe, 1500s?; Ulster flag, Northern Ireland, 1800s?; Fraternal Order of Police crest, U.S, 1900s?; Heineken beer bottle cap, 1900s, Denmark; Top Star brand, Germany, 2005; Texaco Oil Company; Nation of Islam sign, U.S, 1950s?; Macy's Department store, U.S, 1900s/; Turkish flag, 1900s?; Masonic crest, U.S, 1800s?; Masonic Grand Lodge symbol, Britain, 1800s?; U.S. Marine Corps graphic, 1940s?; Hells Angels New York logo, U.S, 1969.

The five-pointed star often appears in combination with other graphic forms to denote memberships and ideologies unassociated with Leftism. These other threads of association include the five-pointed star's use by Masonic groups and other secret organizations. A star logo inherits a rhetorical language of secrecy and avant-gardism from these other kinds of association. Further connections include the five-pointed pentagram that appeared on the coats of arms of crusaders in the

Middle Ages. The pentagram has also often been associated
with the occult. When the sign was turned so that two of its
ends were pointing upward, it is understood to represent the
Devil. Since medieval times in Nordic countries this upturned
star sign was drawn on doors and walls as protection against
trolls and evil. In more recent eras, the five-pointed star has
been used on army uniforms, and on the sides of tanks and
fighter planes in the United States, and a range of other
countries.

As this range of examples indicates, many people in the
West are already on some level aware of prior associations with
the five-pointed star beyond its use as Communist signifier.
This sign has often implied secrecy, militarism, and an
exceptional status.[16] The Communist red star inherits these
earlier associations. This reminds us that a sign's meaning
remains fluid and subject to switches. This inherited
polysemous quality adds to its rhetorical charge.

A Communist graphic with less multivalent
associations is the hammer and sickle, a logo that first appeared
in Soviet symbolism around 1917.[17] The Soviet flag featuring
the hammer, sickle and star was officially adopted in 1923.
Although the hammer and sickle symbolizes the worker and
peasant, also implicit in this logo's visual rhetoric is the
potential of both's use as weapons, suggesting the possibility of
violent insurrection. The hammer and sickle sign was never
used by the RAF. But the RAF's logo substitutes these tools of
industry with the image of a machine gun.

Despite contestation over exact details concerning
specific narratives and meanings, what is clear is that the
Russian revolution, and before it the Parisian uprisings,
produced catalogs of images which were then used to signal
communism and/or a call to violent worker uprising. In the
wake of Marx and Engels' 1848 demand for a global worker
insurrection ("Arbeiter aller Länder vereinigt Euch!" Workers
of the world organize yourselves [18]), red star graphics signaling
Communism sprouted across a range of geographies. These

movements generated a body of internationally-recognizable Leftist signs, which led to the establishment and growth of communism as one of the first multinational visual brands of an ideological and economic nature.

In the context of wildfire global expansion in hostile political environments, the use of these Communist graphics often relied on grassroots, do-it-yourself patterns. These patterns established the permissions for these signs' appropriation in home-made embodifications, creating a tendency toward self-authorization around the usage of all Leftist signs. These signs were understood to be free, shared, and for the use of all. Without the control of copyright, the dissemination of the Leftist logo became widespread across a broad semantic field through its use by a diffuse range of groups and organizations.

Thus Leftist signs were from their inception floating in contexts that were, in terms of ideology and identity, particularly prone to schisms and wild cards. These logos— uncontrolled and untrademarked—lent themselves to insurrectionary movements of almost any hue. Due to this meta-praxis, a semantic fluidity is understood in the conception of all Leftist signs, and this sense of laissez-faire lends a particular rhetorical punch to their understanding. What we gather from all these earlier patterns is that long before the 1960s and 1970s, radical and Leftist signs were already established as markers with less than legitimate public associations. By the Seventies, with the rise of the domestic terrorist, these uncontrolled Leftist logos and ideologies provided the possibility for personally-motivated acting-out in the name of another loose signifier, "the people" (das Volk).

33

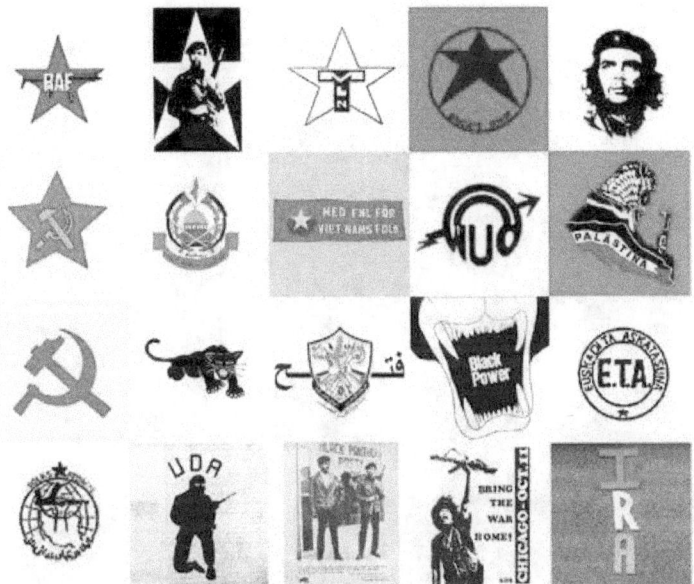

Fig. 7. Leftist, Radical and terror group logos of the 1960s and 1970s: from l-r, starting from top: Rote Armee Fraktion logo 1970; Black Panthers newspaper logo, 1968; Tupamaros logo, late 1960s; Brigate Rosse logo, late 1960s, Che 1965 (courtesy Estate of A.Korda; USSR logo 1920s, Hamas logo (date unknown); Vietcong flag, 1970s; Weather Underground logo, 1970s: Palestina poster, West Germany, 1970s; Soviet hammer and sickle logo, 1920s; Black Panther logo, 1968; Fatah logo, c.1970; Black power poster, 1970s; Basque ETA logo, 1970s; Palestinian-German group, early 1970s; UDA mural, Belfast 1970s; Black Panthers poster 1968; SDS Days of Rage poster 1969; IRA mural, Belfast 1970s.

The RAF adopted this visual style associated with Communist revolution in an attempt to *inszenieren* (insinuate and establish) the idea of their role in a larger ongoing international Leftist movement. What was the part played by the RAF in the dissemination of a free-floating transnational visual language that denoted not only the Left, but now also the urban guerrilla? By the RAF's adoption of this global Leftist visual rhetoric, I argue that this group blurred and shifted the perception of these signs and of the ideology of many other international Leftist groups.

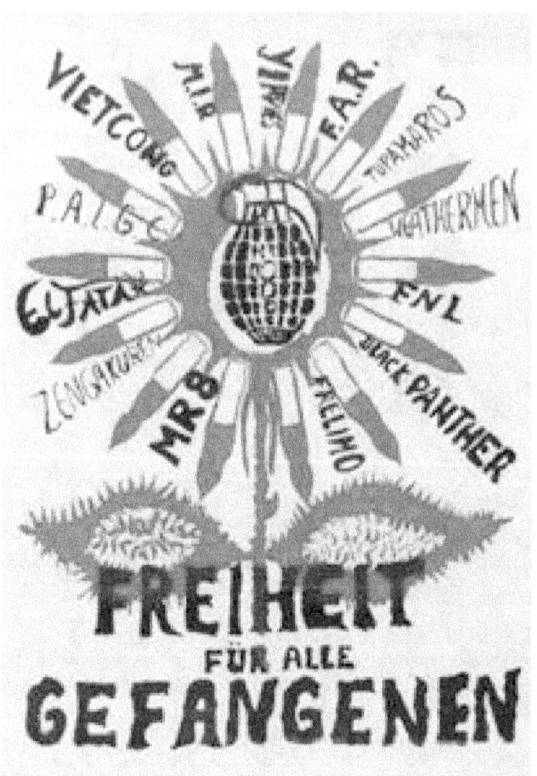

Fig. 8. Holger Meins' "Freiheit für alle Gefangenen" poster. From "883" magazine, 1970.

An early RAF-related poster is particularly useful to understand the RAF's attempts to position their involvement in a global resistance movement. The image above was featured in the West German underground magazine *883* in 1970. The poster was designed by Holger Meins, who joined the RAF the same year.[19] [20] 1970 also marked the official formation of the RAF.

This image is remarkable on many levels—as an object expressing the verbal style of the era, for its graphic cleverness, and also as a chilling forecast of future events. (Meins himself died in jail on hunger strike four years later on bombing charges). The image of a sunflower exploding in bloom is screen-printed in a primitive hippie-esque style. But this is no reference to flower-power. It drives the hippie "peace and love" rhetoric into reverse. On closer inspection the flower is assembled from a hand grenade, names and bullets, and it is red and somewhat-star-shaped. A text below the flower reads "Freiheit für alle Gefangenen" ("Freedom for all prisoners"). The flower is symbolic harbinger of future growth (a probable reference here to Mao's injunction to "Let a thousand flowers bloom"[21]) but also here of imminent violence (the bullets ready to fly). Circling the fourteen-pronged, star-shaped, bullet petals are the names of international radical and terrorist groups of the period who were in the news. Notably no German group is present. The poster suggests that all the prisoners from these political groups should be liberated from jail by violent means.

However we should note that all these groups were involved in activism of many different shades, ranging from community initiatives (i.e. the Black Panthers' free breakfast programs) to spectacular bank robberies (the Tupamaros in Uruguay), or the anti-Vietnam War bombings of state buildings (the Weather Underground in the U.S). Meins conflates the identities and goals of different groups, including national homeland movements, anti-colonial struggles, ideological groups, or armed community initiatives, are all here conflated. The rhetoric of this poster suggests that these groups shared a common goal that was only to be accomplished through violence. The poster implies that all these cells are ideologically linked beyond the release of their imprisoned members. Even in 1970, this appears to be misrepresentative of some of these groups, and a wishful thinking on Meins' part—in his invocation of a global Leftist terror on a monstrous level.

The appropriation of the names of these groups in a poster made in another country renders their names emblematic and mythologizes their identities. What is kept and what gets lost or evacuated in such a re-situating? Whilst Meins' poster acknowledges the semantic power of these identities, and appears to endorse their struggles, his appropriation brings into question the issue of authorization. This citing or co-option of another's struggle—whatever the intent—is part of a pattern of meaning-fragmentation that occurs around all uncopyrighted symbols and is a frequent pattern around signs of the political Other. The appropriation of the names, ideology and tactics of Third World anti-colonial movements by Europeans like the RAF (most of whom were born into West German families who survived the fascist era) opens another set of questions. As noted, one central ideological slippage of the RAF was to imagine that in identifying with Third World struggles, adopting their visuals and their violent strategies, that they, the RAF—despite being white and living in Western Europe under a relatively democratic government compared to say, Argentina—were then entitled to locate themselves similarly as the geo-political "oppressed" subjects of world historical agency.

These issues of authenticity and the appropriation of global Leftist signage brings into discussion the role of this public marker for the terror group. As noted, a logo is of great importance for a terror group's public identity. It is used in their communiqués as an authentifying sign for their deeds. But the broader signification of such a sign is more clearly explained by considering the legal and cultural operations that structure its use and social status.

To explain the role of a terror logo within wider imaging systems, it is necessary to consider the history of logos as social and economic phenomena, and to look at the shifting historical contexts from which they emerge, how they assume currency, and the ways in which they operate.

The Logo in Society

The connection between public signs and a specific social or political identity begins within economies of ownership, shipping, slavery and sovereignty.[22] The shift from the sign as tribal marking develops due to its importance in the emergence of monarchical and institutional contexts. Publicly-identifiable signage makes visible specific compliances or associations with ideologies, memberships, or hierarchies within the civic body. Social and cultural identities in turn grow in stature as these logos develop currency. These visual domains expand in relation to technological and economic advances. Logos accrue associative power through their use in guilds, crests, and uniforms—a language of signage within an economy of paternal "author"-ity.

An example of this power of visual display is the way in the Middle Ages in Europe, court painting was used to show hierarchies of social control and the power of the established economic order. And although the subject matter of court painting expanded over time beyond just symbolizing economic status or portraying the sovereign and court, and began to include subjects whose status was less socially determined, the logo, as seal or mark, retained its imprimatur as an indicator of social status or authenticity.

During this period in Italy, the privileging of certain types of cultural production established a structural hegemony that then affected further economic and social relations. Anthropologist Claude Levi-Strauss talks of the relation between economic elites, cultural objects, and aesthetic hierarchies in these terms:

> For the Renaissance artists, painting was perhaps an instrument of knowledge but it was also an instrument of possession.... Renaissance painting... was only possible because of the immense fortunes which were being amassed in Florence and elsewhere, and that rich Italian merchants looked upon painters as agents, who allowed them to confirm their possession of all that was beautiful and desirable in the world. The pictures in a

Florentine palace represented a kind of
microcosm in which the proprietor, thanks to
his artists, has recreated within easy reach and
in as real a form as possible, all those features
of the world to which he was attached.[23]

Within the world of commerce, signs of "quality" and
"markability" develop as a kind of shorthand—as locations
where they become legitimated to mark off and police
geographic or economic territory.

Later, due to the Industrial Revolution, increasing
power was invested in brand logo in relation to the emergence
of mass-production and commodification culture. A key to the
rising power of this type of sign is the development of print
technology, and the logo's currency for the bourgeois classes of
post-Enlightenment.

Further, an important shift in this semantic field
concerning logos and signs was the introduction of the concept
of "copyright," which began within European state systems
during the eighteenth century. The introduction of mass printing
and copyright changed social and economic relations in a
profound way.

European governments had previously granted
monopoly rights to publishers to sell printed works. An
example of the emergence of the modern concept of limited
duration copyright was the British "Statute of Anne" in 1710.[24]
This statute was among the first in Europe to accord exclusive
rights to authors (i.e. creators) rather than publishers, and this
law included protection for consumers of printed work,
ensuring that publishers could not control their use after sale. (It
also limited the duration of such exclusive rights to twenty-
eight years, after which all works would pass into the public
domain).[25] Similar patterns of legal control and ownership
around print and image reproduction rights began to emerge
concurrently across Western Europe. The "Berne Convention
for the Protection of Literary and Artistic Works" in 1886

began protected ownership over scientific advances and artistic works beyond national borders, thus introducing the concept of transnational copyright. As historian Hernandez-Reguant notes of the impact of the Berne Convention, "over the next century, many other countries followed suit in order to participate in international commerce."[26] The introduction of this type of legislation encouraged broader patterns of control around all visual and verbal signage.

Notably during the twentieth century, communist states did not acknowledge or adopt the transnational laws of the Berne Convention. However in capitalist countries, parameters controlling the visual field continue to develop over time. One recent indication of the ongoing tightening of this copyright control is the introduction of increased levels of trademark infringement legislation. Recent U.S. patent laws now include the protection of the use of particular color combinations, letters and styles in public signage.[27] This legislation prohibits the use in advertising of imagery or color-combinations that are deemed too similar to the logos of established transnational brands in any way close to those used by global franchise corporations such as McDonald's or Federal Express.

What these developing legal patterns suggest is that the level of control around all public signage is constantly growing, and the visual has become a field increasingly defined by legal, economic, administrative and linguistic limitations.

This pattern illustrates the way that institutional and economic systems attempt to control certain types of visual signage. But it is also important to consider the way that other historical developments fracture and redraw the existing roles of the visual sign. In order to better understand the shifting social role of the logo, it is necessary to consider shifting societal relations in the wake of the Industrial Revolution.

Technology and Visual Perception

If the visual was once a locus primarily used for the display of hierarchical power, suddenly in the nineteenth century, due to the advancements of photography and print technology, the role of visuality shifted in significant ways.

Parallel to the logo's emergence as a social and cultural signifier, due to important steps forward in technology, changes concerning visuality began to emerge in institutional contexts. The introduction of photography as a mass tool also altered much in the arena of visual relations.

The "bringing-to-visuality" established in court painting installed one kind of ocular economy where visibility indicated high social status. However due to photography this pattern of "visual-presence-denoting-power" could suddenly be reversed.[28] The reproducibility of photographs introduced the idea that a "bringing-to-visuality" was not always an indication of great socio-cultural power.

Objects such as mugshots used on a "Wanted" posters are emblematic of this redrawing of the parameters of what the visual could now perform. In a somewhat Foucauldian analysis, historian John Tagg argues that in the nineteenth century police photography, along with "the burgeoning sciences of criminology, psychiatry, germ theory and sanitation," redefined the social as the object of their technical interventions.[29]

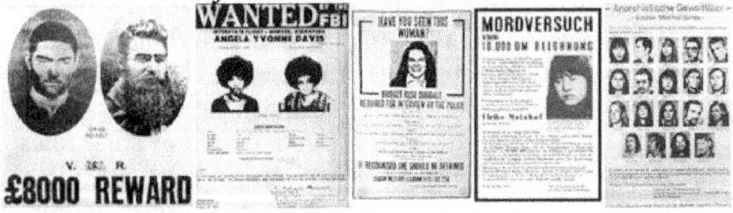

Fig. 9. Police "Wanted" Posters from the Eighteenth Century to the 1970s: (left to right) Ned Kelly Wanted poster, Australia, 1800s; Angela Davis FBI Wanted poster, U.S, 1970, Bridget Rose Dugdale Wanted poster, Northern Ireland, 1974, Ulrike Meinhof Wanted for Murder poster, West Germany, 1972, RAF Wanted poster, West Germany, 1972.

Tagg suggests that parallel with photography came the growth in institutional settings of new "technologies of inscription."[30] The photographic display of a fugitive's likeness on a police poster could now demonize his or her face and name in a way that explicitly marked this identity as separate, sick, or notorious.[31] The "Wanted" poster installed a specific type of visual regime. The mugshot established a new ocular economy —one of policing visuality and of a forensic surveillance of the body.[32] The mugshot precisely renders the human subject "objectified," denatured, "identified," and subaltern. It developed a new "tabloid" print category—the visualized villain.

The enhanced veracity of photography leads to a refiguring of existing social relations and also of public conceptions of the state's stability. In a Wanted poster the criminal is rendered both wanted yet undesirable. This is the Wanted poster's inherent contradiction, it presents the criminal as the portrait of moral ugliness that the state nevertheless needs and desires as symbolic currency. As art historian Rachel Hall points out, the Wanted poster shows the face of a criminal who has successfully avoided the eyes of the police—at least for the moment anyway.[33] But a poster declaring the villain's status as "Wanted" also demonstrates the vulnerability of this new disciplinary power. The Wanted poster is witness both of the domination of the state, and of its own vulnerability. The Wanted poster is not only a tool of surveillance, but also a report of its own functioning—an advertisement of "the one who got away."[34]

Walter Benjamin's essay "Critique of Violence" argues that public admiration for the great criminal arises not in response to his deeds, but to the violence to which they bear witness: the violence of the state. The criminal's violence arouses, "even in defeat the sympathy of the mass against the law."[35] In Benjamin's analysis, the high profile criminal threatens the law by indirectly making a spectacle of the state's exclusive claim to violence—and I contend, the extent of its visual domination.

In this new inter/disciplinary system of state control over identity, besides individuals, certain texts (including both written texts and image-texts) could be marked as "unnamed-able," "unsay-able," "unvisualizable," "ineffable," or demarcated as publicly useable only within specific state-approved parameters.[36]

Outlaw Signs:
The Control and Use of
Copyright installs a sense of legitimacy around specific texts, images, and cultural framings. Parallel to socially-legitimated identity emerges its reflection—the illegitimate or forbidden. An early explanation for this policing of signage comes from the work of Count Goblet d'Alviella, an eighteenth century semiologist who conducted research into the distribution and migration of sacred symbols. D'Alviella suggested that certain symbols were mutually exclusive, i.e. they could not appear in the same country or cultural sphere.[37] If the logo of a crown signifies the sovereign, no other visually-similar marker can be allowed to diminish the monarch's visual sovereignty. The use of similar kinds of sign in such a context would therefore through their very existence, interrupt an established frame of reference. Such a pattern can be noted in the Christianization of pre-existing pagan shrines.

Implicit in this either-or dynamic is the idea that from their first emergence in society, public signs hold a crucial role in dominant regimes that control language, establish agency, and guard territory. The appropriation of any given sign—legal or illegal—interrupts the social order that attempts to dominate the visual sphere.

A contemporary example illustrates how visual control is typically enacted in Western society. The use of the *Federal Express* logo is tightly controlled, and appropriating or misusing it, incurs a fine for theft of intellectual property. If a claim of trademark infringement submitted by *FedEx*, a fine is meted out by the state's legal system, and the offending visual is withdrawn from public display.

However, the appropriation of an uncopyrighted "outlaw" sign such as the red star RAF logo, the Black Panther logo, or for that matter, the Hell's Angels biker gang colors, creates a different kind of uneasiness, because another kind of social control surrounds these signs. Although the state or certain social groups may outlaw such signs at a certain time or place, no clear written ruling controls their use in other settings. Like many other culturally-indeterminate symbols, they are unprotected by legal means, but exist as loaded cultural markers. They exist as signs outside the state's law. But they still have specific understandings and connotations around their public use.

How do "outlaw" or terrorist signs establish themselves and operate as a heretical category amid a closely administered, legitimated, forest of signs?

In the 1970s, systems of communications such as television, newspapers, the underground press, or juridical documents helped to publicly define this type of signage.

Wider public use of these outlaw signs often begins in edge zones such as the underground press, university campuses, graffiti, rock festivals, tourist zones, art galleries, and most recently, the Web. These transitional or countercultural settings are where less-legitimate subject matter can more easily circulate. Border zones are by their nature porous and troublesome—subject to contestation and random policing. Such zones often become locations for struggle over linguistic meaning, and sometimes for an enactment of a discursive performativity.

In such settings, a certain type of mob rule consensus can still exert domain, where certain citizens feel entitled to publicly enact their own regimes of correction, denial, and punishment. Such elements do this (presumably) in the name of maintaining—even essentializing—their notion of respectful social and linguistic order.

This "misuse" of outlaw signs illustrates how a non-juridical control of the visual is enacted. Unlike the state-legitimated "FedEx" model of visual control, the unauthorized use of a terror logo or the Hell's Angels "colors" provokes a different kind of "forbidding" injunction from extra-legal forces —often enacted in a more random way via threats of physical violence from gang members, associates, rivals, or from "lobby groups."

A recent high-profile example of this extra-legal pattern of control around outlaw political signage occurred in June 2007. Hollywood actress Cameron Diaz found herself forced to make a public apology in the media on a trip to Peru for wearing an army green handbag with a red star and a Mao slogan in Chinese that read "Serve the People." To some in Peru, the bag and its slogan evoked painful memories of the Maoist Shining Path insurgency that fought the government in the 1980s and early 1990s in a bloody conflict that left nearly seventy thousand people dead.

According to the Associated Press, one prominent Peruvian writer claimed that "Diaz should have been a little more aware of local sensitivities when picking her accessories." Diaz was compelled to make a public statement to express her regrets for this unintended faux-pas: "I sincerely apologize to anyone I may have inadvertently offended. The bag was a purchase I made as a tourist in China and I did not realize the potentially hurtful nature of the slogan printed on it."[38] Her apology exemplifies how particular kinds of outlawed signage are conceived in the public domain, however unintentional or unknown their meaning to the wearer of such a sign. The Diaz story illustrates the way this pattern of random social policing of outlaw signage occurs. Although renegade signs are not usually controlled directly by legal means, they are patrolled by other forces (i.e. the general public and lobby groups).

In the blame storm of social policing swirling around taboo signs, terror group logos (such as that of the RAF) exist on the fringe of the visual field due to their potentially-problematic, banished, interstitial, and/or redundant status. In his seminal 1936 essay "The Work of Art in the Age of Mechanical Reproducibility," Walter Benjamin famously argued that lesser-viewed signs retain a greater level of "aura" [39] —associative social power—due to their rareness of public display. Benjamin argues that controls exist in the visual field which influence the use of these kinds of "exceptional" signs. But, he adds, mechanical reproduction is a liberatory force, [40] that the new age of print technology will refigure all existing social relations, and liberate the use of such signs.

Three Dominant Visual Systems: The State, Industry, and the Media

Contrary to Benjamin's claim, I argue that the twentieth century has been marked not by a liberatory struggle, but by a power shift between monarchical power and less-explicitly hierarchical forces invested in technological reproducibility for commercial gain—such as industry. And this reshuffling of power is most explicitly enacted in the field of visuality. [41]

The monarchical display of power in earlier centuries indicated visual sovereignty—a sign of civic order unchallenged and undisputed. Such a visual display is performative, and is manifest through public rituals such as the state parade, the political rally, the royal wedding, or the demonstration. Historically these types of events establish or re-assert the dominant force in control of the visual field. But after the Industrial Revolution, a shift in the existing economic relations emerged due to the impact of technological reproduction. Independent economic forces began to vie with the state's monopoly for control of public visual space. As a number of theorists have noted, the impact of industrial revolutions, mass reproduction, and advertising create vast new parameters for dissemination.

New forms of production produce unforeseen distribution possibilities with new technologies to dominate markets, and in marketing, the ability to go global and "colonize" economic markets in an entirely new, less explicitly domineering way than the European imperial model. This challenge to monarchical domination over the visual field is illustrated by the growth of the advertising business in the wake of the Industrial Revolution and in its use of the visual landscape to establish and develop the consumer market.

To further explain this shift in power relations in the visual field, it is helpful to relate these patterns to the social analyses of British sociologist Raymond Williams. He claims that since the Modern Era there is no single dominant ideological formation, but rather a range of competing discourses that define the social sphere. Williams draws distinctions between "residual" ideological formations (ideologies that have been mostly superceded but still circulate in various ways); "emergent" ideological formations (new ideologies that are in the process of establishing their influence); and "dominant" ideological formations (what Louis Althusser termed "ideological state apparatuses"; e.g. schools, government, the police, and the military).[42]

In relation to Williams' analysis, we can conceive of the refiguring of power relations in the post-World-War-Two period as a triangulated struggle for dominance between state, media, and the corporate. During this period, other challenges to the state's domination of the visual field emerged. The development of the news industry during the post-war era can be mapped in parallel to the explosion of commodity culture.

The challenge to the visual dominance of older monarchical systems is exemplified by the emergence of mass media news systems in the second half of the twentieth century. Since the 1960s, there has been an immense growth in the role of both television and the tabloid press in shaping public opinion.

Historian Cori E. Dauber notes television's crucial role in shaping public conceptions, the impact of live television footage in the later 1960s, and how it affected U.S. government 's involvement in the Vietnam War:

> It is…believed that the unprecedented freedom of the press to roam the combat zone at will, to publish or air images with little outside interference, and the status of Vietnam as the first "living room war" contributed to that erosion (of public opinion). For the first time, it is argued, members of the American public saw for themselves…what it was that really happened when we sent young men into battle.[43]

Due to the deregulatory effects of new technological systems like television, the U.S. government was caught off-guard in the Vietnam conflict. The constant flow of gruesome images flooding back from Vietnam is generally accepted as one of the main contributing factors for the public backlash that ultimately led to the withdrawal of U.S. troops in 1974. What this pattern shows us is the way that new technological industries refigured social relations, and developed a new discursive language. However, as Chomsky, Herman and O'Sullivan have noted, the state itself later became more adept at controlling this new discursive forum.

The growing importance of systems such as television, radio, and print news media post-World War Two has led to patterns where all information was increasingly disseminated through massive "mediating" systems. Over the past fifty years, these "top-down" systems have developed nuanced discursive modes of morphing public opinion.

Under such a system, a visual signifying an outlaw identity—such as a terror logo—may enter the arena of news coverage, but it is (re)presented in this forum in a very specific way. As we have earlier seen, a "guerrilla" logo is never an officially legitimated visual marker. But due to new technological developments and framing systems, since the 1970s, terror group logos including those of the RAF, the Brigate Rosse, ETA, Hamas, and Hezbollah often appear on mainstream television and in newspapers. These logos are used to signal "quasi-legitimate" public entities. Through news media use, these logos become widely understood as a type of political signage associated with a particular type of identity outside the law.

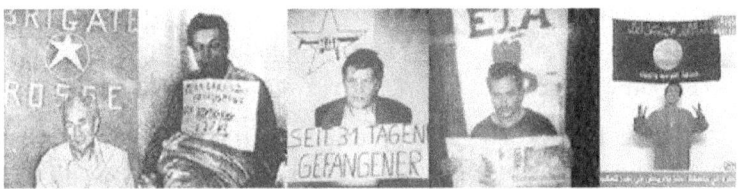

Fig. 10. (left-right) Kidnap Victims with Terror Group Logos: Aldo Moro, kidnap victim with Brigate Rosse logo 1978; Peter Lorenz, Bewegung 2.Junl kldnup victim with group name 1976; Hans-Martin Schleyer, kidnap victim with RAF logo, 1977; ETA kidnap victim with logo 1990s; Iraq kidnap victim with Islamic group logo, 2004.

The RAF logo often appeared in the news media of the Seventies, but within the context of a larger framing construct. The group's logo was displayed as a backdrop in television and newspaper coverage of hostage stories and arrests. In such an arena, the logo becomes synecdochal for the terrorist's ideology, a particular group of "Wanted" persons, and a specific psycho/geography. The logo was heavily programmed—but it was used within specific media structurations where this display of alterity is closely interpreted by the position of the news channel.

Similar to media's use of the swastika sign, a terror logo is coded as notorious and usable only within a particular contextual framing. The media's presentation of the terrorist identity thus both establishes its public presence and also quarantines its perception in further discourse. Although the terror logo retains some of its outlaw understandings, now through television and newspaper coverage, it develops increasingly as a loose signifier, subject to a wider range of interpretations. As soon as this kind of sign moves into wider arenas of public circulation, it becomes subject to freer play and it starts to lose power as semantic slippage occurs around its usage and understandings.

To conclude, this chapter has focused on three aspects to the history of the RAF's logo. The first section looked at the genetics of Leftist visual markers. The second considered the rhetoric of Holger Meins' poster "Freiheit für alle Gefangenen" and issues concerning copyright and identity control. Lastly, this chapter discussed the media's framing and reframing of outlaw signage.

The aforementioned dynamics illustrate the complex linguistic patterns and histories that shape understandings of outlaw political identity. Because of the contexts in which Leftist signs first emerged, I argue that the RAF's visual identity was from its birth an entroubled signifier—one that was hybridized and interstitial due to the political and linguistic operations that surround its referents. This complex background has led to the understanding of the RAF logo as a densely-loaded signifier, somewhat unclear.

Further questions remains in this pre-history of RAF imagery. What occurs over a longer time as the RAF identity moves into broader public settings, and what happens to particular types of underground signs as they enter larger communication systems? As I have suggested, television and the newspapers in the 1970s crucially shaped the initial public conceptions of this oppositional group's identity. An example of the free play that emerges around such a Leftist sign is illustrated by the history surrounding Che Guevara's image.

The following chapter considers socio-cultural tendencies that emerged around Che. As we will later see, what happens with Guevara´s image is similar to patterns that occurred around the RAF´s identity.

[1] Robert Storr, *Gerhard Richter: October 18th 1977,* p.54
[2] Several others also claim authorship of this logo. It becomes a hard point to prove.
re. Baader and von Czettritz and the RAF logo design,
http://www.taz.de/index.php?id=archivseite&dig=2003/04/12/a0229
[3] For a larger discussion of other groups active in West Germany during the 1960s and 1970s, see Varon, p.200-213, Baumann, Peters.
[4] re. Baader's journalistic career, see *Bild* Friday, June 2nd 1972, as displayed in Biesenbach. p.101.
[5] re. Meinhof and Meins' media connections are widely cited, for example, Varon, p.20, p.39.
[6] As likewise, did Hitler and the Nazis, through their choice of visually-hypnotic signs such as the swastika.
[7] It is also important to note the specifically German subtexts to these narratives. There is a connection between some RAF imagery and public images associated with recent national history. Within West Germany, in the context of the Berlin Wall, these narratives relate to National Socialism, concentration camps, national treason and national upheaval. However, these themes are not the focus of this chapter. These domestic, national connections in RAF visuals are explored further in Chapter Three.

[8] The Minutemen was originally the name given to teams of men from the Massachusetts militia in the eighteenth century, who vowed to be ready for battle at a minute's notice. This name has also been associated with a far-right U.S. militia groups active since the 1960s particularly concerned with issues of immigration and illegal border-crossing. See Garry Wills. (1999). *A Necessary Evil: A History of American Distrust of Government*, p.33. New York, NY; Simon & Schuster.

[9] The Black Panther group's "running panther" logo joins a language of signage related to that of sports product brand logo Puma (formed in 1948 in West Germany).
[10] Khvostov, p.32.
[11] During this period Leftist identity also developed as a subject for satire and was subject to loose associative projections within right-wing newspapers. Although even in this context of disparagement, this "Leftist" identity itself is acknowledged.
[12] Ibid.
[13] These are the youth (the future generations), the military (to protect and defend socialism), industrial workers (laborers), agricultural workers (peasantry), and the intelligentsia (to criticize and to improve the ideas and practices of life in order to attain communism). Ibid.

[14] A Russian proverb says that «*красивий — самы красный*» («the more red, the better»). Thus Moscow's Red Square has a double meaning, referring not just to its color but also meaning "Beautiful Square." Furthermore, the most important Russian Orthodox festivity is the so-called Red Easter, when the priests wear red vestments. http://www.crwflags.com/fotw/flags/su.html

[15] Ibid.

[16] One might argue that regardless of color, the eye-catching formal qualities and shape of the star already suggest these particular associations. Its geometric form implies the shining, the heavenly or "star-dom". The star shape intrinsically installs a semantic connection with the special, the remarkable or the celebrated, making it an apt symbol of the avant-gardist or the rupturous. Its "special" form seems much at odds with it as a "red star" to signify the "universal equality" of Communism. As a sign for Communism, the red star has a trace of cognitive dissonance.

[17] http://www.crwflags.com/fotw/flags/su.html Victor Lomantsov.

[18] A quote in German from page 1 of Marx and Engels' *The Communist Manifesto*, "Workers of the world unite".

[19] Varon has cited that the Berlin-based underground magazine *883* was sued in 1970 for the publication for reproducing this Meins poster. During Goldsworthy's paper "Revolt into Style: Images of West German "Terrorism" from 1968 to 1977" at Drew University's "1968: Global Resistance /Local Knowledge" conference.

[20] From *Vorwarts bis zum nieder mit.* p.43.

[21] Citing here the famous Mao's line "Let a thousand flowers bloom."

[22] This point draws from p.4, Davis. *More than a Name: An Introduction to Branding.* Lausanne: AVA, 2006.

[23] This Levi-Strauss quotation drawn from by Berger, p.86.

[24] Reference for Statute of Anne, http://www.copyrighthistory.com/anne.html

[25] Berne Convention. http://www.law.cornell.edu/treaties/berne/overview.html

[26] From Ariana Hernandez-Reguant. *Copyrighting Che: Art and Authorship under Cuban Late Socialism* in *Public Culture*, Duke U P. Vol.16. No.1. Winter 2004. p.9.

[27] Recent legal cases by McDonalds include:
http://internationaltrade.suite101.com/article.cfm/mcdonald_s_sues_copycats

[28] It is important to note here how photographic print imagery develops as a key discursive regime of Modernity. The photographic image is used to police visuality, and yet also simultaneously itself subject to policing, through copyright control and other similar systems of linguistic control. The print photograph is used as part of a complex linguistic and institutional system that both controls its subject and reflexively records its own functioning. The photographic image is both subjectifier of an object, or body, its object of

vision, and itself subject to sovereign power. Related to this, Foucault's "The Author Function" (1970) talks about the history of language and the development of the literary author in relation to punishment. He writes about the period prior the end of the eighteenth and beginning of the nineteenth century when a system of ownership and strict copyright rules were established: "(books or texts') status as property is historically secondary to the penal code controlling its appropriation. Speeches and books were assigned real authors, other than mythical or important religious figures, only when the author became subject to punishment and to the extent that his discourse was considered transgressive." Foucault here suggests the emerging conception of author as individual voice brings into play the issue of control. From Michel Foucault, "What is an Author?" (1969). Trans. Donald F. Bouchard and Sherry Simon. In *Language, Counter-Memory, Practice*. Ed. Donald F. Bouchard. Ithaca, New York: Cornell University Press, 1977. p.124-127.

[29] John Tagg, 1993, p.5. This framing draws from Rachel Hall, p.20.

[30] I am here borrowing Friedrich Kittler's term.

[31] It is important to note that there is a connection between categories of signs defined in the public imaginary as "evil" (i.e. the occult, the taboo, the inhuman) and the development of such a coding through an institutional image category such as the police "mugshot." How do these signs accrue meaning and shift association in the public imaginary? Although on a formal level these two semantic categories are coded separately, can they be differentiated as discrete, or have they become increasingly intertwined in the public imagination?

[32] Of related note here is Warhol's 1964 World's Fair mural artwork, "Ten Wanted Men" and how Warhol's "presences" the constructedness of this image category, through his re-contextualizing and code-switching this imagery through the World's Fair setting. In his book "Outlaw Representations" art historian Richard Meyer discusses the withdrawal of the piece soon after its installation. We can note here the forbidding injunction of the state concerning the public "unvisualizability" of these images outside state control. Similarly there is a semantic connection between Warhol's installation and Richter's paintings of photographs of "state enemies" the RAF and of his uncle "Uncle Rudi' in Nazi uniform, works which de-contextualize and aestheticize these politically-troublesome subjects.

[33] This framing draws from Rachel Hall, p.10.

[34] Ibid.

[35] Benjamin "Critique of Violence," 1978. p.281. Cited by Rachel Hall, p.10.

[36] An example of this tendency, as W.J.T.Mitchell points out, is the "unvisualizability" of U.S. flag-draped coffins in American media reportage on the Iraq war. (Noted during his paper on visuality in the Visual Culture caucus at the College Art Association conference in New York, February 2007).

[37] An example of this pattern concerns the lightning symbol. Fascists in all parts of the world appear to have been in one way or another fascinated by the lighting flash symbol —the ideogram for lightning. Some philologists argue that this sign emerged because this is a symbol for the s-sound in the runic alphabet it has become associated in Germanic countries with sun, strength, victory, words which all began with an S in the Germanic languages. However, during the 1970s, pirate discourses emerged around these fascist signs. In Britain, rock musician David Bowie in 1973, and in the USA the Grateful Dead in 1969 both (inadvertently or not) apropriated logos somewhat similar to the red on black "lighting flash" logo used by Oswald Mosley's 1930s British fascism movement. Both these high-visibility uses refigure public associations with this type of rightist logo.

[38] http://movies.msn.com/movies/article.aspx?news=266698

[39] Benjamin notes "Art in the Age of Mechanical Reproduction" in this regard: "The uniqueness of a work of art is inseparable from its being imbedded in the fabric of tradition. An ancient statue of Venus, for example, stood in a different traditional context with the Greeks, who made it an object of veneration, than with the clerics of the Middle Ages, who viewed it as an ominous idol. Both of them, however, were equally confronted with its uniqueness, that is, its aura." "the earliest art works originated in the service of a ritual — first the magical, then the religious kind. It is significant that the existence of the work of art with reference to its aura is never entirely separated from its ritual function. In other words, the unique value of the "authentic" work of art has its basis in ritual, the location of its original use value. (IV).

[40] Regarding this shift, Benjamin also notes in "Art in the Age of Mechanical Reproduction" that "the masses" changed their perception of themselves. He writes that this shift "began with the daily press opening to its readers space for "letters to the editor." And today there is hardly a gainfully employed European who could not, in principle, find an opportunity to publish somewhere or other ... Thus, the distinction between author and public is about to lose its basic character. ...At any moment the reader is ready to turn into a writer." (V). Benjamin here draws a direct correlation between the development of mass industrial production and the liberating opportunity and commencement of a mass audience to then turn from readers into writers. In the age of mechanical reproduction, anyone can be a cultural producer.

[41] An example of the hypnotic semantic power of such massive symbolic display were the Nazi rallies in Nuremberg in the early 1930s, through the use of the repetition of particular signs and visual configurations, as shown on film in Leni Riefenstahl' *Triumph des Willens* (1934).

[42] Jameson, *Postmodernism. p.6.*

Chapter III

CLONING CHE

In the post-World-War-Two period, alliances developed between Communist states, anti-imperialist movements and those who thought the time was ripe for global Leftist revolution. In this context, Left-wing signage was often incorporated into a broad anti-colonial rhetoric related to specific geographies. Such a pattern was particularly true during this era in relation to South East Asia and Latin America, and most specifically to Cuba and Vietnam, where the image of the "revolutionary face" was often used in public signage as metonymic for a larger struggle.

An iconic face can fulfill a role that no logo can. A face can communicate revolutionary idealism and/or martyrdom. More effectively than any traditional "crest-type" or star, the face logo can establish a more personal connection, and engage specific narratives and demographics. Ideologies can appear more persuasive and personalized when they are embodied by an identity. Unlike the Wanted poster, which has more complex and ambivalent associations, a face on a political poster can be used to identify and mobilize movements around an ideology. In the Leftist canon, graphic designs featuring the face of Marx, Lenin or Mao rendered in stark form on propaganda posters or flags have cast these figures as heroic icons of worldwide revolution.

A key example of this Leftist "face-logo" is the internationally-known image of Argentinian-born revolutionary Ernesto "Che" Guevara, taken in Havana in 1960 by Alessandro Korda. Why should this occur with Che at this temporal juncture, and how did this develop as the archetype of the Cold War Leftist rebel? Che's romantic outlaw legend developed an almost a mythic quality. The construction and development of Che's public image is important to consider because it became the blueprint for the presentation of many other later political outlaw icons of the era, such as the RAF.[1]

The History of Image Che
The famous photograph of Che was taken by Alessandro Korda at a state event in 1960. It was to immortalize Che in a beret with a red star as the archetypal Leftist "guerrilla" fighter. Although there are many iconic images of Che, this photograph became the most famous because of its timing and also because of the strange circumstances of its early public dissemination. The history surrounding the dissemination of this image reveals much about patterns and channels of circulation of Leftist imagery during this era.

Historians David Kunzle and Trisha Ziff have both documented the history and transnational migration of the Korda image. Ziff notes that the Italian radical publisher Giangiacomo Feltrinelli became a key figure in initiating the public dissemination of this image. When Feltrinelli visited Korda's studio in Havana in the early 1960s, Korda gave him a small copy of his Che photograph as a gift. Back in Italy in 1967 a month after Che's death, Feltrinelli blew up and cropped Korda's image and reproduced it as a two-color silkscreen large-run poster. He did this without Korda's permission. Feltrinelli wheatpasted these posters free throughout various Italian cities in public spaces, and likewise in Paris during May 1968.[2]

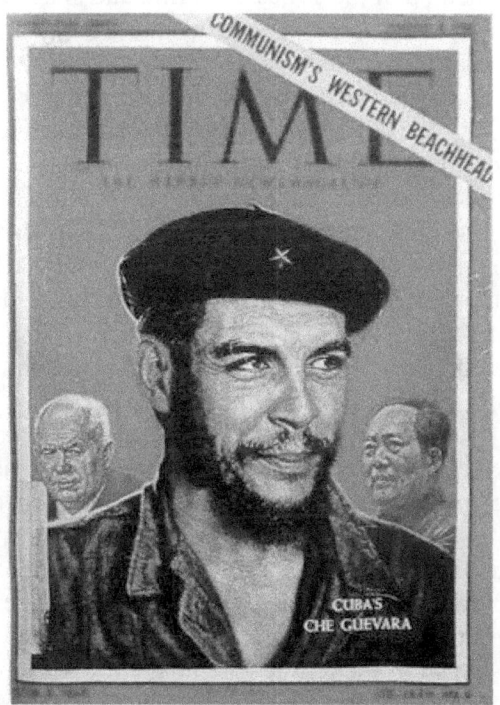

Fig. 11. "Cuba's Che Guevara," Time magazine cover, 1960.

In such a charged political climate, Che's image, mysterious and powerful, spoke with a language of revolutionary fervor across borders and time. Its meaning in such contexts was not explicit. It marked an identity that was mythic and unclear, something akin to the mark of Zorro. But, beyond disseminating this mythic identity, can we explain other reasons why Che posters based on the Korda image such as Feltrinelli's, made this image become and remain so resonant as a public image?

Designer Nick Bell gives a revealing insight into the natural suitability of Che's image to the print technology of the era: "Converted into a stark black cut-out, Korda's photograph became easy, cheap and superfast to copy using the favored material and method of the 1960s: Lith film and silkscreening."[3] Bell points out here that the popular medium of the era affects the specific types of icons that gain currency.

Bell adds that "Had Che Guevara been murdered in the airbrushed '70s, his face might not have made such a lasting, iconic image." The graphic punch of the Korda Che image made it the ideal subject for Lithography. Photo-lithography and silkscreen using photographic imagery on both canvas and paper developed popularity in the fine art world in the 1960s in the Pop Art movement, particularly through the work of Warhol and Rauschenberg.

Emerging print technologies such as Lith film or mimeographic printing, were quickly adopted by Leftist movements in the 1960s for their speed and budgetary ease. Suddenly, even grassroots activists could print graphically-commanding posters to disseminate their dream of anti-imperialistic revolution. Feltrinelli's image and similar posters of Che promoted (and joined) a pre-eminent linguistic style in Leftist iconography, which was stark, crude, idealistic, iconic, and above all, masculinist.

The spread of the pin-up Che image reveals how newer printing processes, and the Leftist tradition of self-legitimating appropriation "in the name of the revolutionary struggle," allows a key countercultural icon to develop currency as a free-floating signifier, loosely denoting the "Radical Left." Acts such as Feltrinelli's established Che as a key "Face of the Revolution" within a larger Leftist economy of images. But an important detail to note is that Feltrinelli released his Che poster under his own copyright name, giving no credit to Korda. Feltrinelli then died in mysterious circumstances not long after.

Due to such piratical patterns, the famous Korda Che image was from its inception orphaned, ubiquitous, and seemingly unclear in legal status.

The circumstances surrounding Korda's image and the Feltrinelli poster copy raise issues of authorization and copyright similar to those mentioned earlier in relation to Leftist signs, and to the 1970 Holger Meins "Freiheit fur alle Gefangenen" poster. As all these cases show, key Leftist identities remain subject to wide play, and to subject piracy within broader image-text economies due to their moral/ uncopyrighted status.

Through appropriations like Feltrinelli's poster, Che's image and story begin to be widely disseminated in the late 1960s from city walls to college dorms. Added to this, state propaganda campaigns such as Cuba's "Organization in Solidarity with the Peoples of Asia, Africa and Latin America" (OSPAAAL), produced a large number of images of Che, which OSPAAAL circulated worldwide. These Cuban government-supported poster magazines were distributed via various independent channels throughout Western Europe and the States, and appeared across campuses internationally during this period.

Che in the Cold War

The question at hand here concerns control of an image's meaning, and what framing encompasses, embodies and evacuates. The image of the Latin-American martyr of the Communist anti-colonial movement (who died at the hand of undercover CIA agents in Bolivia), takes its position in public discourse as a major signifier of "the Leftist struggle." Did the wide adoption of the image of the dead heroic Che, as the metonym sine-qua-non of the "Revolution" occur in the Cold War context because of appropriations like Feltrinelli's or because of its political convenience? A confluence of elements contribute to this pattern.

In the Communist canon, Che updates the pantheon of Leftist revolutionary icons who preceded him—such as Marx, Lenin, and Mao or Vietcong leader Ho Chi Min. But Che renders a new paradigm in this canon of Leftist icons. Whereas earlier "Faces of the Revolution" who preceded him were ruling powers, ideologues and orators, Che is a folk hero—a man of action not words. He updates this pantheon to produce the more glamorous figure of the 1960s "guerrilla" revolutionary. He endorses "propaganda through the deed" rather than word. In the production of Che as a key Leftist icon, there is a shift from specific geographies and ideologies, toward the global, toward a more mythic status and narrative. Although Mao's Long March was part of his populist mythos, it was his Little Red Book that really disseminated Mao's ideas worldwide. But it is Che's photogenic magnetism rather than his words that captured the public eye. His redoubtable courageous gaze seems to advertise the authentic spirit of the "true" revolutionary.

This semantic shift is emblematic of a key change within Leftist circles during the late 1960s, from a verbal to a visual/non-verbal discursivity. Parallel with Che's image dissemination, there was a shift in strategy worldwide within younger Leftist circles from theorizing revolution to practicing it through the urban guerrilla ethos. This tendency during the period can be recognized through the prevalent use of images of guns in Leftist group logos—such as that of the RAF in 1970—and also in their linguistic rhetoric. The vocabulary for describing the Left expanded to include the radical Left, the militant Left, and now also, the urban guerrilla—the latter re-labeled by the Western media as the "terrorist."
After Che's death in 1967, his image reached global coverage due to its specific temporal juncture in the Cold War. Beyond the Communist pantheon, over time "Che" develops as an icon of nostalgia, associated with myths of the young dead Jesus and of a tragic idealistic death. Che's legend creates in its wake many visual echoes. "Che"'s *identity* seems reminiscent of romantic narratives associated with folk archetypes—spectral

figures like Zorro or Robin Hood who return in a crisis situation to exert social justice and then disappear, leaving only their visual markers. The Che myth disseminates the idea, first and foremost, that a true Leftist guerrilla should die tragically —a subtextual narrative that already establishes a romantic trace within his legend.

How did Che's legend impact public conception of the RAF? Due to the posthumous display of his poster on a million college dorm walls, Che's identity has become entwined in broader populist narratives, like those of glamorous outlaws, martyred saints or tragic U.S. icons like Martin Luther King, James Dean, or Marilyn Monroe, a star that burned so brightly but extinguished itself too soon, leaving only its beautiful visual trace, an iconic after-image.

In such contexts, Che's image often becomes inked with more nebulous ideas of freedom, outlaw status and rebellion, rather than with genuine political praxis. To the younger and less-informed, Che's Leftist guerrilla identity was easy to confuse with reckless romantic "live fast, die young" fantasies similar to those projected around 1930s bank-robbing fugitives Bonnie and Clyde (whose story became a major Hollywood movie in 1967).

As noted, 19th century worker movements and 1920s Communists both generated catalogs of images and a visual grammar that developed wider public currency. These signs became widely established in public discourse as associative markers and reference points. 1960s Leftist movements adapted some of these signs and introduced further signifiers, employing new iconic faces such as Che's, or gestural poses, such as the clenched fist—to update the transcontinental language of radicalism. This new lexicon of imagery gains currency through its presence in emerging communications systems.

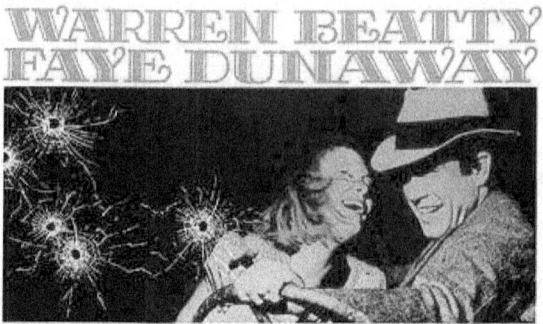

They're young... they're in love

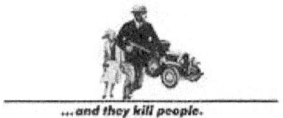

...and they kill people.

BONNIE AND CLYDE

MICHAEL J. POLLARD · GENE HACKMAN · ESTELLE PARSONS

TECHNICOLOR® FROM WARNER BROS.- SEVEN ARTS

Fig. 12. Movie poster for "Bonnie and Clyde" 1966.

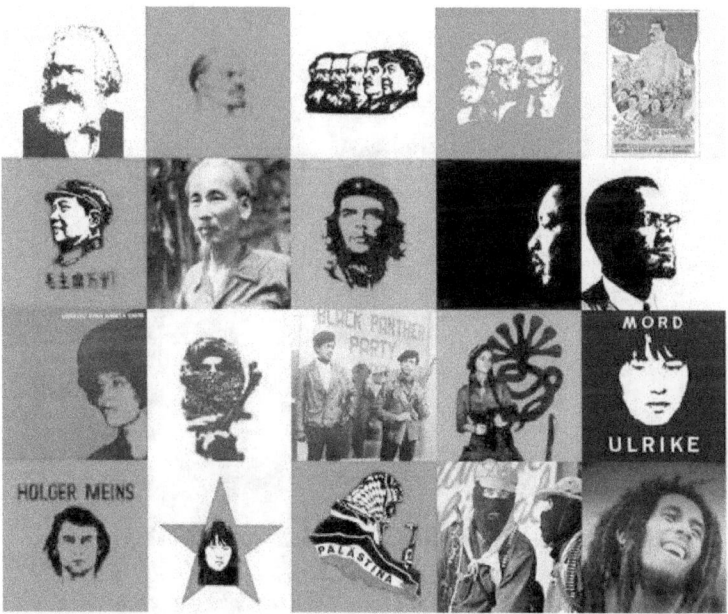

Fig. 13. Leftist and Third World icons from the1800s to the present: (Left to right, top to bottom): Marx; Lenin; Leftist pantheon featuring Mao and Stalin;, Marx, Engels, Lenin; Stalin; Mao, Ho Chi Minh; Che Guevara; Martin Luther King; Malcolm X; Angela Davis; unknown Palestinian figure; the Black Panthers 1968; Patty Hearst in 1974; Ulrike Meinhof, 1970s; Holger Meins, 1974; Ulrike Meinhof star; German pro-Palestinian poster;1970s;Subcommandante Marcos of the EZNL, 1995; Bob Marley, 1980.

These signs move across geographical terrain during the late 1960s via both the underground political press and television. In media coverage of radicalism in the wake of Che, there is a developing currency of Che-related symbols such as the beret, the raised fist, the raised cigar, and of a "revolutionary pose" rendered in stark iconic form to signal the new Leftist rebel. This archetype is not a man of words, his likeness embodies the spirit of the revolution, and his ethic is "Propaganda by the deed."

60

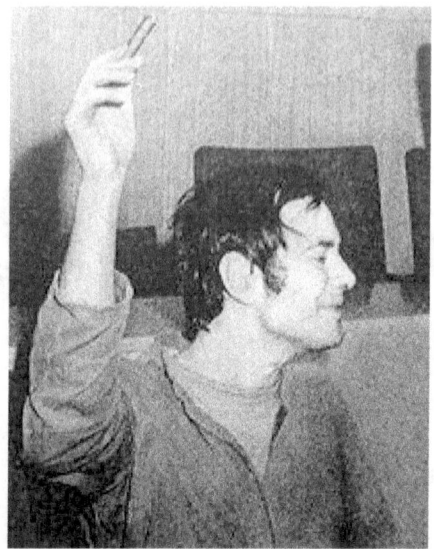

Fig. 14. Andreas Baader in court in Frankfurt in 1968, on Vietnam-related arson charges. Note the raised cigar gesture à la Che. (From Der Spiegel magazine, May 1970).

Visual Rhetoric and Leftist Icons

Although most Left visuals remain free-floating in the public domain, as critical mass is attained, iconic figures—such as Che—become metonymic for broader ideas and move into wider systems of economic exchange.

Since Che's death in 1967, Korda's photograph is relentlessly employed in pop culture, entertainment industries, and publishing to wordlessly conjure up the zeitgeist of the 1960s. Like 1960s Beatle imagery, the Korda "Che" now appears emblematic for a spirit of utopian idealism, rather than any specific Marxist agenda. Complex realities and much broader socio-cultural narratives are sewn together in specific eye-catching iconic figures used to signify an era. As we can note from the patterns developed around the early dissemination of Korda's Che image, these types of iconic "Leftist" signs enter a global level of visibility through their migration from grassroots campaigns into larger systems of commerce and cultural play.

Che emerges during the late Sixties as a symbol of global revolution. Just as Mao declared "Let a thousand flowers bloom," Che's archetype appears in its wake to generate a wave of visually similar icons, who likewise seem bent on violent revolution.[4] In the Cold War context, Che's image was deployed in the Western media to signal a specific type of Leftist rebel identity. During this era, further catalogs of figures emerged in the press who were presented in a way similar to the "Che" archetype. Such icons in the U.S. news included the Black Panthers, Angela Davis, the Weathermen, Jane Fonda, and Patty Hearst. In West Germany these figures were student leaders such as Rudi Dutschke, or later, terrorists such as the RAF. (This pattern in West Germany is discussed further in Chapter Four). In the Cold War climate, images of these figures were presented in various media forums in relation to endless stories of imminent Leftist revolution.

As Che's legend grew in relation to his imitators, critical mass reflectively developed around his mythic status. Whenever complex narratives emerge around a key symbol (like Che or the red star), its successors appear to solidify the original's semantic resonance retrospectively. What this pattern shows us is how once a "catchy" icon or story becomes established in public discourse, related ones often appear to emerge in its wake. At this juncture, due to such patterns, Che's image now appears as an Ur-symbol of the "Leftist revolutionary" vocabulary. His stature as THE archetype of the guerrilla martyr solidifies through patterns of replication.

Image Overkill: Che

Examples of patterns of replication around Che and other Leftist icons can be witnessed in visuals associated with black Civil Rights leaders in the U.S in the 1960s. One reason for some of this intertextuality is that Cuba's propaganda poster campaign OSPAAAL not only produced images of Che, but included many iconic black U.S. radicals of the 1960s. It should be noted that all these OSPAAAL posters share a similar "Che"-like, devotional, religious, and melancholic quality in their formal and stylistic representation—particularly of those considered martyrs, such as Martin Luther King, Malcolm X, and Angela Davis.

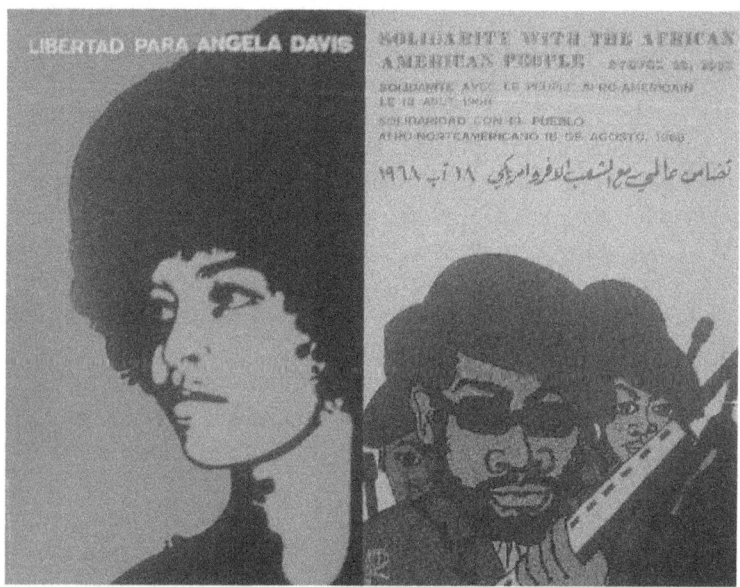

Fig. 15. OSPAAAL global solidarity posters from 1970 and 1968. "Freedom for Angela Davis" "Solidarity with the African-American People." Produced in Cuba.

It is revealing to compare the construct of Che's image —a state-endorsed, patriotic embodiment of the Cuban revolution—with those of figures from the U.S.'s black radical (non-state) movement during the same period.

Angela Davis, a militant black Communist, is a similarly visually iconic figure from this era. Tellingly, most American rebels (political or not) usually reach public visibility and notoriety via their Wanted posters. In 1969, Davis became internationally-known as a high-profile fugitive, involved in the Soledad case, (a controversial legal drama involving a courtroom shoot-out by two young black men). Implicated in the case for gun possession, Davis went on the run for two months, provoking international debate concerning her innocence. During her flight, Davis' FBI Wanted poster was disseminated nationwide. The FBI poster shows the young black activist with large Afro hairstyle and a defiant pose. This image of Davis shares some of the rhetorical punch of the Korda Che photograph. In her FBI mugshot, Davis' resolute face seems similarly to embody the "authentic" spirit of the revolutionary. She looks as telegenic as a pop star. She is in fact a political fugitive, pursued, and later jailed on dubious charges, which were later to be dismissed. During this time, images of Angela made her a globally-recognizable figure. This emergence as a high-profile Leftist icon is due to a confluence of forces, firstly the nationwide dissemination of her FBI Wanted poster and then the consequent television coverage of her arrest—but it is also due to Davis' natural photogenic qualities, to an OSPAAAL global solidarity poster and grassroots campaigns for her freedom. For all these reasons Davis' image became internationally recognizable—like Che— as a global symbol of Leftist revolt.

In relation to Walter Benjamin's writings on mass technological circulation (see Chapter Two), it is important to consider how long these types of visual icon can retain their politicized "aura." Most people at this point best remember Davis or Che's visuality, rather than their history or political ideas. Davis herself noted in 1994 of the later perception of her 1970s public image:

> It is both humiliating and humbling to discover
> that a single generation after the events that

constructed me as a public personality, I am remembered as a hairdo.[5]

The issue Davis alludes to here is how public conception of controversial political figures often becomes so contested, and so *decontextualized* that any coherent, generally-accepted association becomes hard to ascertain. Saturation coverage of global Leftist icons like Davis or Che makes them become over-determined subjects, evacuated of any earlier rhetorical association due to media and pop cultural overkill— objects that are seen but ignored, present but discursively invisible and/or exhausted. Due to the endless de-connotated pop-culch recycling of images of Che and Davis, a dumbing-down has occurred and their *identity* has become metonymic no longer for any political standpoint, but for the particular ideological impasse of the cultural Cold War—a world-historical moment from which no clear result or meaning appeared to emerge.[6]

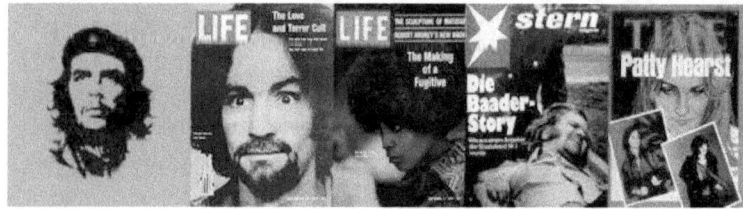

Fig. 16. Che and other 1970s Outlaw Icons: Che, 1967 courtesy Estate A.Korda, Charles Manson on LIFE magazine cover 1969, Angela Davis on LIFE magazine cover 1970, Andreas Baader on STERN magazine cover 1972, Patty Hearst on TIME magazine cover 1974.

In relation to the discussion of Che and Angela Davis' image-association and its "diminishing" return, a second tendency can also be noted that once a powerful symbol (understood as) signifying outlaw identity reaches a high level of public visibility, a cross-over occurs, less bona-fide representatives of the Leftist struggle appear to pick up or mimic the "authentic" lingua-franca associated with "sincere" guerrilla fighters like Che, Davis and the Panthers—to project a somewhat disingenuous embodiment of revolutionary zeal.

How are such Ur-symbols of revolution and terror defanged in the media? Terror theorists Herman and O'Sullivan discuss shifts in news formations in the 1970s and the emergence of the "terror industry" as a growth area within the media during this era. Within this system of "terror news" coverage, a particular visio-linguistic code for "radical" or "terrorist" develops.

Since the 1970s a stereotypical "terrorist story" journalistic style has developed, which is simple, direct and stark in style and palette. This presentation often uses the color coding of red and black. The urgency of this subject framing is further *signalled* by a font which is **bold**, `hard` and CAPITALIZED.

The spectrality of a terror act creates the public need to put a face to their deeds, to create a stereotype on whom to hang these horrific acts. There is a need to use the visual to mediate these traumatic events. Presentation and framing is curiously similar across a variety of Western countries during the Cold War, stereotypical archetypes of terrorist identities/identikits are introduced, the subject's clothing is militaristic and black, and like Che, they often wear a beret. The men are usually long-haired and bearded and wear a leather jacket, and the women sometimes pictured holding a gun. The terrorist figures are often portrayed in spectacular poses—their expressions defiant, or reflecting the pain of arrest or death. The entire graphic presentation communicates a direct rhetorical punch.

The Raised Fist: Media Hijack and Authenticity

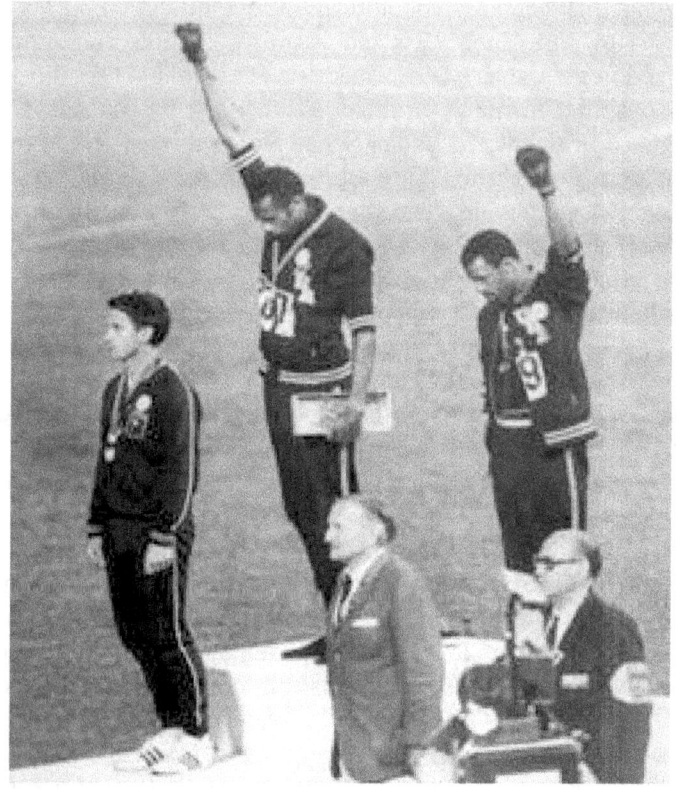

Fig. 18. The Raised Fist at the 1968 Mexico Olympics: U.S. athletes John Carlos and Tommie Smith after receiving their medals at the Olympic Games.

In an infamous image of the 1960s, African-American athletes John Carlos and Tommie Smith, are shown giving the "Black Power" salute with gloved fists as they receive their medals at the 1968 Mexico Olympic Games. In this shock media intervention, witnessed live worldwide, the athletes take the symbolic raised fist of the imprisoned martyr and bring it into the supposed non-political world of TV sport. This politic of gesture was to become emblematic of the "Black Power"

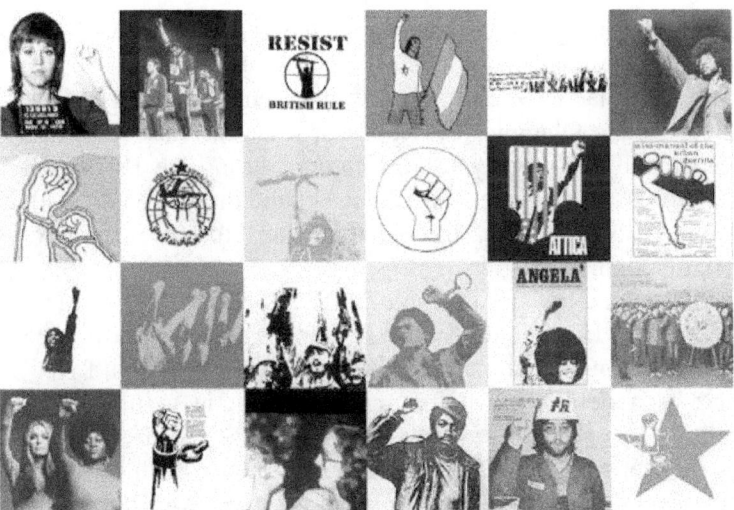

Fig. 17. The Raised Fist Gesture: Radicals and leftists giving the raised fist (left-right, top to bottom)- Jane Fonda in Cincinnati airport, 1970, US athletes at the 1968 Mexico Olympics, IRA graphic, 1980s, Belfast IRA solidarity mural, Shankill Road, !980s; U.S. underground magazine graphic "Rising up angry"; Angela Davis 1973?; Belfast mural in solidary with I.R.A. H-block prisoners, 1980s; Iranian Leftist group logo,circa late 1970s; Viet Cong poster used by Weather Underground, 1969, U.S; Rised fist graphic, Britain, mid-1970s;Attica prison solidarity poster,U.S, 1970s;Carlos Marghinella, Mini-Manual of the Urban Guerrilla, late 1960s, U.S; West German radical women's solidarity poster, 1970s; West German women prisoners solidarity poster, 1970s; Fidel Castro triumphant in Cuba, circa 1960; Black Panther Bobby Searle, U.S, 1968?; Angela Davis, "Portrait of a Revolutionary" book cover, Britain, 1971; Chinese Cultural Revolution, late 1960s, Beijing; Erica Jong? and Angela Davis, New York, early 1970s; Anti-colonial poster, South Africa, 1970s; Patty Hearst giving the raised fist gesture on her arrest, U.S.1975; Black Panther giving black power salute, late 1960s; John Lennon single "Power to the People," 1970; Prisoner solidarity logo, West Germany, 1970s.

movement. The "authenticity" of this image-byte bears some rhetorical similarity to the Korda Che photograph.

In the context of 1968, the athletes' gesture raised uproar. Smith stated at the time that the gesture was intended to draw attention to the Atlantic slave trade and the under-acknowledged history of black oppression in the U.S. It was "for those thrown off the side of the boats in the Middle

Passage."[7] This gesture of revolt was telegraphed worldwide via its media coverage.

The tactic of live "on-air" intervention used by black athletes at the Olympics developed broader currency for white radicals and controversy-seeking figures during the 1970s (i.e. for terrorists such as the SLA, the RAF, and the Brigate Rosse), as television became the predominant forum for news dissemination.[8] [9]

A famous later example is the notorious 1992 incident when young Irish singer Sinead O'Connor ripped up a picture of the Pope on US national television on "Saturday Night Live." There is a deliberate attempt in such a tactic to hijack the medium.

During the 1970s the political currency of this "raised fist" gesture soon starts to lose its semantic power due to an increasing inclusion in broader secular settings.

Two years after the Olympics scandal, even a white middle-class "celebrity rebel" such as actress Jane Fonda famously adopted the raised fist pose in a mugshot taken on her arrest in 1970 in Cincinnati airport for possession of prescription sleeping pills.

Likewise in 1975, kidnapped-heiress-turned-urban-guerrilla Patty Hearst is photographed taking the same stance on her arrest (—a gesture that Hearst then disavows in court very soon after).

Is there is a contextual shift between the genuinely shocking Black Power salute by the Olympics athletes in the context of 1968 in the "non-political" sports world, and the resonance of Fonda or Hearst posing for their arrest photographs, has the gesture now developed into a cliché? And if so, how does such a pattern occur?

In the late 1960s, Fonda's very public opposition to the Vietnam War was seized upon by the right-wing American media, who nicknamed her as the traitorous "Hanoi Jane." She was presented in the media as the embodiment of simplistic Hollywood liberalism. The actress, who had recently played sci-fi comic-strip rebel-heroine "Barbarella" (1966) in a movie, had now cast herself as a real-life revolutionary. A dialectic is established between these two image categories, the "authentic" (black) raised fist gesture, and that of white radicals such as Fonda who were considered by some to be exhibiting a synthetic defiant pose. [10]

The dialectical construct of Western media established between those considered genuine revolutionaries and those deemed inauthentic radicals seems to start to both distract from and debunk the whole notion of "Leftist revolution." A pattern of aestheticization of Leftist signifiers emerges around such over-determined media-oriented acts by Fonda, or other mainstream white radicals who appear to ape the "authentic" struggle of the Black Panthers and Che.[11] [12] The emulating of the *genuine* radical expression of the unarguably oppressed "Other" displaces the discourse of radicalism with a dialectic concerning authenticity. The discussion in play moves away from considerations of black oppression and resistance to what constitutes valid white political engagement. It switches to a distinctly less-threatening discourse concerning authenticity, or the lack thereof, of the privileged white liberal elite.

These patterns of aestheticization, often meaning-substitution and image-overkill start to confuse and deflate the resonance of any real or "serious" public Leftist visual identity in the 1970s. The loose rhetoric of Leftist imagery and its media framing conflate into a language and visual identity marked mostly by its sensational pose, understood as signaling the simplistic idealism of white middle class rebellion. (A pattern of re-programming and reloading of linguistic signs is similarly apparent in the re-use of RAF imagery in later eras).

Outlaw Imagery and Transcultural Drift

This chapter attempts to demark prevalent patterns in the history of Leftist imagery and "guerrilla" icons.[13] It considers their genealogy and their relation to historical shifts in the functioning of the visual. The text offers some visual precursors, paradigms, and antecedents that relate to the RAF's public image—figures and identities that were current in international Leftist milieus in the 1960s. A particular language of signage appeared to interpenetrate and mutate in meaning across geographies during this time to create a transnational, global lingua-franca understood as symbolizing an identity of Leftist radicalism—and later Leftist terrorism. These patterns are particularly apparent during this era in Leftist visuals in the U.S. and West Germany.

Across many other Western national contexts during the 1960s and 1970s, Communism provided an ideal ideological reference point on which to project the specter of imminent threat. In this period of the Cold War, Western media and state systems tried to define Leftist identity through vocabularies of *charged* iconic visual symbols, such as the red star or the image of Che. These ciphers were then used in media circuitry as emblematic of a mythic Leftist identity—an identity constructed predominantly as evil and dangerous, but also aestheticized, malleable and somewhat romanticized.

During an era of intense discursive contestation in the visual arena in the Cold War, many of these signs became *public* images, and around them much mythology grew. No one knew exactly what was meant, and further, this iconography meant many different things to different people based on its geo-contextual setting. For these kinds of reasons, such signs could become the focus of much projection, and in some cases, moral panic.

In the Seventies, a range of somewhat-vacuous Leftist signs seeped through mainstream national media systems and transnational underground propagandist networks. To some viewers, images of Che and Davis were avatars of rebellion for an era (envisaged by theorist Herbert Marcuse and termed the "Great Refusal")[14] when led by a renegade guerrilla element the whole of society would rise up and overthrow the repressive structures of industrialized state capitalism. Within such contexts, particular visual icons and aesthetics became emblematic of a grassroots radicalism. As we can see, groups such as the RAF appeared to adopt this underground visual rhetoric in the construction of their group's identity.

Parallel to such patterns, as illustrated by the history of the Feltrinelli Che poster or of images of Angela Davis and her hair politics, the unstable element of much Leftist "Radical" imagery gave it a tendency toward meaning-erasure, uncredited plagiarism, and debates around what constitutes authenticity.[15]

It has been necessary in this chapter to map and unpack the history of early Leftist signs. This backstory informs the imagery of the RAF in the 1970s. Emigratory tendencies were prevalent around Leftist imagery both during the late 1960s, and before and after. As we shall see in Chapter Four, in the West German context both the RAF and the media borrow from specific Leftist image-banks and a visual language that emerges from these milieus.

In the West German press as early as 1968, what was not yet happening at home could be drawn from contemporary image-libraries worldwide to build up a fantasy of Leftist terror growing in West Germany. This myth was generated in the media for a number of years before the RAF formed or any terrorist attack had begun.[16]

[1] As noted in Chapter One, images of left-wing *radicals* such as Che, are often assigned an esteemed place in culture. This framing of imagery becomes coded with specific types of nostalgic associations. This dissertation considers the ways in which imagery of particular Baader-Meinhof members have—like Che—become floating signifiers for rebellion, and also for nostalgia. I argue in this section that a better understanding of the history of the constructions and patterns of dissemination about Che's visuality and that of other particular 1960s countercultural icons, can provide us with a clearer perspective on similar tendencies that later occur around the RAF.

[2] Kunzle, p.56.

[3] Cited in Ziff, p.42.

[4] In Chapter Four we later witness the beginning of a similar Che-like "massifying' pattern around RAF-related imagery in the wake of Richter's painting series *October 18th 1977.*

[5] Angela Y. Davis. "Afro Images: Politics, Fashion, and Nostalgia," *Critical Inquiry.* Vol. 21, No. 1 (Autumn, 1994), pp. 37-39, 41-43 and 45. Davis discusses how she is remembered for the "arrested moments" of her featured in the popular press during the 1970s. Davis remarks that that the interpretive contexts in which contemporary spectators view these iconic photographs render her Afro hairstyle the most salient element of these images, "understood less as a political statement than as a fashion (1994, p.173). In the early 1990s, her hairstyle and general fashion sense were recycled as revolutionary glamour in a "docu-fashion" spread in *Vibe* magazine. Davis finds the spread disturbing for the way it empties the particular history of her legal case of content "so that it can serve as a commodified backdrop for advertising" 1994, p.177).

[6] Public figures like Che and Davis illustrate how in the Cold War context, particular founding archetypes were used by the media across a range of countries. These types of media uses had a broad cultural impact as a fabricated "other": the left-wing radical—the diametric opposite, the antithesis of bourgeois values—a threat to the capitalistic consumer lifestyle of post-War West. Over a longer period, the original images themselves have become decontextualized, abstracted, exhausted, evacuated of meaning and normalized through their continual public saturation, and through patterns of endless reproduction. Writing in 1990 in *Postmodernism,* theorist Frederic Jameson has talked of similar patterns in relation to what he terms the postmodern turn. Jameson argues that "non-Marxists and Marxists alike have come around to the general feeling that at some point following World War II a new kind of society began to emerge (variously described as postindustrial society, multinational capitalism, consumer society, media society and so forth). New types of consumption planned obsolescence: an ever more rapid rhythm of fashion and styling changes the penetration of advertising, television and the media generally to a hitherto unparalleled degree throughout society;" Relevant to our discussion of meaning slippage is the way the initial public construction of Che and Davis' imagery in the media is from its inception, by its nature, fractured and unstable, prone to rapid change

in political valence. Jameson's analysis frames our contemporary era as one where "the disappearance of a sense of history, the way in which our entire contemporary social system has little by little begun to lose its capacity to retain its own past, has begun to live in a perpetual present and in a perpetual change that obliterates traditions of the kind which all earlier social formations have had in one way or another to preserve. Think only of the media exhaustion of news: of how Nixon and, even more so, Kennedy are figures from a now distant past." By extension we can also here include radical icons like Che and Davis. Obsolence is an intrinsic aspect to contemporary communications systems and it often leaves these earlier visual icons as destabilized, emptied signifiers.

[7] Cited at http://www.famouspictures.org/mag/index.php?title=Black_Power
[8] We witness here how porous the medium of television is and how these kinds of interventions shift our perception and viewing of this medium. Yonah Alexander writes in "Terrorism, the Media and the Police" in *Terrorism: Threat, Reality, Response* (edited by R.H. Kupperman and D.M. Trent), Stanford, California: Hoover Institution Press, 1979. "Modern technology has provided terror groups groups with a critical communications instrument—the media—which willingly or unwillingly serves their specific or general propaganda and psychological warfare needs."
One can see in the 1968 Olympics scandal, within the forum of television an emerging pattern of the on-air political intervention. Famous later examples include the scandal surrounding the London punk band, the Sex Pistols swearing on an early evening chat show on British television in 1977. And also the on-screen flip-outs as often witnessed on national U.S. television since the 1990s, such as those on the "David Letterman Show" by Christian Slater, Madonna and others.
[9] A contemporary manifestation of a similar pattern is, as Murphy notes, "how grainy, low-resolution video images often shot in black and white now regularly alert the viewer to the fact that they are watching a representation of an unscripted and illicit performance." Murphy, p.15
[10] During this time the U.S. media continually lampooned Fonda's romanticized pose of "radicalism."
[11] The canonization of Che as the symbol de rigeur of the Leftist "Revolution" embodies him as a paradigm for the archetypal 1960s outlaw-rebel-martyr. But we also need to consider what other texts, other legends which inform the construction of the "Radical" and/or terrorist identity in the media during this era. The media's framing of the terrorist identity often alludes to archetypal figures within the public imaginary which include the bandit, the trickster, the criminal, the hunted, the "evil", the piratical, the stateless, the traitorous and the "inhuman". As both Campbell and Jung note, these mythic archetypes exist across a range of popular narratives as talismanic figures of misrule, lawlessness, vengeance, justice or the unresolvable. Many of these archetypal entities continue to be played out by the media in their presentation of particular figures in news stories. The U.S's media's representation of a figure

such as murderous cult leader Charles Manson in the late 1960s can be compared with that of a political figure like Che. There is a strong intertextuality between the conception of these two figures in the public imaginary. There is a shared visual grammar between the Korda Che image and photographs of Manson from 1969. Both bearded, long-haired, anti-establishment figures, perceived to be fugitives, surrounded by an outlaw group and involved in violent acts. Similar framings are deployed in the construction of these two public figures as the embodiment of the dangerous outlaw. As portrayed in the media, both figures seem to embody a total opposition to bourgeois normalcy. Although Che was clearly not identified with the hippie movement, those such as Manson, who were identified by the media as hippies, adopted a visual style similar to Che. They also had the scruffy beard, the straggling hair, the look of "all-or-nothing" utopian idealism and free-wheeling air. The media's portrayal of Manson fractures the image of the hippie as innocent and naïve figure. On his arrest in 1969, Manson was presented in the U.S. media as a messianic wild-man. Images of Manson used by the media during this time draw an eerie parallel between the aura of certitude and extremism of Che, Jesus and that of Manson. It is no chance coincidence that the media's representation and framing of Manson draw on such associations. A key event in this period was the gruesome murder of movie star Sharon Tate by the Manson family in 1969. This killing refigured global perception of the burgeoning hippie movement in the West. In the wake of the Tate-LaBrea murders, all hippies were re-cast in popular conceptions. No longer just cast by the media as harmless peace-loving communards, hippies, they were now seen in more sinister terms, as anti-social threats to civic order and potentially murderous cult members. At the time of the Tate-LaBrea murders, a *Los Angeles Times* reader Norman Howard pointed out in a letter to the editor regarding the Manson murders, that in the news youth groups were "stereotyped in popular prejudice as "hippies" and therefore murderers. It would be tragic if an inflamed public opinion now took vicious revenge against any young person classified as a "hippie," but I'm afraid the news media is contributing to just that end." Howard points out that the media's role in fanning the flames and skewering public opinion around margin social groups. Certain news agencies report such events in the most theatricalized terms. They present oppositional social groups (such as hippies or Leftists) in such stories to keep their audience's attention engaged with their constructed tabloid worldview. For these agencies during this era, a figure such as Manson plays out particular media fantasies that leads to a broader public consensus about youth behavior and control. In this forum, like a Greek tragedy enacted, the media villain is portrayed as a violent Oedipal child must symbolically be seen to be captured and imprisoned (and/or killed) for their transgression against the national and familial order. It is important to note that Che's image presents a visual archetype for many such figures. As we have seen, Che's outlaw stature is key to the media construction of many politically-oppositional figures, such as those of Manson and the RAF. These figures and media patterns around them

71d

fragment conceptions of radicals, and the understanding of Leftist outlaw identity.

[12] Stanley Cohen has discussed the media's influence on public opinion in *Folk Devils and Moral Panics: The Creation of the Mods and the Rockers.* Studying the media's depiction of two marginal British groups in the 1960s, Cohen argues that the rest of society received a distorted view of who they were and what they did. Since these groups were an "other," segregated from the rest, it was up to the media to define them and the picture they presented was distorted. By distorting the image of a fringe group, the media can create scapegoats for problems with which they may have little or nothing to do.

[13] Chapter Four draws visual connections between the global media's presentation of Che and Manson in the late 1960s with the contemporaneous West German right-wing media's representation of SDS leader Rudi Dutschke. Dutschke was vilified by the West German right-wing media empire Springer Verlag as the "Red Terror." Such a portrayal draws on these internationally-recognized figures like Che, Angela Davis or Manson as icons of revolt and disorder. In West Germany, the Springer Verlag intentionally misrepresented this moderate Leftist student leader as such a personality—a figure intent on outraging the bourgeoisie. It is important to consider the similarities between Manson's representation in the U.S. press, and the way a similar rhetoric was used in the West German media's vilification of Dutschke. Chapter Four discusses these patterns.

[14] The term "Great Refusal" is a term often used by Marcuse at the end of *One-Dimensional Man.*

[15] Chapter Four explores the exact geographies of the 1970s West German experience and the role of the visual in the constructed presentation and enactment of a domestic Leftist "terrorism." Through their terror campaigns, the RAF provided a local visual enactment, a domestic theatrical performance of global Cold War struggles and ideological strategies. These "enactments" were certainly framed in the West German media as part of an ongoing global wave of Leftist terror. We might describe such an interpretation of events as related to a Marxian Media Studies analysis, focussing on framing struggles in the field of the visual in relation to wider patterns associated with the rise of technology and mass society. Helpful as this model is, within a national context this type of reading tends to diminish some key aspect to the debacle. Given the complex history of Germany from the 1930s to the 1970s, the RAF terror phenomenon can also be viewed as enacting unresolvable psychic longings within the collective unconscious of a deeply scarred nation. A Freudian reading would interpret these events and the "weaponizing" of desire in relation to familial dynamics. Given the domestic (West German) media's tendency to "personalize" events and manipulate public opinion, this type of interpretation is useful to this study. Although the West Germany Leftist terror debacle was related to wider global events such as Vietnam, it was also driven by complex, specifically "German" narratives related to unresolved recent national history, uncovering Nazis still in power, and to deeper issues

72

concerning national identity, family, democracy and race. In the following chapter we focus more on the domestic aspect to the RAF debacle.

[16] There is a distinct difference between this earlier "pre-terror" warning period in the Cold War West German terror debacle and the 2001 Al Qaeda bombings termed "9/11." The West German media drew from a lexicon of other global 1960s news stories that influenced their negative coverage of Leftist student activism at home. When terror really did emerge in the early 1970s in West Germany, prior media coverage made it appear as if it were entirely to be expected.

Chapter IV

"DAS IST TERROR!":

VILLAIN IN POST-WAR WEST GERMAN PRESS

The Cold War was the first media war where propaganda battles between supposedly opposing political systems deployed media images with particular symbolic currency in a climate of political détente. Images of Che Guevara, the U.S.S.R's Sputnik, or dancer Nureyev's defection to the West competed in an "image war" with photographs of the U.S. moon landings, the "black power" salute at the 1968 Mexico Olympic Games, and the inauguration of a Polish Pope in Rome in 1978. All these images circulated in the public imaginary during the Cold War as Soviet and Western states and their citizens witnessed the effects that powerful photographs could have in morphing the mindsets of the masses. These propagandist images were disseminated through newspapers and television. Both capitalist and communist states were involved in this game of visual one-upmanship. Both types of regimes attempt through media display to present their systems as the most advanced.

This image war in divided Germany can be exemplified by two competing architectural statements in 1960s Berlin. With much fanfare and hype, the East German government built a 365-metre high Fernsehturm (television tower) in 1964-69, as a monumental symbol to Eastern Bloc technological advancement. Simultaneously in 1966, the West German conservative publishing giant, Springer Verlag, had a nineteen-storey gold glass-plated office monolith built within a few feet of the Berlin Wall—virtually opposite, *mirroring* the media transmitter tower—attempting to upstage it and to highlight the rich "freedom" of the media in non-Communist countries. Thus a capitalist news corporation symbolically and provocatively challenged "the power statement" of East German Communist technological progress.

The Cold War as an Image War: "Image is Everything"

The chapter in progress zooms in on the intimate relations between the West German media, the student movement, and the war of "terror images" played out within the media battlefield. I suggest that the 1970s terror debacle in West Germany was a negative propaganda campaign for both Leftists and for the government.

Beginning in the late 1960s, in the context of the Cold War, beyond architectural challenges, the conservative Springer Verlag began an intense campaign of anti-Leftist rhetoric in their newspapers. Springer's continuous invocation of the imminent threat of Leftist revolution during widespread Vietnam protests led to a confrontation that ultimately gave the state the permission to install huge new public surveillance regimes and create great losses of civil liberties.

The RAF developed over the 1970s as public enemy number one in the West German media. However, in most of the written histories of the RAF, conventional wisdom has underplayed the importance and centrality of the news media's role in this terror drama. There has instead been a strong emphasis in RAF studies on focusing on the lives of RAF members, the motivations for their bombing attacks or the cultural milieu from which they emerged.[1] Contrary to their emphasis on biography, I suggest that the RAF debacle was a planned series of media events.

Support for this argument comes from the testimony of Michael "Bommi" Baumann of West German terrorist movement "Bewegung 2.Juni," who in his 1975 autobiography, *Wie alles anfing,* stated that the RAF personally told him that a key element to their strategy was media intervention. Baader told him that "the revolution wont be built through political work, but through headlines."[2]

Through bombing, the RAF aimed to create media spectacles, promote a climate of terror, and a crisis in the state's visual authority. A further indication of this intent is that before joining the group, some members of the RAF had previously worked within the media themselves. Ulrike Meinhof was a prominent journalist, Andreas Baader was involved in Fassbinder's theatrical circle in Munich and had previous media experience, and filmmaker Holger Meins had made the incentiary 1968 film *Wie baue ich einen Molotow-Cocktail?* on making a Molotov cocktail.

It is time for new interpretation of the history of the RAF, by focusing on the relation between the RAF and the media in West Germany during this period, the media's goals in reporting the RAF's acts, and also the complex rhetoric of the media-orientated strategies of the RAF themselves. What does the media construct of terrorism reveal about this era and the visual procedures that emerge around such a terror group? I use these questions to explore and to pinpoint the interdependent relationship between media and terrorist group.

To unpack these complex dynamics, it is necessary to begin by considering post-war Germany's historical context. This chapter develops an argument around roles of visuality in a terror debacle and the "weaponization" of imagery. I discuss the West German media's *projections* around public villains and its portrayal of non-violent 1960s student leader Rudi Dutschke. I follow the trope of the RAF's innovative strategies of media intervention and focus on the media's role in a terror debacle. In post-war West Germany a struggle emerged in the 1960s between a conservative media conglomerate and the anti-Vietnam student movement. This led to a battle of violent symbolic display. To fully understand this process of events, it is necessary to briefly consider the historical and cultural settings from which 1970s West German terrorism emerged.

The Role of the Media in Society

Media theorist John Thompson argues that the systemic growth of the media has been an "integral part of the rise of modern societies."[3] He claims that the media is "constitutive and transformative" of Modernity, and its progress is complexly interwoven with all other major developments.

In order to understand the nature of Modernity—the institutional characteristics of modern societies and the life conditions created by them—it is crucial to analyze the growth of the media and its backstory. Thompson maps the "mediatization of culture"[4] which grew through the development of industries such as printing in the second half of the fifteenth century.[5]

It is relevant to consider in relation to Thompson's analysis, the earlier concepts of Italian theorist Antonio Gramsci, born 1891, on the role of culture and its maintaining of the "established order." Gramsci argues that society is dominated by a cultural elite who try to rule the rest of the community. For society to run smoothly it is necessary that the majority acquiesce to their own cultural domination. In a Gramscian analysis of the U.S. press, American media scholar

Marshall argues that "hegemonic ideologies are disseminated through culture: through news production, art, literature, theater, and other cultural forms of expression."[6] Similar to the U.S in the 1960s, in Western Europe despite widescale student revolt, no major systemic change occurred precisely because there was no mass effort to change the opinions of the broader population. And further the "dominant system" under attack was heavily involved in the media from which most citizens got their information. Powerful media outlets helped dampen the flames of any revolutionary spirit in West Germany in the 1960s by "recruiting those initially uninterested persons into a conservative position that would help preserve the status quo."[7]

Since Modernity's dawn, shocking media events have increasingly been conceived of as both sites of commodity and also as locations for re-affirming cultural norms. Historian George L. Mosse notes the introduction in Western Europe, and in particular Germany, during the nineteenth century of the parallel concepts of Modernity and respectability (Anständigkeit) —concepts which have been key to the production of contemporary cultural mores, and of constructs such as media, scandal, spectacle and celebrity culture. Within the media menagerie, criminals and celebrities are coded as outlandish. Scandalous events concerning such figures enact and re-confirm broader cultural values for a wider population.

In his 1946 essay *The Culture Industry*, Adorno points out that social *conditioning* is manifested through the exhibiting of accepted social mores and roles: "In so far as cartoons do any more than accustom the senses to the new tempo, they hammer into every brain the old lesson that continuous friction, the breaking down of all individual resistance, is the condition of life in this society. Donald Duck in the cartoons and the unfortunate in real life get their thrashing so that the audience can learn to take their own punishment." [8] Adorno spotlights that Disney cartoons condition the public to expect similar treatment themselves as part of the natural condition of life.

Likewise, public crucifixions of tabloid animals are used to reaffirm the normative cultural scripts of the time.

Marshall also argues that the media tends to act as one body that can shape the way a populace thinks or views the world by a careful selection of themes, "thereby creating an impression among its viewers or readers that may or may not be true." He adds that "since Man's behavior is more often than not steered by a person's impressions of what the cultural norms may be, the media could serve to influence the way people behave by molding their views of the world."[9]

Discussing a slightly later era, but also of relevance here, Fredric Jameson argues that the media constitute one of the most important elements in late capitalism. He speaks of "new forms of media interrelationship"[10] leading to the increased capitalist take-over of our lives. Due again to this "mediatization of culture, we become increasingly reliant on the media's version of our reality, a version of reality that is filled predominantly with capitalist values."[11]

To understand the role of the media in the outbreak of terrorism in West Germany in the 1970s, it is important again to consider the post-war psycho-cultural climate. These settings of circumstance arose from the many unresolved threads of World War Two.

The Post-War West German Media and Springer-Verlag

In West Germany in the 1950s the popularity of a cinematic genre known as *Heimatfilme* can provide a sense of the social and cultural atmosphere of the post-War era. These family-oriented films featured stories conveying a strong sense of traditional order. Reminiscent of the 1960s Disney genre of familal melodramas (not the animated cartoons), they were marked by narratives which culminate in the restoration of patriarchal order, typically with a traditional family wedding as the final "happy ending" salvational sequence. Idealized hetero-normative values and small town mores were valorized, and an imaginary "Gemütlichkeit" cocooned pre-Nazi Germany.

Common to most *Heimatfilme* was the complete avoidance of any awkward or uncomfortable topics like Fascism, World War Two, or East Germany (the DDR).[12]

Such sugary texts try to define the cultural and moral climate of 1950s West Germany, and their cloying normative agendas set the prevailing tone for much mainstream West German cultural production well into the 1960s. Similar types of cultural production and exchange are prevalent in many post-war countries during eras of huge technological change and political upheavals, as order and the family's sanctity are portrayed as key to national survival. In post-World-War-Two West Germany, these traditionalist cultural scripts appear to act as a psychological balm for a particular generation of war-torn citizens. Such broadly played *family fare* reassured older audiences, but disenfranchised some of the younger generation, contributing during this era to an increasing sense of generational gap within society.

After the construction of the Berlin Wall in 1961, some conservative West German news agencies also turned their national and local news coverage to integrate narratives similar to those of the *Heimatfilme*—including stories of domestic upheaval and familial redemption. The tone of these news stories shares a rhetorical language already established in this cinematic genre.

Political theorist Benedict Anderson has noted how key newspapers are to shaping and consolidating a national consciousness. They help to create a sense of confidence in community and nation states, which is essential because the state needs the confidence of their citizens in order to appear successful. As Marshall notes regarding Anderson's ideas on nationalism and collective consciousness, "reading newspapers helps foster that confidence in society because it is a daily activity in which the reader knows others are participating." Newspapers help maintain social cohesion; they can give their readers hope in the system and faith that their political, social and economic institutions are functioning securely.[13]

In Cold War contexts, West German newspapers were attempting to preserve their readers' belief and confidence in the state and its institutions. As we shall see, by the mid 1960s some of these papers chose to do this by marginalizing anyone or anything that appeared to threaten the state's fragile order. They particularly focussed on villainizing figures from the West German student movement.

It would be misrepresentative to suggest that the *whole* of the post-war West German media and other forms of cultural production presented a partisan or unified voice. A plurality of opinions and issues were articulated and a range of constituencies addressed. Rather than dismissing the entire West German media in the post-World-War-Two era, I focus on the mainstream tabloid press predominantly owned by the Springer Verlag publishing empire, which exerted considerable influence in framing and disseminating domestic news to a mass audience.

Emerging first as a local paper in Hamburg in the 1920s, by the 1960s the Springers' light and sensational Verlag had developed into unprecedented levels of public influence and popularity throughout West Germany. Springer newspapers included *BILD, BZ, Berliner Morgenpost, Hamburger Morgenpost,* and many others. Sales statistics on late 1960s West German print media show that 39 percent of the newspaper market and 18 percent of magazines bought were produced by Springer.[14] It controlled 81.5 percent of the sales of the daily national press and 90 percent on Sunday editions. Springer publications accounted for 66.5 percent of the total West Berlin market alone.[15] This was clearly a huge share of the West German newspaper market.

The rampant growth and influence of Springer Verlag did not go unnoticed. In response to this increasing media monopoly, some within the West German intellectual community expressed concerns about Springer's "massification" and heavy-handed reactionary political rhetoric. In 1966 historian Golo Mann remarked that "Die Springersche

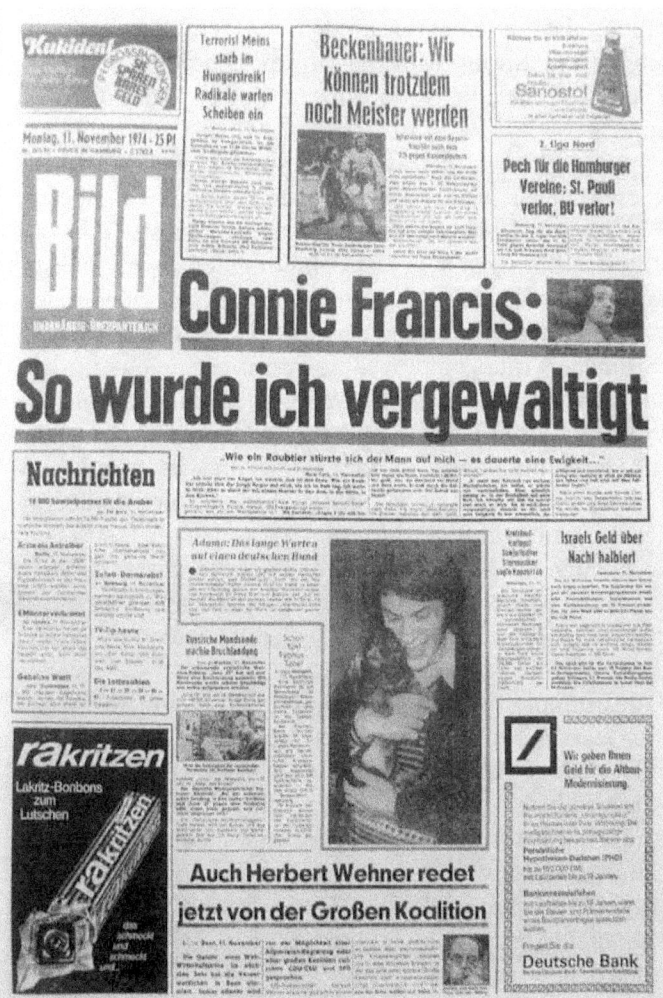

Fig.19. BILD newspaper cover from November 11th, 1974. The headline reads "Connie Francis: How I was raped." The subtitle continues "Like a wild animal he threw himself on me. It lasted an eternity." Also of great note here is that above, a smaller news item states that RAF member Holger Meins has died on hunger strike and that stones were thrown at memorial demonstrations. The juxtaposition of these two news items says much of the editorial agenda of Springer publication BILD during this era.

Machtballung ist zu einem zentralen Problem der Republik geworden." (The Springer media power conglomeration has become one of the key problems for the West German Republic).[16]

Springer newspapers were unpopular with Mann and many others because of the way that their reporting relentlessly adopted hyper-traditionalist standpoints and partisan editorial perspectives. Springer stories highlighted nationalistic conservative views, and were aimed at an imagined West German "moral majority" who supposedly shared Springer's values. Springer writers employed powerful personal narratives and installed particular kinds of psychological panic to intrigue their newspapers' burgeoning audience. (One might compare Springer's growing power in the 1960s and its reactionary invective with that of the global media channels now owned by Australian mediamogul Rupert Murdoch).

Although the histrionic tone of Springer stories may not have been taken entirely seriously by its readership, this type of continual anti-Leftist propaganda clearly colored public opinion.

An example of Springer's strange obsession with such moralistic fear is this 1974 *BILD* front-page story which graphically details the rape of white U. S. country singer Connie Francis in a New York hotel room by a black intruder. The headline reads: "Connie Francis: So wurde ich vergewaltigt" (How I was raped), Springer then quotes Connie: "Wie ein Raubtier sturtze sich der Mann auf mich—es dauerte eine Ewigkeit." (Like a wild animal the man threw himself on me. It lasted an eternity).

Springer headlines often dwelt on themes of domestic violation, of Oedipal urges enacted, or of the threat of national order torn asunder—traumas similar to those Germany itself had already experienced at the end of World War Two, through the 1949 establishment of the DDR, and the consequent schitzophrenic splitting of the country's body politic by the Berlin Wall in November 1961.

Beginning in the 1960s and continually thereafter, Springer news stories never failed to contain similar narratives both horrifying and intriguing—often featuring invective against transgressive youth and the threat of domestic killers.

The Nu-Tabloid Villain: Leftist Student

By the late 1960s, through the concave lens of Springer's press, the distant war in Vietnam appeared to have boomeranged back into violent, out-of-control, anti-Vietnam student rebellion at home in Germany. In this context, certain non-violent figures from the SDS or the Ausserparliamentarische Opposition (A.P.O)[17] student movements were actually villainized and continually termed as "terrorist" by Springer (a number of years before any actual bombings took place).

Beginning around 1967, Springer began a campaign of whispers and smears against high-profile young moderate A.P.O member and SDS leader, Rudi Dutschke. This campaign deliberately invoked a rhetoric of terror around Dutschke, although he was completely non-violent."Dutschke was famous for advocating "die lange Marsch durch die Institutionen" (the long march through the institutions). Dutschke's views echo much moderate Leftist analysis of this period, changing "the system" from inside rather than through violent means. Through most of his life Dutschke remained an outspoken opponent of the RAF's violent strategies).

During 1967 and 1968, amid widespread anti-Vietnam demonstrations, Springer stories continually and misleadingly singled out Dutschke as a hardcore Leftist troublemaker, an "Unruhestifter" (rabble rouser), "Krawallmacher" (riot starter), referring to him in relation to "Meinungsterror," meaning ideological terror. Tabloid photographs of Dutschke's face became sensationalized and made notorious in Springer's papers as he was repeatedly labeled "Rudi the Red Terror."

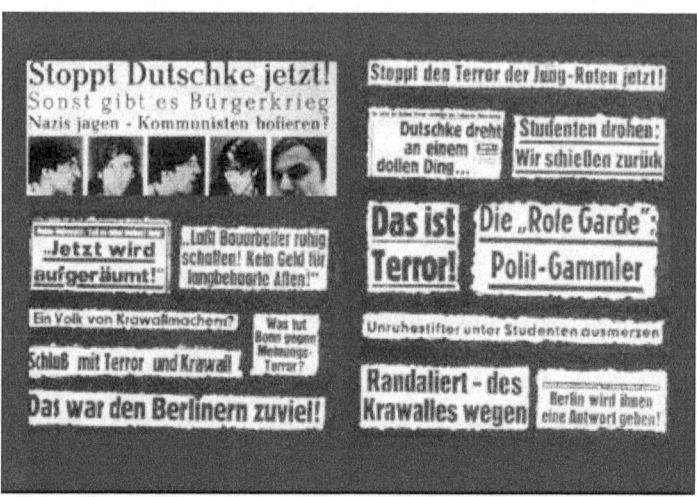

Fig.20. Springer headlines from 1967-68 concerning Rudi Dutschke.

Prior to the actual emergence of the bombing attacks in West Germany, the Springer press were associating the term "terror" with images of Dutschke. In this political theater of the absurd of the late 1960s, Left-wing "terror" was here invoked as a loose signifier for the oppositional and imaginary, even though "real" terror did not yet physically exist.

Springer employed languages of "monstrosity" in the construct of a political and moral witch-hunt against West German Leftist student leaders. Such locii become sites for excess of meaning and wild projection, a fabricated "axis of evil" which would then provide the discursive framing and literal potential for an act of monstrosity.

In April 1968, spurred by a Springer headline imploring its readers to "Stoppt Dutschke Jetzt!" (Stop Dutschke Now!), an unhinged right-wing youth attempts to assassinate Rudi, shooting him on a Berlin street near Dutschke's home. Dutschke recovered from his wounds but spent the remaining ten years of his life severely handicapped. In a response to what many perceived as a Springer-incited attack, large groups of outraged students attacked the newspaper's offices in Berlin and Hamburg, and riots ensued.[18]

The Dutschke episode illustrates the media's role in the provocation/incitement of student violence during this period. The fuse had literally been lit.

The Rhetoric of Monstrosity: "Die Ungeheuerlich" and Springer

Why did a cultural agency like Springer intentionally promote the idea of Leftist violence? What role did this anti-Leftist terror rhetoric play for a media conglomerate such as Springer—which creates and then manipulates public images?

Springer's smearing of Rudi reveals much about the political bias and wide influence of this one particular media channel. Springer had a particular investment in promoting this "Leftist terror" "Reds under the Beds" red herring. It distracted from another "specter still haunting" the West German news— other "ghosts of Old Europe"[19]—Nazi war criminals still at large and undetected within the society. A notorious case of the time was the Kiesinger-Klarsfeld circus. At a state gathering in 1968, the twenty-nine-year-old anti-Nazi activist Beate Klarsfeld publicly slapped the face of Chancellor Kiesinger, publicly "outing" him as a former Nazi Party member.

The neo-myth of a Leftist domestic threat was promoted through headlines such as "Stoppt den Terror der Jung-Roten jetzt" (Stop the terror of the young Reds now!) which created a convenient distraction from the increasing drive by the student movement to investigate hidden ex-Nazis within the then-ruling conservative government. Such fabricated cartoon-like stories of the young "enemy among us" conveniently shifted the blame game from old Nazi war criminals to Leftists.

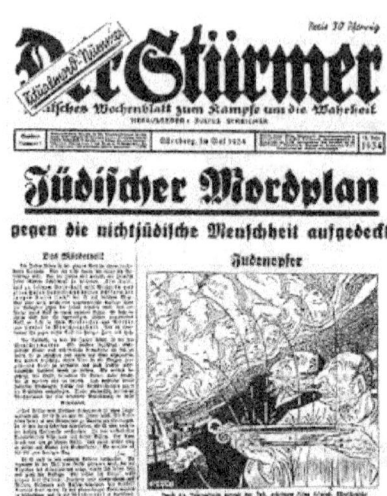

Fig. 21. Examples of anti-Semitic propaganda in Nazi Germany: (left-right) Front cover of "Der Sturmer," May 1934, a far right-wing German newspaper. The headline reads "Jewish murder plan" and "The Jews are our misfortune"; Film poster for "Jud Süss" (1940), a violently anti-Semitic German movie, directed by Veit Harlan, which was a box office success in Germany and France during the early 1940s.

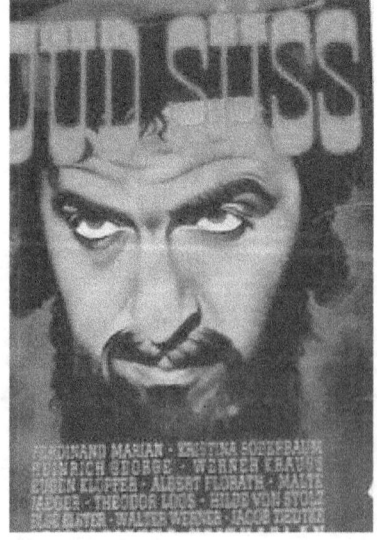

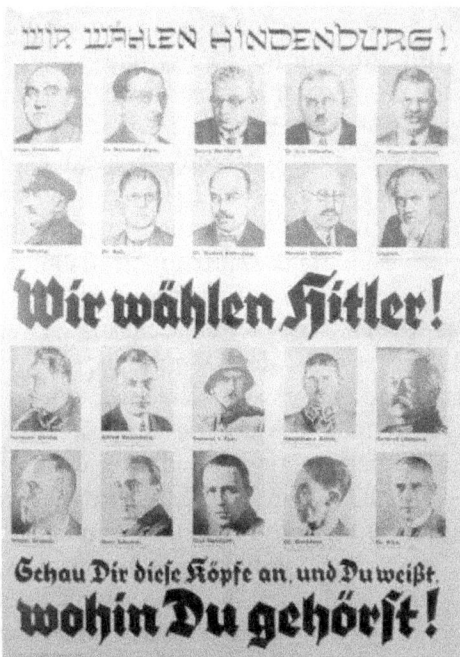

Racist propaganda poster from the 1932 German election, making reference to Nazi ideas concerning phrenology and the body of the "Other." The text reads: "We vote for Hindenburg." We vote for Hitler," "Look at the heads and you know to whom you belong!"

Writing in 1946, Adorno notes that pre-Springer, Mosse Verlag and Ullstein Verlag had been "the two largest press combines of German-Jewish capital in the Weimar Republic, controlling newspapers, magazines, and publishing houses. Both were taken over by the Nazis."[20] Adorno here pinpoints an important intersect in the post-war West German situation.

One reason that a conservative publisher like Springer would be unsympathetic to investigation into former Nazis still at large, was that a large section of the newspaper market that had formerly been in German-Jewish hands, had now been taken over by a non-Jewish generation of publishers in the post-war period who directly benefited from their absence. Although

88

neither Axel Springer nor his father, Springer Verlag's founder had been affiliated with Nazi Party and were pro-Israel, Axel Springer's greatest mentor in the post-war publishing world was a former leading Nazi era publisher. [21]

In the cultural "year zero" context of post-war West Germany, Springer presses built new myths around specific social groups, that were constructed as inherently "oppositional" and "evil"—promoting them as new public threats, new categories of social pariah. This negative-stereotyping was curiously reminiscent of Nazi-era newspapers in the 1930s, when Jews, gypsies, homosexuals and Communists were relentlessly demonized in news stories. A similar linguistic trace is viewable in Springer headlines in the 1960s through construction of categories marked by their projected physical Otherness (Flagged by headlines such as "Kein Geld für langbeharrte Affen," No money for long-haired apes, "Polit-Gammler," Political lowlife hustlers, or "Wie ein Raubtier" Like a wild animal). In the aftermath of the shooting of Dutschke, some commentators detected this textual haunting.

In May 1968 after the Dutschke shooting, the Berlin Evangelical Student Union release a statement concerning the editorial bias of Springer newspapers, *BILD* and *BZ*:

> Since the Third Reich, the object of attack has been switched: the hooked Jewish nose in [the famous weekly] *Der Stürmer* has been replaced in the cartoons in *BILD* and *BZ* by the beard of the student, considered subhuman like a gorilla. [22] [23]

The Evangelical Student Union text shows how prevalent the physical demonization of Leftist students had become in Springer newspapers in the late 1960s, and how reminiscent it was of earlier anti-Semitic rhetoric of the Nazi era, positioned in relation to the "obscene" body of the Other. By focussing on this projected bestial, regressive, "ungeheuerlich" (monstrous and/or inhuman) physicality, the specter of 1930s racial "Otherness" was now re-purposed in the West German media to villainize the identities of young white German demonstrators.

At this historic and fragile juncture in the new West German democratic republic, Springer could escalate public fears with this kind of feral invective. As one conservative media group controlled close to 70% of the newspaper market during this era, it was a major player in appearing to present a consensus of opinion. Springer did this through privileging certain information and suppressing other key details (such as the underplaying Dutschke's clearly stated non-violence).

Linguist Noam Chomsky argued that the media has the ability to manufacture (public) consent. With similar dynamics, media theorist Colin Seymour-Ure states that the "timing of communication processes is probably one of the most important determinants of mass media effects."[24] Theorists Watson and Hill also discuss the power of the media to shape opinion:

> If the timing is right, the media can often be the arbiters of crisis, by being in the most prominent position to define it. Because of their agenda-setting capacity, the media have influence over the criteria that, in the public domain, decide what is important and what is not, what is normal and what is deviant, what is consensus and what is dissensus, what is significant or newsworthy, and what is marginal.[25]

In his study of 1960s US news coverage *The Whole World Is Watching: Mass Media and the Making and Unmaking of the New Left,* American historian Todd Gitlin analyzes examples of the mass media's distortion of American New Left movements in order to marginalize these groups. Gitlin argues that the major media outlets, "consolidated into a corporate identity" are committed to issues at odds with the Left, such as maintenance of private property rights, a strong national security state, maintenance of certain moral codes and a free market system within a clearly defined corporate or bureaucratic structure." [26]

As Marshall notes concerning Gitlin's argument, "the media did not need to create fantasies or falsehoods about the Left; they simply distorted and shaded their meanings and aims, often making them seem more radical, extreme and dangerous than they really were." Gitlin points out how the American media covered issues very selectively: "Journalism's more regular approach is to process social opposition, to control its image and to diffuse it at the same time, to absorb what can be absorbed into the dominant structure of definitions and images and to push the rest to the margins of social life."

Gitlin lists examples of how the U.S. media frames news stories in such a way as to re-assure Establishment views and draw the "silent majority" together.[27] Although Gitlin's focus is primarily on the U.S, his analysis also rings true in dominant media patterns in West Germany during the same period, similar tropes of media framing can be seen in Springer's distortions of "Dutschke."

As we witnessed in Chapter Three, the media harassment of moderate Leftist figures such as Dutschke was not specific to West Germany alone in the Vietnam era. Gitlin notes that slanted representations of domestic Leftist "threats" were also prevalent in North America and other Western European states during the Cold War era. However unlike the U.S, in West Germany for historical reasons, (the proximity of the DDR, the shadow of fascism)the fragile political climate creates an environment specially favorable for increasing confrontation.[28] By the end of the 1960s in West German, the convergence of reactionary conservative voices in the media, and a vocal New Left student movement spurred by Vietnam, and also the many unresolved post-war historical threads, all together generated a profound sense of imminence.

The Dutschke debacle exemplified how Springer press' anti-Communist witch-hunt manifests in West German society during this era, and due to such combustible dynamics how, by the end of the 1960s, this ongoing Cold War propaganda war escalates to new heights.[29]

The War of Terror Begins

Around the time of the 1968 Dutschke shooting, Andreas Baader confided to fellow nascent terrorist Bommi Baumann his embracing of the theory that "the revolution wouldn't be built through political work, but through headlines."[30] Through bombing attacks, Baader intended to create a theatricalized media spectacle against Vietnam that he hoped would then help kickstart a wider Leftist revolution across Western Europe.

Ten days before Dutschke was shot, on April 2nd 1968 Baader, his girlfriend Gudrun Ensslin, and two others planted fire-bombs in two department stores in Frankfurt to protest against U.S. involvement in the Vietnam conflict. All four were soon apprehended and jailed.

Four years later, in May 1972 the RAF exploded across the global headlines when they bombed American army bases in three different cities—Munich, Augsburg, and Frankfurt.

As noted, some members of the RAF had worked in various elements in the media and were aware of the agenda and political machinations of the Springer empire. In the climate of escalating harassment, the RAF's decision to make media-centric terror attacks engaged Springer's continual provocations against the Left.

Conceivably inspired by Marcuse's concept of "the Great Refusal"—meaning the rising up of society against the repression of Western industrialized/mechanized capital, the RAF's aim through bombing was to utilize, through spectacular display, mainstream media news channels to publicize their views. By attacking domestic army bases, the RAF hoped to "bring back home" the reality of the ongoing violence in

Vietnam and draw a parallel, intentionally aiming to promote a climate of local shock and panic. In his study of RAF communiqués, art historian Robert Storr stated that their meta-praxis "was based on the Maoist notion that the triumph of the revolutionary Third World over the reactionary First World depends on bringing the battle from the margins to the center of the empire."[31] Storr quotes how Hans-Joachim Klein, member of the RAF's second generation, explained the group's struggle:

> From the beginning the RAF has always said: the important thing is to exacerbate contradictions in such a way that the situation becomes more and more openly fascist. The important thing is to make the latent fascism that's predominant in West Germany clearly visible. After that the masses will rally round..
> [32]

The RAF's strategy of violent symbolic display aimed to enter the ongoing "image war" of the Cold War—projected on to the global screen of the media. However, this was a location where the RAF themselves were also soon to be portrayed by their enemies—the conservative press.

Minutes after the 1968 department store arson attacks, future RAF leader Gudrun Ensslin anonymously called the police to inform them that the attack was "a political act of revenge," and not a mere performance art "happening."[33] The RAF were keen to distance themselves from what could be conceived of as a "cultural" act.[34] Ensslin's fears of misinterpretation proved to be well-founded.

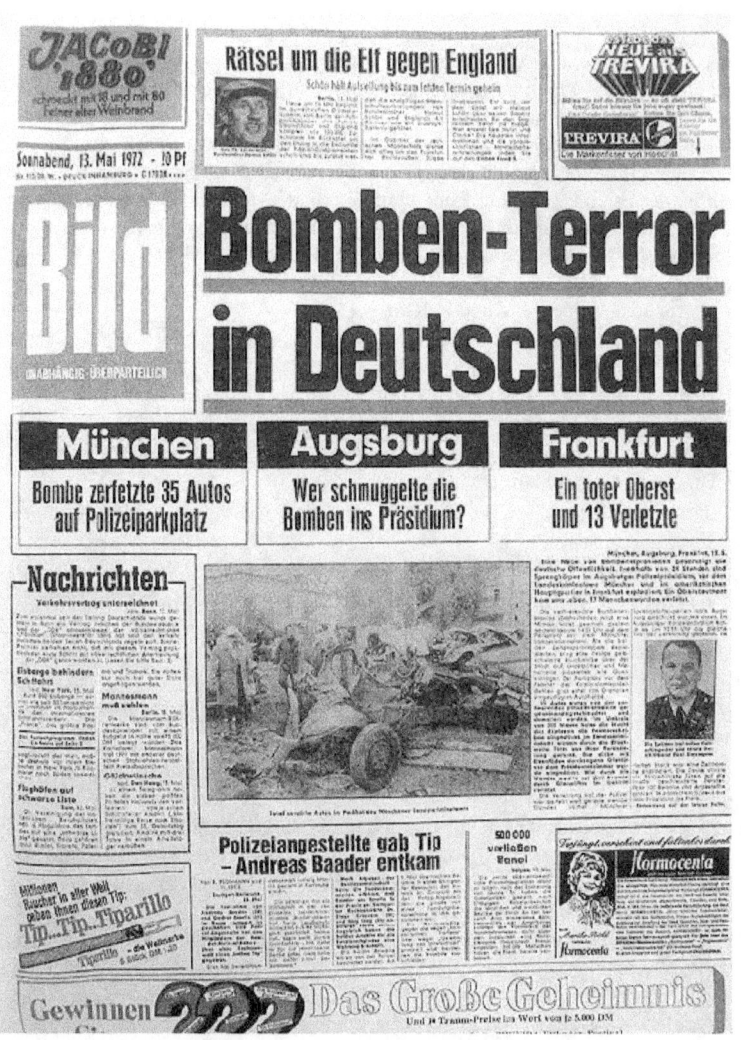

Fig 22. The front-page of BILD newspaper on May 13th 1972. "Bomb terror in Germany: Munich, Augsburg and Frankfurt". Note reference to Baader as the perpetrator already on the same day.

[1] Examples of such a tendency to underplay the media's role and the RAF's deliberate media-oriented strategies are apparent in the works of all the accepted canonical works on the RAF. Aust, Varon, Peters and Phillips. A cinematic work which acknowledges the importance of the media's role in the RAF story is the semi-documentary film *Deutschland in Herbst*, (1978) by the Verlag der Authoren. This film features a fictional section where television producers get into a heated debate concerning the Greek play *Antigone* which is to be cut from a public broadcast for its political sensitivity in the RAF terror context. This scene spotlights the role of the West German media and state in the control and manipulation of the RAF story.

[2] Baumann, p.110.

[3] Thompson, 1995, p.3. Cited in Kim, p.15.

[4] Ibid.

[5] Ibid.

[6] This framing of Gramsci's ideas draws from Marshall, p.6-7.

[7] Drawing from Marshall's phrasing of similar patterns in the U.S.

[8] P.138.

[9] This framing draws from Marshall, p.7.

[10] Jameson, *Postmodernism,* p.xix

[11] Ibid.

[12] *Heimatfilme* are noted for their sentimental tone and simplistic morality, and centered about love, friendship, family. Famous examples of this genre include *Der Förster vom Silberwald* (1954) or *Schwarzwaldmädel* (1950).

[13] From Benedict Anderson, *Imagined Communities.* Draws from Marshall, p.9.

[14] From Springer biography: *50 Jahre Axel Springer Verlag* (1996) by Claus Jacobi. "Nach Bonner Berechnungen stammten 39 Prozent der in Deutschland verbreiteten Zeitungsauflage und 18 Prozent der Zeitschriftenauflage aus diesem (Springer) Verlag."
http://www.axelspringer.de/inhalte/geschich/inhalte/kampf/kampf.htm

[15] Varon, p.39.

[16] http://www.axelspringer.de/inhalte/unterneh/frame.html. from: *50 Jahre Axel Springer Verlag* 1966 by Claus Jacobi

[17] For further discussion of the APO movement and the 1960s West German political context, see Varon, p.31, p.60.

[18] re. Dutschke shooting, Varon, p.40-41.

[19] A reference to Marx and Engels, the Communist Manifesto" and "the "heilige Jagd" (holy hunt) of Communism during the nineteenth century.

[20] Related to this theme, Adorno notes in *Minima Moralia*, #35, p.57, "it is an injustice to the editors of Mosse and Ullstein or to the reorganizers of *Frankfurter Zeitung*, to reproach them with time-serving under Fascism. They were always like that." A footnote beneath notes that "Mosse-Verlag and Ullstein Verlag were the two largest press combines of German-Jewish capital in the Weimar Republic, controlling newspapers, magazines, and publishing houses. Both were taken over by the Nazis."

[21] Springer's mentor.

[22] *Der Spiegel*, no.34. May 5, 1968. As displayed in Biesenbach, p.80-82

[23] The Evangelical Student Union was not alone in blaming the media for Dutschke's shooting. Intellectuals, among them Böll, Adorno, and Mitscherlich, drafted a statement asserting: "Fear and an ability to engage the student opposition seriously have created a climate in which the intentional defamation of a minority provokes acts of violence against it. This climate has been systematically created by a press that presents itself as a guardian of the constitution and claims to speak in the name of the majority and of order, but that means by order nothing more than its domination of an immature populace and the way to a new, authoritarian nationalism." Solidaritatsbekundung namhafter Intellektueller vom 13. April, 1968," In *APO: Die Ausserparlamentarische Opposition,* ed. Otto, 264. Cited in Varon, p.40.

[24] From Watson and Hill, p.93.

[25] Ibid.

[26] This Gitlin quote drawn by Marshall, p.8.

[27] Ibid.

[28] Notable here is a tendency for conservative media opinions and perspectives to seep into and become common in mainstream popular discourse through their repeated circulation.

[29] Seen from the perspective of the next generation of radical students, the Springer propaganda campaign had a further currency. Von Dirke (p.87) cites this group: "We belong to the generation of those who were fascinated by the distorted portrayal of the radical students, of those who identified with the stone-throwing hordes, but we found the reality to be much more harmless. The exaggeration of the media lifted us up, encouraged us. Reality was disappointing." Through their myth-making, distortions and exaggerations, the press arguably inspired a larger wave of responsive violence.

[30] Baumann, p.110.

[31] Robert Storr, *Gerhard Richter: October 18th 1977,* p.54

[32] Storr, p.134.

[33] Scribner, "Buildings on Fire: The Situationist International and the Red Army Faction." *Grey Room* 26, Winter 2007. MIT, p.32.

[34] Ibid, p.38.

Chapter V

GIRLS WITH GUNS:
THE RAF IN THE MEDIA
-THE CRIME LOCATION AND THE FEMALE TERRORIST

By making front-page news with their U.S. army base
bombings in 1972, the RAF initially appeared to have
succeeded in their aim of producing a shocking visual spectacle
in the media.

However the desired intent remained unclear to the
public. Media images showed that buildings had been bombed
and that all that remained were the ruins. Viewers look into the
void of this image, searching for clues to suture the wound of
incomprehension. Photographs of bombed locations produced erasure
of visual coherence, giving the reader the feeling of having missed
something—a sense of unknowing, of indeterminacy.

The mysteriousness of a terror-attack image incites public discussion. Normal life has been interrupted, and may be again. In such a context, there is a need to negotiate such confusion by returning repeatedly to the photograph of the trauma in search of meaning. The bombing photograph now provides a location for excess—both in viewing and in interpretation.

The anonymity of a terror attack fractures existing frames of reference—voyeurs need time and further information to digest its meaning and cause. The terrorists have succeeded in evacuating public space and creating a no-go zone within the state's territory, but what substitutes what has been destroyed? No clear indication of meaning is apparent. No insurgent troops have taken over the location and beyond the bombing itself, no signatory marker is immediately present. Police guarding the site of the attack are all that can be seen.

The bombing aftermath photograph shows a space under close surveillance and the carnivalized re-assertion of governmental order around a state "wound." Earlier attempts at guarding this government location have failed and new guards have now arrived. They are too late to protect this space or any possible victims, and besides, a further attack at this location is unlikely. Bombing aftermath photographs show attempts to reclaim state territory, but the guards protecting this crime scene are the only actors visible in this scenario. Tabloid visuals of post-bombing sites thus record an ameliorative gesture, commemorating that protection occurred here too late.

The relation of the tabloid terror-"event" image to the rest of the front-page layout of the newspaper is key to understanding its rhetorical punch. Amidst the monotony of everyday life, the terror "image" provides a locus for linguistic excess. Located between the banality of advertising images (in Fig. 22, for cigars, alcohol, and hormone cream) or coverage of tax reforms, distant external affairs, celebrity gossip, or scantily-clad "Page Three" girls, the picture of a domestic terror attack performs a specific function within the framework of the newspaper.[1] It acts both to explode the continuum and to reassert its necessity.

In a tightly administered bureaucratic society like Cold War Allied-occupied West Germany, the scandal of a terror attack permits a new discursive space to emerge within the newspaper's parameters, as the terror image becomes awash with an aporetic overflow of rumored meanings and explanations.

In a discussion of the visual prosthetics of the crime scene and the "modern anti-spectacle," media theorist Nick Mirzoeff cites philosopher Jacques Ranciere on the constructed-ness of such a setting: "The police above all provide a certitude about what is there, or rather, about what is not there. "Move along, there's nothing to see." The police try to assure the public that what is here is neither worth viewing nor permissible to view."[2]

But in fact, the state's façade of daily order has been removed by the attack, so there is now much to witness. The terror site shows the state's regulatory system in disorder. The act of terror by its very nature intentionally challenges and intervenes into the circuitry and normative procedures of everyday life. This "anti-spectacle" is the terrorist's art.

Ranciere sees the urban crime scene as a stage. "Politics consists in transforming that space of circulation into the space of the manifestation of the subject." The terrorist act *politicizes* space, media photographs of a terror site transmit a symbolic hole in the state's "visual domain." Terrorists hijack civic order, shifting perceptions and controlling uses of public space. Cordoned-off zonas and quarantined space interrupt the circulatory flow of capital.

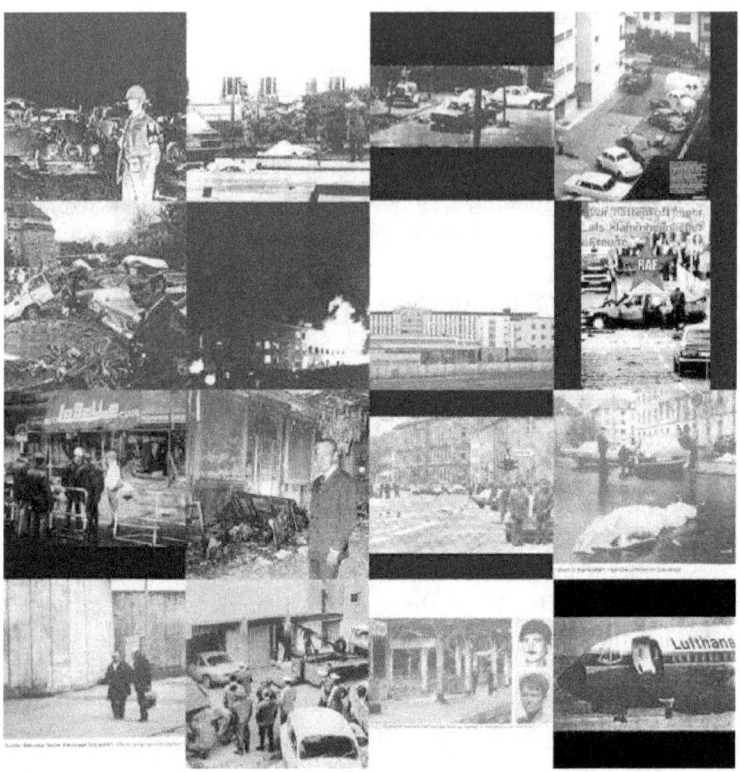

Fig. 23. Evacuated spaces related to the RAF from the 1970s and 1980: Frankfurt U.S. army base bombing, May 1972; Murder of Buback, 1977; Schleyer kidnap site, 1977; Baader, Meins and Raspe arrest site, Munich, June 1972; Augsburg U.S. army base, May 1972; German Embassy in Stockholm, April 1975; Stammheim High Security prison; Assassination of Alfred Herrhausen, 1989; LaBelle Disco, Berlin, 1986; Augsburg U.S. army base, May 1972; Buback murder, 1977; Jean-Paul Sartre visits Stammheim prison, 1976; Baader, Meins and Raspe arrest site, Munich, June 1972; Site of police shoot-out with RAF members Grams and Hogefeld at Bad Kleinen, 1993; Mogadishu hijack, Somalia, October 1977.

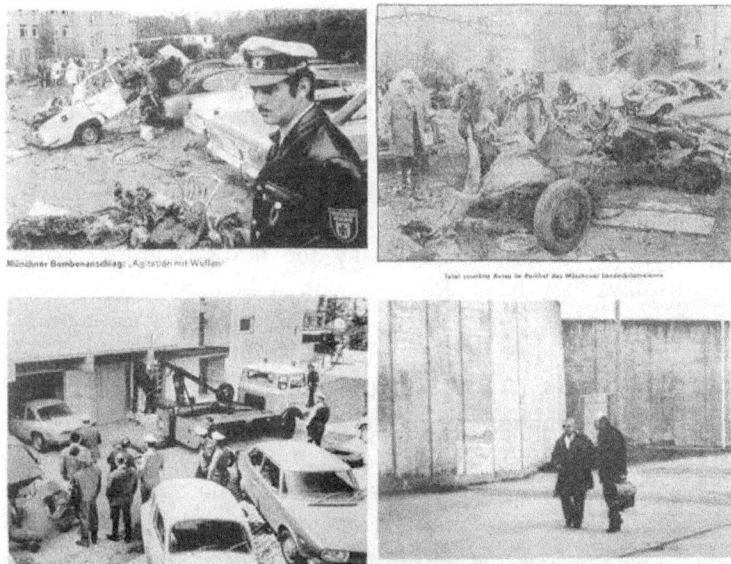

Fig.24. Four RAF-related evacuated spaces in the 1970s: 1972 -Two images of the car park of the U.S. army base at Munich after the RAF bombing; the arrest of Baader, Meins and Raspe in Munich, in June 1972; Jean-Paul Sartre goes to visit the RAF in the high security Stammheim jail in Stuttgart in 1976.

The bombing image awakens the *reader* of the media to the fact that the state's visual order has been fractured, intentionally and symbolically violated. The newspaper reader, television viewer, and next day's passer-by witness only empty space and demarcated territory. Images show buildings lying in rubble, cars mangled, and if there are victims, their corpses are shrouded in white sheets. Their identities are un-viewable, as if, their deaths are being hidden.[3]

Media coverage of a terror event installs a specific, ritualized language to negotiate its representation. In such settings, the press structures the *meanings* of these events.[4] [5] The initial response of the state to a bombing attack is to release *specific* information to the press, but withhold other details from the public and decry "senseless" violence. Then identikit witch-hunt suspects are fed to the media.

In a terror scenario, rumors and gossip circulate at hyper-speed as the public attempts to regain equilibrium. In response to this violence, visuals such as terror photographs provide the central mediating toolbox for framing comprehension of the attack. Although the terrorist has temporarily succeeded in hijacking the news headlines with their display, they have done so with only partial success— because the nature of this event is then branded for the public by the media.

The anonymity of a terror act is a deeply disturbing aspect for the public, and in response the state and media gesture to this sense of unknowing by providing images, first of the event, and then of identities for the bombing's supposed culprits. The face-icon now becomes a central motif in all further coverage of the terror phenomenon. Photographs of bombing suspects are presented as a palliative act, in an attempt to re-establish visual order and to regain the control of illusion. Rarely after such an event is the terrorist's communiqué reproduced verbatim in the media.

Photobooth Hooligans: The RAF as the Face of Terror

The flood of newspaper images of bombed U.S. army bases in the West German media was swiftly followed by Wanted posters for the RAF. The viral spread of these mugshots turned the RAF, as their subjects, into instant outlaws. These posters proclaimed the bombing's culprits as "Anarchistische Gewalttäter" (violent anarchists).

The RAF were now cast by the media in a live docu-drama human interest story which featured them cast as tabloid villains, renamed by the police and media as the "Baader-Meinhof-Bande"—a criminal gang coded as the embodiment of terror and notoriety, the faces of evil incarnate, of the true terror that the media had earlier suggested lay behind its portrayal of Dutschke. [6] [7] Through this nickname "Baader-Meinhof-Bande"

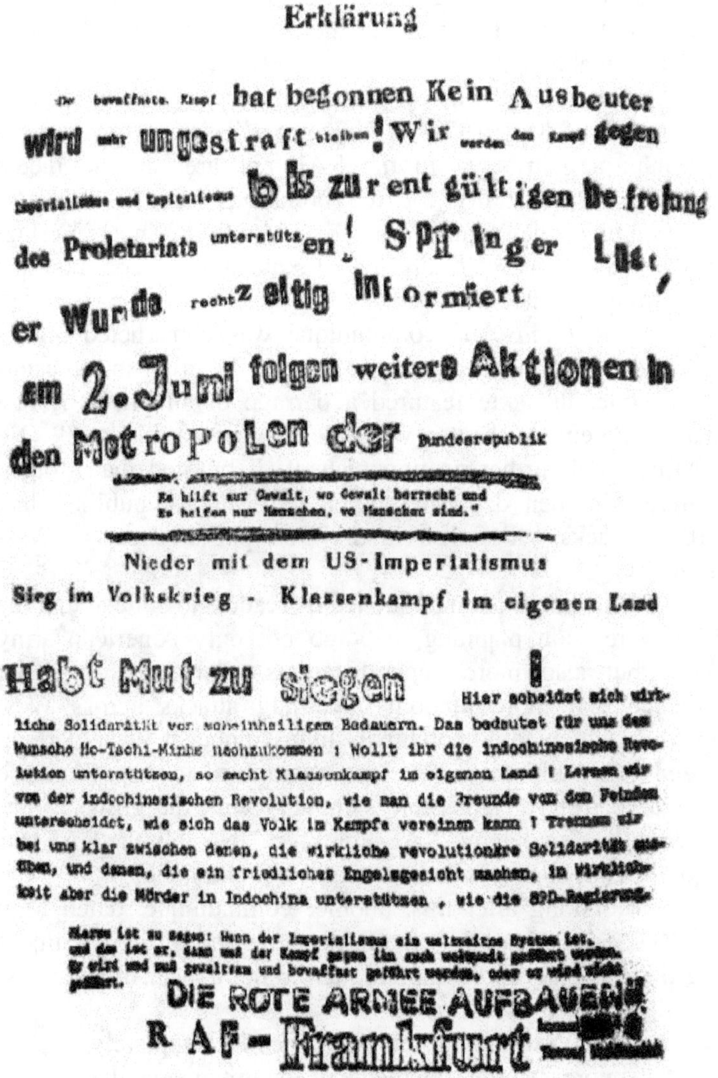

Fig. 25. Fake RAF "Erklärung" communiqué from May 1972. Printed in the moderate newspaper Frankfurter Rundschau after the U.S. army base bombings.

the group were pathologized public entities. The bombings were framed not as political acts but those of a Bonnie and Clyde-style criminal gang.[8]

Parallel with the progression of the events, soon after the attacks of May 1972 on U.S. army bases in Germany, a communiqué attributed to the RAF appeared in the media claiming responsibility for the bombings. The *Frankfurter Rundschau* (a newspaper unaffiliated with Springer Verlag) printed a "RAF" *Erklärung* (explanation) communiqué concerning the attacks.

The *Rundschau* communiqué was constructed out of collaged newsprint, using "ransom note" lettering in gangster-esque style, its texte featured a barrage of simplistic Leftist rhetoric "Kein Ausbeuter wird mehr ungestraftbleiben!" (No exploiter will further go unpunished). It boasted that "folgen weitere Aktionen den Metropolen der Bundesrepublik" (that further attacks will follow in the metropolitan areas of West Germany).

This faux communiqué led its readers to believe that the RAF were soon planning to bomb not only American army bases, but also more general targets—alarming newspaper audience that more random upcoming attacks across West Germany which could potentially injure innocent West German citizens were imminent—an idea guaranteed to disenfranchise the public from any possible sympathy with the group cause. This text was signed by "RAF-Frankfurt." Notably the RAF star logo does not appear anywhere on the communiqué.

Not long after this, another communiqué, dated May 28th 1972, was released by the RAF outing the earlier document as a fake. The second communique did not appear in the press. It read:

> The West German press has nearly completely suppressed the statements of the urban guerrilla commandos. Instead the *Frankfurter Rundschau* published a letter stuck together out of cut-up newsprint, which, when compared to

authentic RAF communiqués, can clearly be
seen to be a fake, to create the impression that
the bombers are brainless twits generating
nothing but chaos—in an effort to create
uncertainty amongst the people regarding the
actions.[9]

Few of the general public actually knew of or ever saw
this second RAF communiqué. This RAF's response
communiqué of May 28th 1972 begs the question of the group's
own naiveté, as in the wake of their bombing attacks, many in
the West German establishment and media would have
presented the RAF's identity in an equivocal manner. If the
press printed the RAF's communiqués verbatim after the
attacks, it would have appeared that they had conceded to the
RAF's bombing tactics, or even expressed tacit support to the
RAF's cause.

From this perspective, the escalation of violence in
West Germany during this period could be seen as a "self-
fulfilling prophecy" of the media's earlier "Red Menace"
projections around Dutschke. [10]

Discussing state control and the power of the media,
American Students for a Democratic Society leader Tom
Hayden remarked in the late 1960s that "Rulers first fantasize
their devils, then create them." In a way similar to the myths of
Leftist terror that had been projected around a moderate figure
like Dutschke in the 1960s, in the aftermath of the 1972 army
base bombings, covert elements (e.g. the anonymous fabricator
of the fake communiqué) tried to define public conceptions of
the intent of the RAF.

By the summer of 1972, simultaneously with the
campaign of misleading information against the RAF in the
media, the fierce nationwide manhunt leads to the arrest of most
of the group's leaders.

At this point a shift of visual categories occurs in RAF
media coverage. Press focus shifts from images of bombing

sites to mugshots of the suspected bombers. To supplement its portrayal of the "Baader-Meinhof-Bande" serial, the press digs up more dirt: personal photographs of suspected group members and of their families or friends.

From this *image-intersect*, a sub-genre of RAF imagery emerges, seeded from two overlapping fields. Firstly, there is imagery produced by the terror group themselves, such as their logo, their communiqués, or spectacular visuals produced by their actions, (i.e. photographs of the aftermath of bombings or of terror victims). Secondly is the category of imagery that is state and media-generated, including mugshots of suspected group members or fake communiqués. Supplemented to the media/state output is a more vernacular style of photography—childhood snapshots of suspects, their families, or images of arrested members at earlier points in their lives. This body of personal RAF imagery is widely circulated by the police and media during this era.

This image-harvesting has a strange corollary effect. The RAF's bombing campaign intended a visually rhetorical double-bind—to control public vision through spectacular acts that involved both an erasure of visual space and a reversal of "normal" visual procedures.

However, instead, as Guy Debord noted in 1977, the RAF themselves "became fodder for the media machine,"[11] cast as spectacular

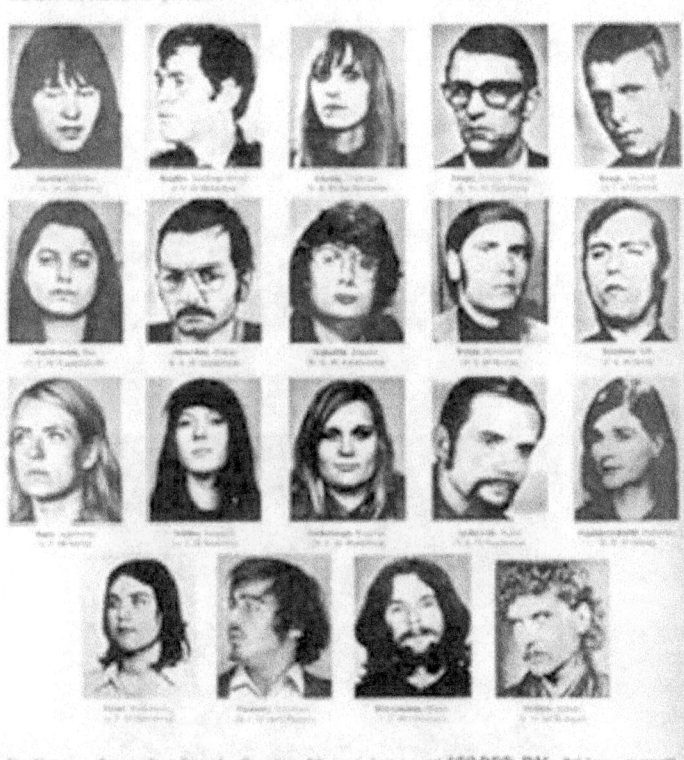

Fig. 26. Police Wanted poster for the RAF from May 1972. "Anarchistische Gewalttäter" (Violent anarchists)

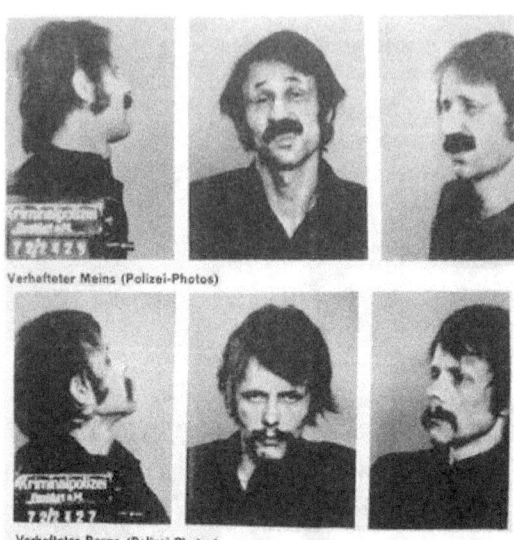

Verhafteter Meins (Polizei-Photos)

Verhafteter Raspe (Polizei-Photos)

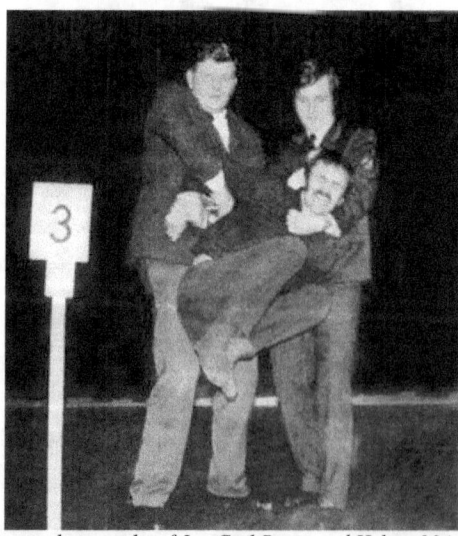

Fig. 27. Police arrest photographs of Jan-Carl Raspe and Holger Meins in June 1972. Both deliberately avoid the camera, grimacing and struggling.

young criminals, emergent, enraged celebrities in an ongoing, long-running serial, domestic terror drama.

Due to the constant use of personal images of RAF members during this era, it becomes possible to chronicle their lives "as imagined," in disguise, as arrestees, as prisoners, as hunger-strikers, as corpses. Did the endless display of their faces "before turning terrorist" and becoming *terrorized,* actually humanize the identities of RAF members?

Identity Theft: "I Am A Camera"

The RAF's intent to control the media through bombing is an important fault-line in discussions of the group's aims. So what specific role did the media hold for RAF strategies? Although their bombings did deliberately provided spectacular visual displays, some RAF watchers argue that the praxis in which the group was truly engaged was mostly manifested in the written word (i.e. their communiqués)—and that their bombing attacks had only aimed to "enact an opposition" to spectacular economy by erasing normal vision and manufacturing an "anti-spectacle."[12] RAF bombing attacks aimed to produce a vacuum of visual urban space—interrupting "the spectacle of everyday life"—to symbolically bring home the violent reality of the Vietnam War. Another indicator of their anti-visualist intent was that on their arrest, RAF members would frequently attempt to a-void the camera or grimace menacingly.

There is clearly an "anti-visual" intent to RAF strategy, and an ambivalence toward the imagistic, but contrary to this aim, some of the RAF leaders were renowned (at least in media coverage) for their flamboyant personal style, expressed in their taste for fancy clothes, fur coats, expensive cosmetics and a very particular choice in high-class stolen cars such as BMWs (renamed in popular legend as "Baader-Meinhof Wagons"). And despite an earlier conviction for targeting two Frankfurt department stores in 1968 as symbols of the

"Konsumgesselschaft"(consumer society), when RAF leader Gudrun Ensslin was finally re-captured in June 1972 for the army base bombings, she was caught while shopping in a high-end fashion boutique.[13] Likewise, Andreas Baader was known to keep two fur coats with him at all times—even in high-security jail.[14]

These *accessories* indicate that some at least in the RAF's leadership invested in luxury, in the currency of the imagistic and the invocation of a gangster-esque mythology. [15]

In discussing the relations between glamorous style and West German terror, it should be noted that there is a strange intertextual seepage between the RAF's Wanted posters and pin-ups from the burgeoning hippie culture of the period. The two "image categories" appear somewhat elided in collective consciousness. The preponderant styling of long hair and dark sunglasses makes it difficult to differentiate between images of "Wanted" RAF terrorists and pictures of contemporary hippie "pop stars." There is a similar notoriety, social interstitiality and transitory *quality* to both pop celebrity and terrorist. The young entertainer's continual secretive flight from hysterical fans provides a strange parallel to the youthful fugitive living in the underground—good-looking terrorists, dressed in stylish leather jackets and sunglasses exude a similar air of deliberate inconspicuousness. There is an inherent connection between the romantic figure of pop celebrity and outlaw—as fluid, shape-shifting, Protean figure. Continuous media photographic coverage of RAF members developed their identities as strangely double-coded figures. On the one hand, they appear as murderous outlaws and criminals, and also as oddly glamorous and even heroicly misunderstood, young renegades.

In the struggle over definition of public identity there is complicity between terrorists and media in the construction of such outrageous public identities and *sensational* "symbolic violence," and how these theatricalized image-based terror news stories were so successful in fascinating the *vampiric gaze* of the public.

In this arena, the visual becomes a site for intense battles for power and assignment of meaning, a locus for both ocular stimulation and wild hysteria. As the RAF TV drama escalates throughout the 1970s in increasingly violent spectacles, the stadia of the media increasingly becomes the central location for these compelling events. The terror story increasingly develops as a highly-commodifiable news product.

The villainization by the press of "Dutschke" in the 1960s demonstrates its bi-partisan representation of the Left. During the media pursuit and the arrest of the RAF leaders in 1972, this theatricalized visual and verbal language around Left outlaw identity was hyped to new levels. Similar to the rhetoric constructed around Dutschke, Springer press stories at the time concerning the RAF were printed in the most extreme terms, polarizing public opinions, covering events relating to the group in the most *theatricalized* of terms (such as "Die Gesichter des Terrors" The faces of terror).

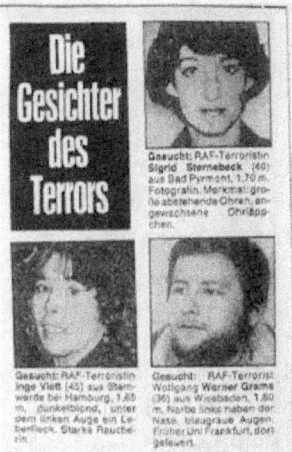 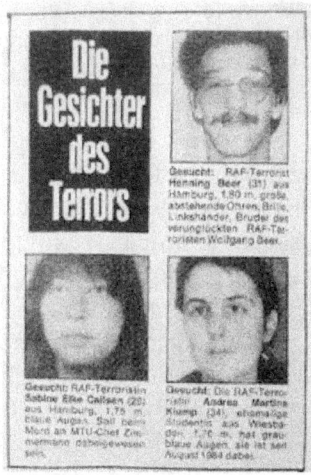

Fig. 28. "Die Gesichter des Terrors" (The Faces of Terror), 1980s BILD picture captions for RAF members still on the run.

This *polarized* language is mirrored in the linguistic framings of RAF texts with increasing vehemence, as the state, media and terrorists all argue in visio-verbal rhetorics of extreme and concreted oppositionalities. In 1974, RAF member Holger Meins' final communiqué from prison just before his death from hunger strike ends with the words "Entweder Mensch oder Schwein" (In the final analysis, you're either human being or pig).[16]

In such a discursive climate, all other voices become silenced, reduced to spectators in a constructed war of no compromise.

Public discourses concerning terror are often cordoned off into binary paradigms—the struggle between one element and another, i.e. the sovereign and their opposition. In much terror discourse, such a linguistic model is mapped onto the terrorist versus the technology of the state. It is hard to escape such binary framing in the rhetoric of terror. This doubling theme becomes a recurrent feature in discussion of the subject.

Phallic Woman, Oedipal Daughter, Mother with Gun: Media Demonization of Female Terrorists

In the same way Springer press villainized moderate left-wing leader Rudi Dutschke as a figure of monstrosity in the 1960s, in the 1970s news coverage of the RAF, gender was invoked in a similarly extreme and binary manner, to suggest outrageous or inhuman identity. This *monstrosity of evil*, of violence unsurprisingly had a sexual component.

This identity was embodied for Springer in the out-of-control woman terrorist. Endless news stories focused on the high proportion of RAF members who happened to be female.

A peculiar dialectic is established within Springer's linguistic matrix, between its endless confectionery parade of topless Page Three "beauties," and the portrayal of their opposite—armed terrorist women —encoded as figures of fearsome irrationality and danger, sigils of aberrant gender performance.

This evil woman archetype is hardly a new category. Foucault highlights medical institutional discourse and the emergence of the "female" as an hysterical object—a subject for the "scientistic" and (particularly) forensic conception of women's bodies—a location for study and control. In the printed press, since the first half-tone photograph entered the newspaper format in 1873, [17] discursive media structurations have emerged where imagery of women's bodies is often used in a decorative or illustrative relation to news narratives.

In media throughout history a category of imagery of "bad females," often defined as troublesome and political, remains a constant news feature from Joan of Arc to Jane Fonda. A genealogy of figures demonized in the press during the twentieth century tars almost all key female political activists from those associated with Suffrage and human rights to socialism, women such as Sylvia Pankhurst, Emma Goldman,

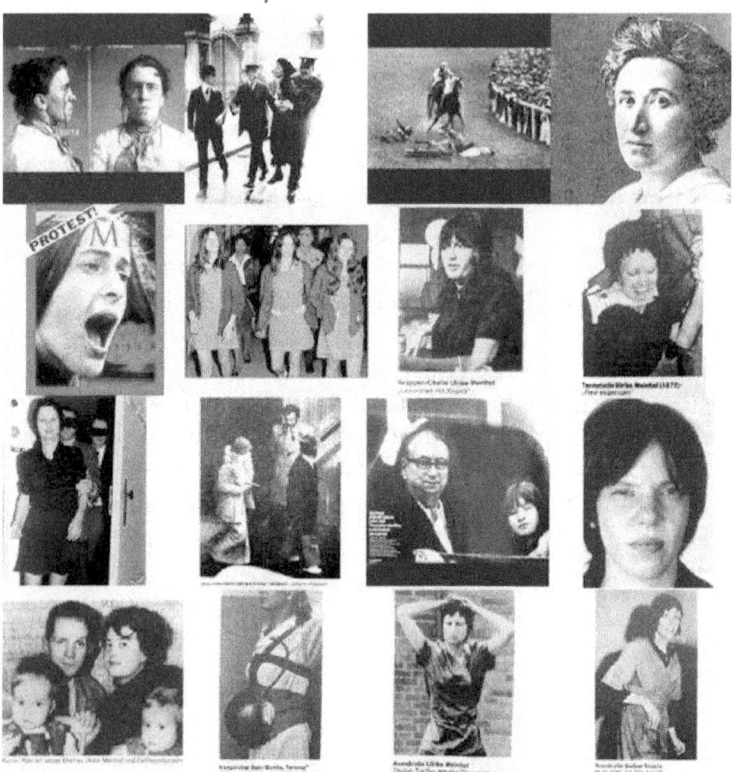

Fig.29. Scandalous and political women in the press since 1900: (left-right, top-bottom) Emma Goldman in an arrest photograph, 1916; Suffragette Sylvia Pankhurst being arrested outside Buckingham Palace in 1914; Suffragette Emily Davison killed by the king's horse at Epson in 1913, Rosa Luxembourg, circa 1910; Time cover, 1968; the Manson girls go to trial in California in 1970; Meinhof in court, late 1960s; Meinhof on arrest in 1972, Gabriele Kröcher-Tiedemann kidnapping OPEC ministers, 1972; Susanne Albrecht, mid 1970s; Meinhof with her husband and daughters in the mid 1960s; The threat of women terrorists with "baby-bombs" became a popular news story during the mid 1970s; Meinhof in jail in the mid 1970s; Ensslin in jail in 1976.

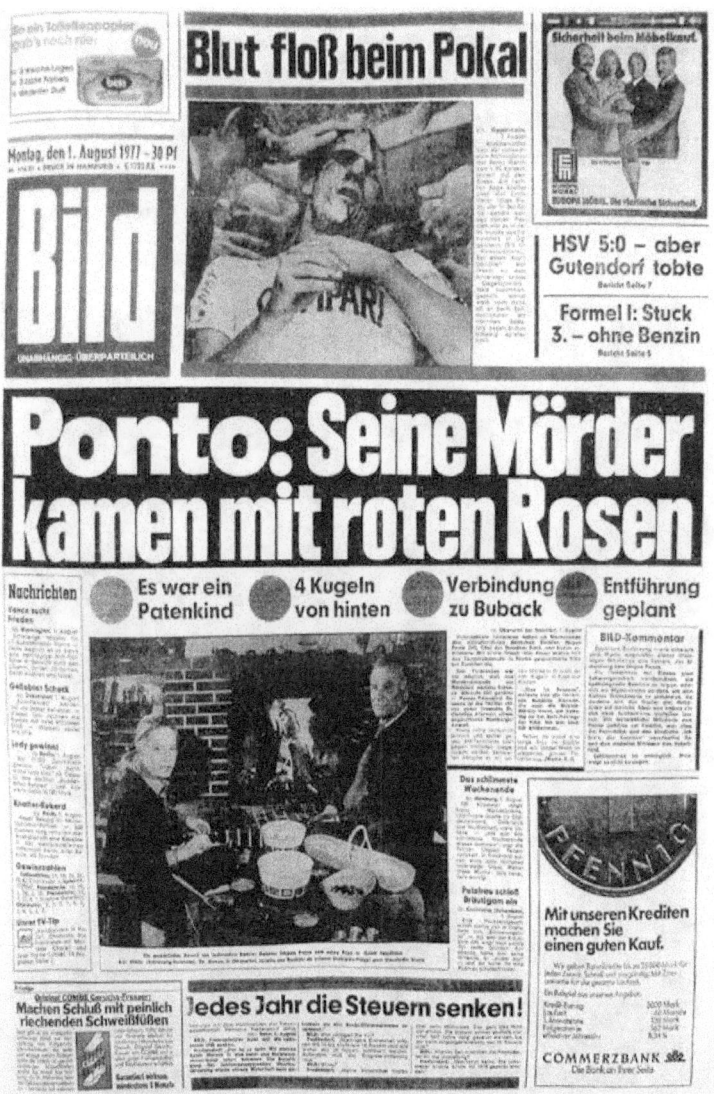

Fig. 30. Front-page of BILD, August 1ˢᵗ 1977. "Ponto: His killers came with red roses," "Es war ein Patenkind" (It was a godchild).
BILD's narrative accentuates the Oedipal drama of the story, juxtaposing text on the gruesomeness of the act with imagery of RAF member Susanne Albrecht's uncle, banker Jürgen Ponto and his wife at home sitting before an open fire.

114

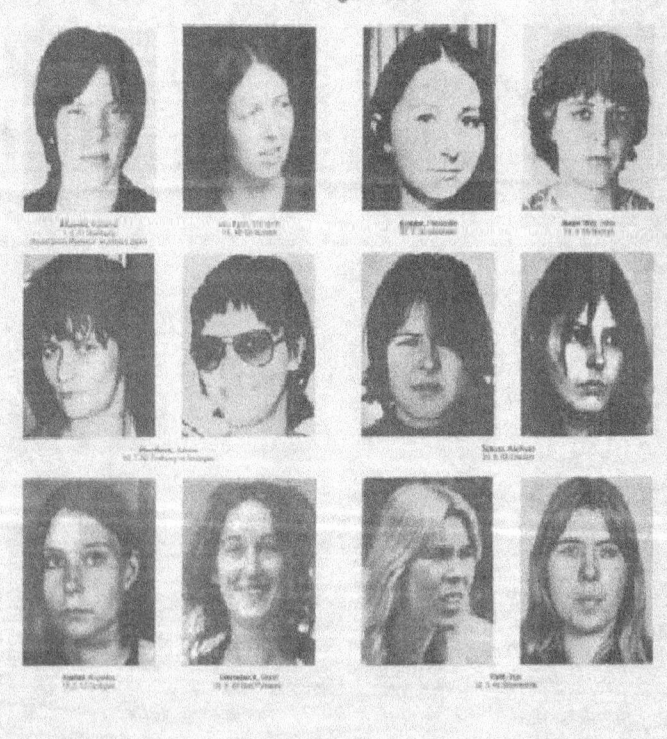

Fig. 31. Wanted poster for female RAF members in 1977 after the murders of Buback, Ponto and Schleyer

and Rosa Luxembourg. The media has often demonized images of oppositional female political leaders to objectify them as "scandalous" and/or denatured.

Concurrent to this by the 1970s, triggered by the explosion of feminism, a new type of troublesome political woman emerged as a category for the media—the "armed female terrorist." Stories concerning women "out-of-control" become a popular news item/product in the media. Patterns are visible in this period in the lurid coverage of the trial of the shaven-headed Manson girls in the U.S. in 1971, responsible for the gruesome murder of pregnant Hollywood star Sharon Tate.

Then, in 1974, press-heiress-kidnap-victim-turned-terrorist Patty Hearst was captured on newspaper front-pages posing with a gun—having switched channels to join the black male revolutionaries, the Symbionese Liberation Army. Blazoned across newspapers worldwide in this decade such images projected narratives of young politicized women running wild. Stories of violent women, mothers unfit or terrorist women with "baby bombs" were blown up to massive proportions to enhance the myth of "emancipated" women going "out of control."[18]

In the West German government of the time a topic of serious discussion was whether the recent emergence of a large number of female terrorists suggested that the current wave of feminism had progressed "too far."[19] An amusing play on this rhetoric is featured in an image caption from the magazine *Stern*, which features a photograph of the West German terrorist Gabriele Kröcher-Tiedemann kidnapping OPEC ministers at gunpoint in Vienna in 1972. Her photograph is jocularly captioned "Gänzlich emanzipiert" (Fully emancipated).[20].

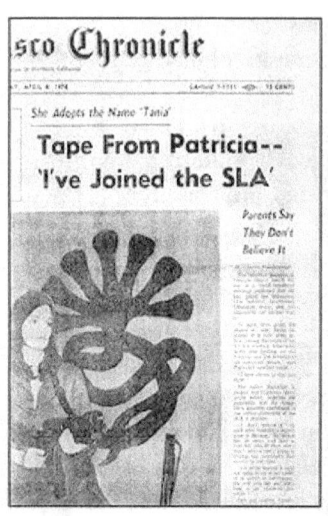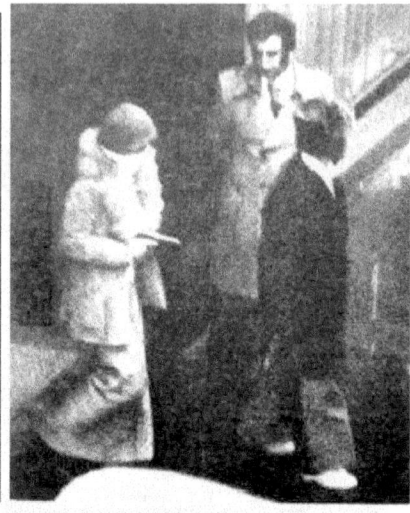

Opec-Attentäterin Gabriele Kröcher-Tiedemann: "Gänzlich emanzipiert"

Fig. 32. (left-right) Girls with guns: Hearst and Kröcher-Tiedemann. Patty Hearst on the cover of the Hearst-owned "San Francisco Chronicle," April 1974. Gabriele Kröcher-Tiedemann kidnapping OPEC ministers in Vienna in 1975. From "Stern" Magazine. The caption beneath her image reads "Gänzlich emanzipiert" (Fully emancipated)

Framed by rhetoric, the identitikit "terrorist woman" on the tabloid page presents an entroubled figure, a monstrous creature that *exceeds* society's boundaries. Located on the news paper adjacent to pictures of compliant Page Three girls, images of gun-toting females seem to stir up psychosexual panic for its readers.

For enhanced understanding of media representation of female terrorists, it is useful to consider the press framing of RAF members. Springer press coverage displayed its voyeuristic fascination with the person-ality and psychological make-up of RAF leader Ulrike Meinhof, a former magazine editor, whom Springer credited as the group's leading ideologue. In 1970 aged thirty-six, Meinhof, former editor of konkret, the leading left-wing journal, deserted a high-profile career in the media, playing a key role in the escape of Andreas Baader from jail, to go underground and help form the RAF.

To her peers in the press, Meinhof was a privileged person, someone who should have known better. They felt that she had *betrayed* her career, her marriage, her young children, and her class. As one of the older and more established figures in the RAF, she was portrayed in the press as one of the group's key ringleaders. Ulrike was centrally involved in a string of RAF actions including the U.S. army base bombings in May 1972. Her *outlawed* life on the run ended in arrest and imprisonment in June of that year. Meinhof was to die in prison four years later, allegedly by her own hand.

In relation to understanding media *representation* of Meinhof, it is important to note the way that gender and gender panic were enrolled in the construction of Meinhof as tabloid villain. During her time on the run, from 1970 to June 1972, Meinhof was constantly presented in the press in ways that accentuated her unfeminine qualities, her "unnaturalness." (Fig.32 is captioned "Group leader Meinhof, a Leninist with a gun"). The press were totally fascinated by the fact that Ulrike had given birth to twin daughters, eight years before she turned terrorist, and that she had deserted these poor young children when she went "renegade." "How could she?" Meinhof as the highest-profiled member of the RAF was *vilified* in the tabloid media as a figure of outrage—the monstrous Jocasta.

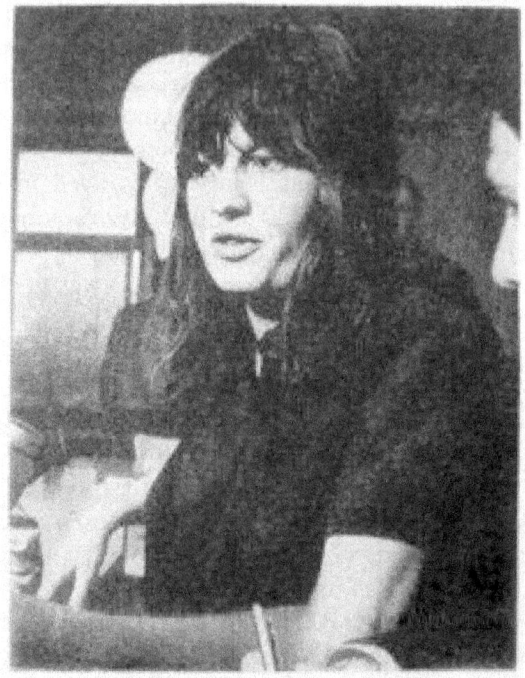

Gruppen-Chefin Ulrike Meinhof
„Leninisten mit Knarre"

Fig. 33. Meinhof: A "Leninist with a gun." From "Der Spiegel," June 5th 1972.

One theoretical *lens,* for considering tabloid media's representation of female terrorists, is to view the dynamic in relation to Lacan's model of the "Phallic Woman.". This identity is *symbol*-ized in the media by Meinhof whom they portray as a violent androgyne, an *entity* who had substituted motherhood for a gun. For the press through her embrace of terror Meinhof had become a Phallic Mother.

In her essay "Representation and Sexuality"(1983), psychoanalytic theorist Kate Linker discusses Lacan's "Phallic Woman" archetype in relation to post-partum trauma, [21] arguing that for the post-partum mother "the experience of having the phallus pertains to the Imaginary, resulting from the mis-recognition of the child as belonging to the mother's body. [...] Thus there is instability in the relationship—and difficulty, occasioned by the mother's inability to accept the child as "whole," as a-part from, rather than part of herself." In her analysis, she notes "the mother's desire to remain the omnipotent Other."

Linker sees the shift from the dyadic to the triadic relationship—through the re-integration of the father—as a threat to the narcissistic identification of the mother. The terrorist gun now replaces the child as source of the mother's empowerment.

As a rebel armed, Ulrike attempted to attack the state, but Lacanian theory conceives that Phallic Woman violates nature and must *necessarily* be stopped. From such an interpretation, the press perceives Meinhof's desire for armed revolt as an unnatural post-partum fantasy of re-empowerment that transgresses against the natural order. The responding paternal rupture can come either organically or through the state´s intervention.

Another theorist, Marcia Ian, argues that Lacan's "Phallic Woman" archetype represents the wish for the end of contradiction and ambivalence, particularly—although not exclusively—in the arena of sexuality. Phallic Motherhood becomes "an act of idealization by means of which some 'other' is endowed with transcendent wholeness, autonomy, and power that the self lacks."[22]

In Ian's reading, the nursery crime, "this fantasy of union is ruptured by the ultimate necessity of division, required both by the processes of the child's maturation, and by the Oedipal prohibition of the Father and the Law."[23]

In both these interpretations, Ulrike is portrayed in the media as a deranged mother who has overstepped her parental role, and instead of relinquishing her maternal desire for union, has re-phallicized herself through terrorism, transgressing against normal gender scripts. Hyperbolic press coverage of Meinhof subtextually played on this psychological panic. States can only restore natural order by castrating—literally disarming —the monstrous armed Phallic Woman, through chaining them.[24]

In a consideration of *outlaw female identity*, another useful model for analysis can be found in film scholar Laura Mulvey's seminal Feminist essay "Visual Pleasure and Narrative Cinema"(1973), which discusses gender in relation to scoptic [25] desire. Her work considers cinema's ocular regime and the Hollywood projection of "feminine" qualities of "to-be-looked-at-ness"—as a figure for objectification and fetishization.

In Mulvey's classic, binary, Feminist reading, visuality is split into the active "determining male gaze" and the passive "female object" who "holds the look." She discusses the *role* of women in adverts: "Traditionally, the woman displayed has functioned as an erotic object for the spectator ... isolated, glamorous, on display, sexualized."[26] Images of women "can be said to connote to-be-looked-at-ness... they play and signify male desire." In the tabloid mind of a "male" reader, through the spectacular projection of "femininity" in advertisements or in images of Page Three girls, the body politic of woman is signified as an *object* that "holds the look," and is a prize to be won if a product is purchased.

In relation to media portrayal of "terrorist women," it is interesting to note the Hollywood narrative concerning out-of-control females that must be pacified. In Springer's framing of RAF female terrorists, these troublesome women must be shown to be brought symbolically to justice, under control, in displaying them on camera in arrest or imprisoned poses. 1970s West German media images repeatedly display girl RAF members posed in submissive positions of arrest, vain struggle, and complete humiliation and defeat. These images attempt to de-empower and re-code this "rogue" agent of female identity —reducing the figures to a status similar to that of Page Three

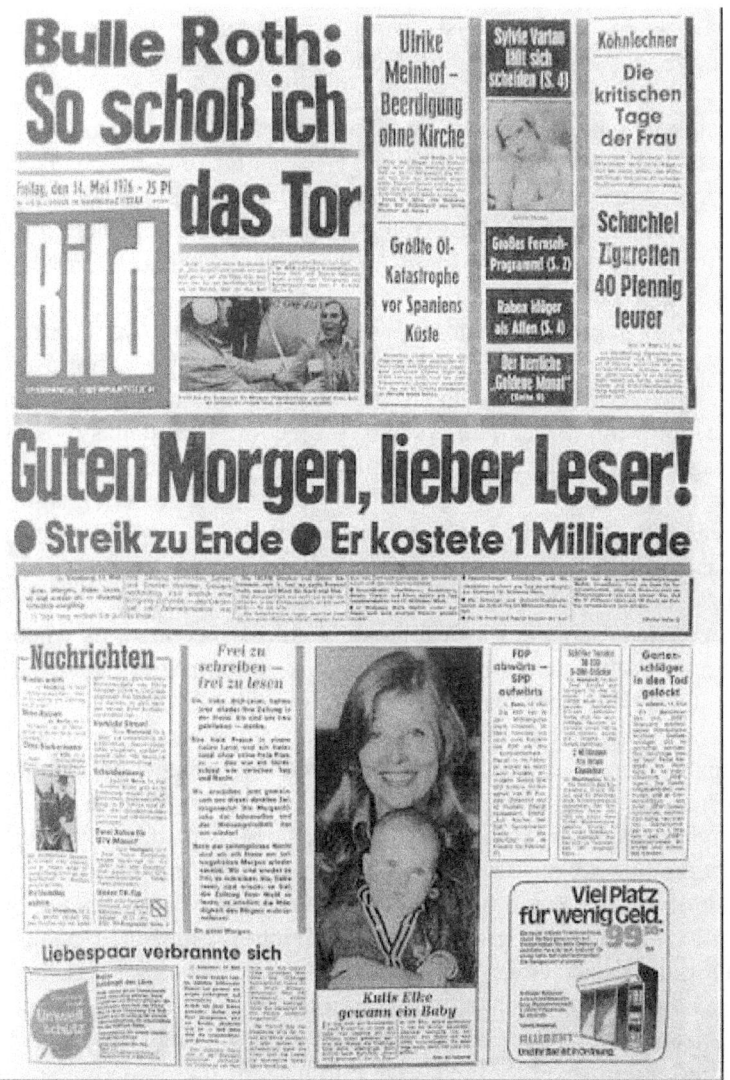

Fig.34. BILD May 14ᵗʰ, 1976.

The BILD on the day of Meinhof's funeral. The frontpage seems to juxtapose and compare the divorce of French pop beauty Sylvie Vartan, German actress Kulis Elke adopting a baby, with the detail that Meinhof's burial did not include a church service.

girls, where the "terrorist" woman is forced to pose for the camera in a posture of submission.

In the 1970s, news images of the arrest of Ulrike Meinhof, Gudrun Ensslin or other female RAF leaders were presented as a tabloid spectacle, a type of "terror porn." Images of apprehended "women terrorists" send out a sigil, a subtext to other female citizens: "Liberated women are crazy, violent and will be arrested, tortured and, in some cases, killed. Don't let this happen to you."

Looking at photographs of Meinhof thirty years after her death, it is difficult to disengage from these projections. In the media, Meinhof's likeness becomes a location for the specular, for voyeurism, ocular projection and fantasy. Her image was repeated ad infinitum in the press. No images of Meinhof seem denied public viewing, press images diachronically document the forty-one years of her life—from high-school student, to magazine editor, to mother with two small children, as demonstrator, as fugitive, as arrestee, in jail, as corpsed, and even as a forensic medical specimen, as when Meinhof's brain was removed for post-mortem after her death to investigate clues for her turn to "criminality." [27] [28]

Post arrest images of her body are used to play out a fetishized, on-camera, live, ritualized enactment of public correction by the state in the public's name. As Ulrike is symbolically and literally humiliated, transfixed newspaper readers and television viewers *experience* the imagery with a mix of repulsion and ocular fascination—observers winessing a modern-day lynching. Completing Meinhof's mediated public abasement and violent death, the camera's control over her visual presence is absolute. The consumer of the newspaper featuring Meinhof-related stories becomes complicit in her public humiliation by their very purchase of these newspapers. Watching of television coverage explicitly marketed around the voyeuristic exhibition of her torture, decline and death almost implies *access*oral complicity.

Such surveillant viewing is relentlessly compelling, yet in the end the entire subject becomes overwhelmed and overwhelming, exhaustive and exhausted, ghostive.

As can be noted in recent U.S. media, image catalogs of terrorists are endlessly regurgitated by the news, the repetition closing off any genuine discourse, rendering the subject overdetermined, evacuated of meaning, repulsive, and ultimately unviewable, undigestible, and almost invisible. Media representations of female terrorists in the 1970s can be seen as related to the birth of a new news product/category.

The voyeurist, relentless obsession of the press in focusing on *humiliated* female terrorists bears a similarity to the later emergence and naturalization of what is known as "stalkerazzi"/vulture culture. A famous early example of this press obsession was the spatial harassment of Jackie Kennedy by New York paparazzi piranha Ron Galella. The press stalking of the fugitive/celebrity/ woman during the 1970s has since become completely normalized as a media business. Famous public figures are routinely hunted as public quarries, chased down and aggressively documented by the vigilante camera eye in a draconian assertion of media power.[29] [30]

[1] The newspaper format is a complex embedded rhetorical space.

[2] Mirzoeff cites Ranciere in *Watching Babylon.* p.16.

[3] Notably in contrast the state's covered-up victims, the mortality of the RAF terrorists is prominently displayed in the tabloids in the mid-1970s--brought to visuality, as scalps in a grisly imagistic war.

[4] The RAF's "terror act" can be viewed at core as a technologically-recorded-and-mediated performance by non-state actors. It is a challenge to the nation-state through spectacular bombings (or later by abduction and/or murder of state officials or military personnel). Symbolic destruction is performed by terrorists in an attempt to display a challenge to the state's power. The terrorists do this by interrupting its visual and social order. Terrorist "refusals" of the democratic process are visually-enacted manifestations of "rogue (non-state) power" within non-combat, civilian zones. These terror acts are framed and made concrete by the media's photographs of damaged buildings, partially destroyed cars and bombed army bases strewn with broken glass. The media's presentation of terror acts is crucial to their public perception. And then, rather than allowing such acts to be perceived as random acts of violence (or perpetrated by "foreign" intruders), the terrorists later leave various trace markers--such as communiqués. The group's communiqués explain their ideologies and demands. These clarify that the attack has been made by "activist" national citizens, acting under the exegesis of a "political" association—in this case, that explain that they are acting in response to Che Guevara's injunction to "create two, three...many Vietnams." The communiqué argues that "the fascist state's" monopoly of violence and control of visual meaning has been broken. But how many in the general population had access to, or chose to read, or understood the RAF's dense diatribe-filled communiqués?

[5] Notable regarding RAF communiqués and their descriptions of political violence and the visual is their inherent unreadability. They are theoretically and densely written so to exclude any easy interpretation-- in a manner similar to Debord and Adorno's cryptic writing styles.

[6] The name "Baader-Meinhof-Bande" was used by the police and newspapers from May 1970 after Baader's jail escape to refer to the RAF to diminish the group's identity and also to suggest the group were led by Baader and Meinhof. This term was used in the media throughout the 1970s to imply the RAF were a non-political, criminal gang, but also to further personalize and this terror group's identity. The name "Baader-Meinhof" is sometimes used in popular culture in English-language discussion of the group. However Storr, Varon, Scribner and some German scholars use the group's official name, the RAF.

[7] It's important to note how the tabloid media push the bounds between private and public information. Since Modernity's dawn, scandalous events

have been ritual enactment of societal mores and been increasingly conceived of as sites of commodity. In recent years these tendencies are exemplified by tabloid constructs involving humiliating public spectacle involving "troubled" celebrities.

[8] It was immediately assumed by the press and state that Baader and Meinhof (the RAF's best-known public figures) were the group's leaders.

[9] From http://www.germanguerilla.com/red-army-faction/documents/72-05-28.html

[10] From "Trial" by Tom Hayden. As quoted in John Sinclair's book, *Guitar Army*, 1972.

[11] Scribner, "Buildings on Fire: The Situationist International and the Red Army Faction." *Grey Room* 26, Winter 2007. MIT, p.32.

[12] An example of this type of study is Bowman Howard Miller's 1983 *The Language Component of Terrorism Strategy: A Text-based, Linguistic study of Contemporary Terrorism*, which focuses primarily on the RAF's communiqués. But a tendency to underplay the media aspects to the RAF debacle and instead concentrate on their ideologies is also apparent in the work of Varon, Peters and others.

[13] Ensslin 1972 arrest cited in Varon, p.215. Ironic to note here is how the 1968 arson attacks of 1968 intended to target "commodity culture." Varon, p.41.

[14] From *Der Welt*, "Wer war Andreas Baader wirklich?" by Marco Stahlhut. January 3rdd 2007. "Selbst in Stammheim besaß (Baader) noch zwei Pelzmäntel und mehrere Sonnenbrillen. "Ein Kerl wie ich", bittet Baader nach einer Verhaftung, "ein Kerl wie ich braucht sein Rasierwasser". http://www.welt.de/print-welt/article705594/Wer_war_Andreas_Baader_wirklich.html

[15] In this relation to glamour, Baader and Ensslin are reminiscent of other "Leftist" terrorists active in Western Europe during this time, such as the dandified Carlos the Jackal, a.k.a. Illich Ramirez Sanchez, the notorious terrorist/gun-for-hire, involved in the 1972 OPEC hostage crisis in Vienna. For a further discussion of his tangential relation to RAF terror, see Varon, p.68.

[16] This extract from Meins' final letter is widely quoted. The full letter is available at http://www.germanguerilla.com/red-army-faction/documents/74-1—31-meins.html.

[17] *The New York Daily Graphic* was the first newspaper to include a half-tone photograph, on December 2nd, 1873, an image of the city's Steinway Hall appeared on the back page. From *Dictionary of Media and Communication Studies*. 6th Edition, James Watson and Anne Hill. p.325. London: Arnold, 2003.

[18] Of further interest related to this theme is Eileen MacDonald's *Shoot The Women First*, a study of female terrorists across a range of countries during the 1970s.

[19] This issue is discussed at greater length as the cover story of *Der Spiegel*, "Die Terroristin: Frauen und Gewalt," August 8th, 1977. P.21-33.

[20] Within an ongoing flow of media-generated myths during the 1970s, the RAF members were presented as the embodiment of a "red terror" archetype. Narrative threads played on particular myths and fears around such ideas. By enfolding RAF images with other narratives evoking deeply troubling subconscious associations, the media profoundly shaped public opinion of the group. There is intertextuality between the horror imagery of the emaciated RAF members in 1974 in jail on hunger strike with the ghostly images of World War Two concentration camp victims. (explain re. von Trotta) West Germany was still haunted by the visual grammar of Holocaust imagery in the post-war era. Certain public images like these can appear to act as cracks in a society's facade that threaten to rupture the domestic. It can be argued that West German media channels used certain types of framing on particular imagery to erase others and to regulate the society.

[21] Kate Linker, "Representation and Sexuality." 1983. p.403.

[22] Ibid.

[23] Ibid.

[24] However there are shortcomings in trying to consider Meinhof in relation Lacanian theory. Although from the government's perspective, Meinhof is the gun-toting mother who violates the natural order. But from the terrorist's perspective, her actions can also be portrayed differently. Instead, she is reacting to a government that is out of control. She imagines herself as "the Law" correcting imbalances in German society. The "Phallic Woman" is an abstract term, useful but limited because almost anyone in this dynamic could be seen as the "Phallic Woman" overstepping their position. Against this, although this theory provides an interesting analytical model for considering the phenomenon of the female terrorist, it cannot offer any explanation for the psychological drives of the male terrorist.

[25] Scoptic relates to the psychosexual term, scoptophilia, the pleasure of looking.

[26] Mulvey, p.62-64

[27] Meinhof's brain was removed for post-mortem to investigate clues for her turn to "criminality."

[28] Notably after her death, some posthumous posters of Meinhof portray her in a style similar to the Korda Che image.

[29] An example of this pattern was the "gay-celebrity-with-AIDS story" tabloid genre of the early 1980s, and how it established the new patterns and

permissions for the, unremitting close surveillance of celebrities we now take for granted.

[30] Stranger still concerning images of West German terrorists which were produced in the media in the 1970s, is the way that they have developed as objects oddly associated with nostalgia and aestheticization. This commodification and consumption of terrorism are subjects I return to further in Chapters Six and Seven.

Chapter VI

THE PEOPLE'S COURT:

VISUAL HIJACKING, THE CORPSE AND THE HOSTAGE

Bomb attacks were just one of the RAF's media-oriented tactics. By the mid-1970s, the RAF changed channels to a program of deliberately bombarding the media and the public with imagery that was much more explicitly terrorizing. Seemingly in response to continual media pillory of RAF members such as Meinhof, the RAF appeared to shift to different media tactics—techniques intentionally producing images that were profoundly more disturbing and horrifying to the public.

These new tactics upstaged the endless news stories of subjectified terrorist women. In response to Springer's

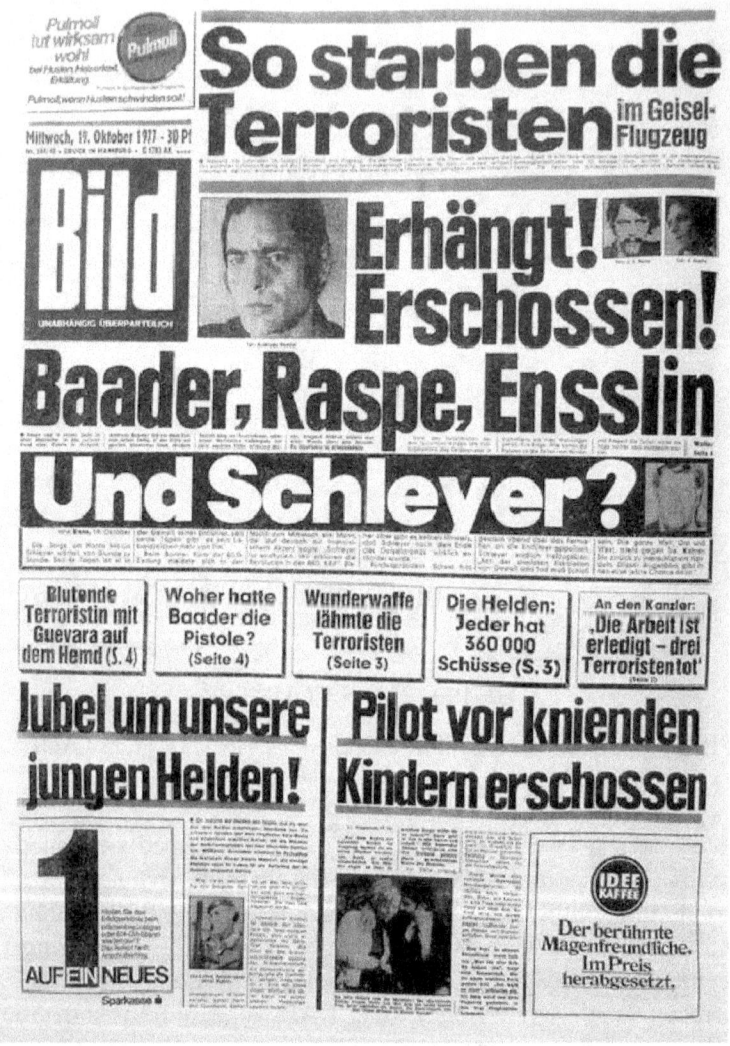

Fig 35. Front-page of BILD, October 19ᵗʰ, 1977. Baader, Ensslin and Raspe dead. Note the mention of the Che Guevara T-shirt worn by the one surviving Palestinian terrorist at Mogadishu who survived and was captured.

127

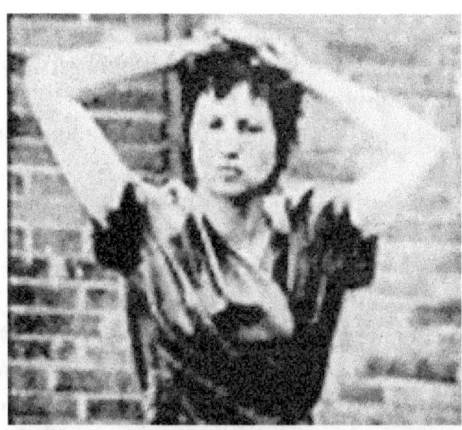

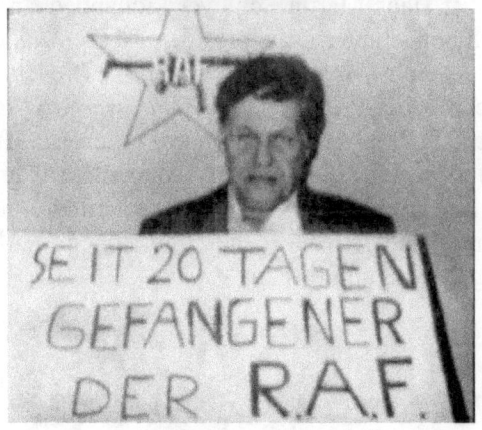

Fig. 36. Two Captives in the RAF Debacle: Meinhof and Schleyer. Meinhof in jail in the exercise year, 1975, Hans-Martin Schleyer in the RAF kidnap video in 1977.

spectacularized chained females, West German terrorists now *reversed* these procedures—deliberately queering traditional media cultural scripts—showing men, rather than women, in poses of *display*, vulnerability, of objectification.

RAF strategies in the mid-1970s turned the tables on the media, producing an image-reversal—by generating disturbing images of male RAF prisoners on hunger strike in 1974. Their emaciated bodies provided an unsettling visual terrain, reminders of sunken faces of concentration camp victims. As RAF member Holger Meins slowly wasted away and died on hunger strike in November 1974, his shriveled corpse was to be shockingly displayed "on camera" via the media's lens.

But, beyond this press-oriented horror tactic, in 1977, the RAF produced equally visceral media imagery in the kidnapping of a male high-level state official and then displaying him on camera in "hostage videos." The RAF then virally disseminated these videos at the press.

This new RAF *tactical* attack is exemplified in their most *famous* televisual intervention—the release of the video of industrialist Hans-Martin Schleyer kidnapped. In August 1977, RAF members abducted the president of the *Bundesvereinigung der Deutschen Arbeitgeberverbände* (Federal Union of Employer Association) and the *Bundesverband der Deutschen Industrie* (Federal Association of German Industry). By kidnapping such a high-ranking state official and former SS officer like Schleyer, the RAF aimed to pressurize the government into freeing the imprisoned RAF leadership, including Baader and Ensslin.

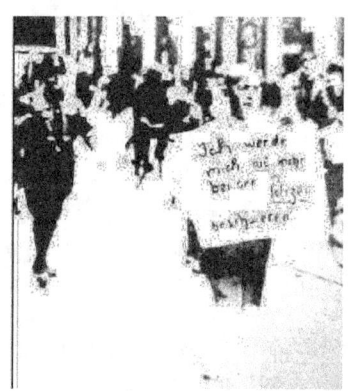

Fig. 37. (left-right, top-bottom) Victims of "the People's Court." Jewish citizens in Germany in the late 1930s being public humiliated by black shirts.

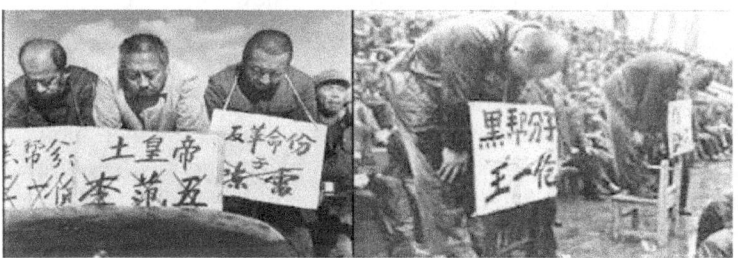

(left-right)Images from the Chinese Cultural Revolution, 1960. Disgraced farmers and bureaucrats: Placards around their necks read "Counterrevolutionary revisionist element," "Local despot," "Black gang element."

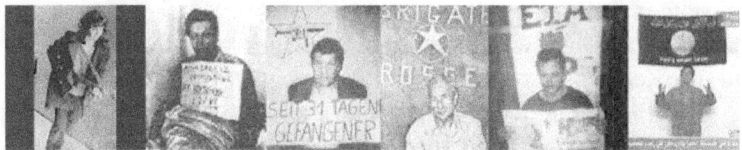

(left-right): Patricia Hearst caught on closed-circuit video, robbing the Hibernia Bank, San Francisco, 1974; Peter Lorenz, Berlin mayor, Bewegung 2.Juni kidnap victim with group name 1976; Hans-Martin Schleyer, kidnap victim on video with RAF logo, 1977; Aldo Moro, kidnap victim with Brigate Rosse logo 1978; ETA kidnap victim on video with logo 1990s; Iraq kidnap victim on video with Islamic terror group logo, 2004.

In a series of videos. the RAF posed Schleyer holding a placard documenting the number of his days as an on-screen hostage. This mirror-war image repositioned the state itself being on trial in the RAF's televised "People's Court." The reflective haunting image of Schleyer, himself a former Nazi, seemed to intentionally draw reference to historic images from the Fascist era (anti-Semitic lynching during the 1930s), or the Chinese Cultural Revolution (images of publicly disgraced professors and party officials). In visual locations like these, *citizens* deemed renegade or inherently "base" are shamed ritually on camera in public, made to wear placards that proclaim their "crimes." [1] In reversing totalitarian visual languages of these regimes, and in appearing to explicitly play on gruesome riffs of state terror, the RAF attempt to intentionally shock and horrify their audience.[2]

The Schleyer shockvideo was a new engagement with the "theater of cruelty." In a response to these "acts," the state re-acted with its own even more conspicuous displays of violence—releasing to the mass media gruesome photographs of corpses of Baader and Ensslin lying dead in their own blood in state cells and simul*casting* real-time executions of three plane hijackers in Mogadishu. This imagistic "war/porn" was vaingloriously paraded across the press. Scalps in a grisly imagewar, these photographs of dead terrorists (similarly to the famous image of the dead Che) identify and confirm their defeat and erased threat. The contract between viewer/media and state is fulfilled.

In this psy-war, three known parties—the media, state, and the terror cells—deliberately attempt to psychologically terrorize the public They manufacture and recycle visuals with troubling subconscious connotations, trawled from psychic, cognitive associations of humiliation.

However, media images of bombings, hunger strikers, kidnap victims with the RAF's logo, or dead prisoners, start after a while to eschew any coherent reading or interpretation. The image itself became fascinatingly horrific—producing an *incapacitating* visceral overload.

Theorist Roland Barthes used the term *punctum* in explaining the inherent ability of certain photographic images to *arrest* the intention of the viewer. It is relevant here to consider the power of media images of hunger strikers, kidnap victims and corpses, to arrest the attention of the individual—to horrify, to interrupt, and to deliver a specific type of rhetorical punch. Barthes' *punctum,* the *qualité* of an image that shocks the viewer and makes them pause, allows the image to "puncture" their conscious-ness. As Barthes describes it, "(F)or me, the punctum takes the spectator outside its frame," "The punctum, ...is a kind of subtle beyond."[3]

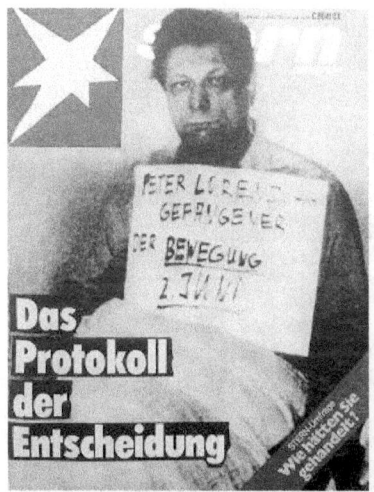
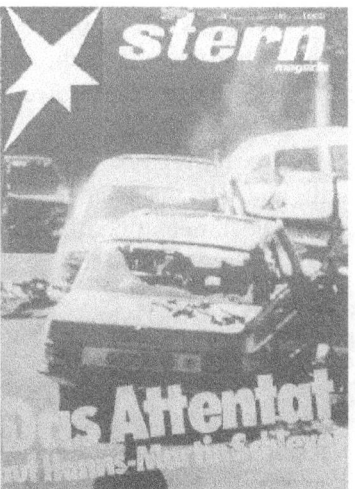
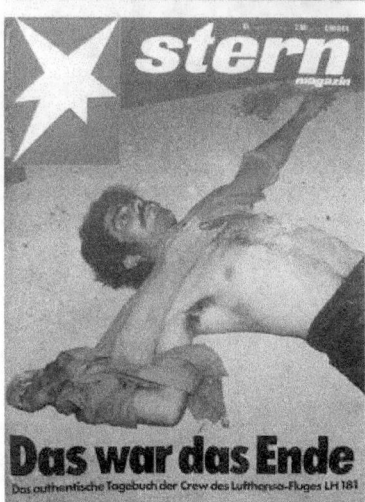

Fig 38. Stern magazine covers from 1975 and 1977: (left-right) February 1975 (Berlin CDU mayoral candidate Peter Lorenz kidnap); from October 1977 (Hans-Martin Schleyer's car after his kidnap; and also a dead terrorist after the failed Mogadishu airplane hijack).

132

In discussions of imagery relating to terror, it is crucial to consider how the viscerality of the *punctum* to an image of a terror scene sutures the viewer into the psycho-mythological matrix of terror. Often, what the viewer searches for in an image of terror is not present. The actual terror event has passed, and all that remains is shadow—the hypnotic and gruesome documentation of aftermath.

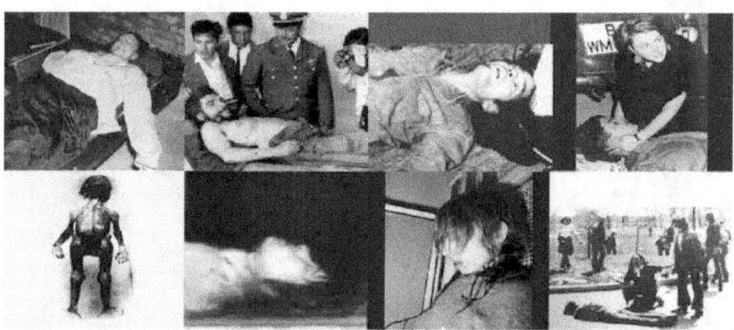

Fig.39. The Political Corpse: (left-right, top to bottom) Goering dead in prison, 1945; Che dead in Bolivia, 1967; Andreas Baader dead in Stammheim prison, 1977; Benno Ohnesorg dead outside the Deutsches Oper, West Berlin 1967; Holger Meins dead from hunger strike in prison, 1974; Ulrike Meinhof dead in Stammheim prison in Richter's painting, 1976; Gudrun Ensslin dead in Stammheim prison, 1977; Jeffrey Miller student demonstrator lies dead at Kent State campus, shot by the Ohio National Guard, 1970.

The horror tactics of RAF kidnapping videos of 1977 exemplify the ongoing power play for visual dominance between state, terrorists and the media as the Cold War thaws.

Examining these patterns shows proof of the way that the terrorist succeeded during this era in developing parasitic relations to the media. Although in achieving this, "the terror struggle" engenders another type of struggle—between sensational terror news reportage and the control of the state — between government mandate and commercial incentive.

In a discussion of terror strategics during the 1970s, media theorist Melani McAlister notes that in the first wave of televisual terror:

> coverage of hijackings and bombings offered a "magnifying effect," similar to "a form of political advertising." Like the sponsors of early television who produced shows as vehicles for their commercials, media terrorists now provided drama—murder and kidnapping, live—in return for advertising. More or less consistently, the media gave the hijackers and bombers the kind of political status they were seeking.[4]

McAlister highlights the para-osmotic interrelation between terrorist cells and mediocrats. Terroristic media interventions of the 1970s produce sensational live news feeds that became eye-catching cogs of the "info-tainment" industry.

The RAF's Schleyer videos and their freeze-framed stills provoked outrage and huge media coverage as they were broadcast publicly in 1977. Literary theorist Charity Scribner recently proposed that the RAF made "television history" by distributing this kidnap footage to the media,[5] However, given the reach and range of similar global media-oriented interventions in the late 1960s and 1970s, it remains debatable to what degree the RAF were breaking entirely new ground.

Two years earlier in West Germany, in February 1975, RAF-related terror group Bewegung 2.Juni kidnapped and photographically displayed the captive CDU mayoral candidate for Berlin Peter Lorenz in a manner very similar to the RAF's presentation of Schleyer.

Scribner's suppositions bring up further questions concerning transnational migration of terror mise-en-scene d this period. There is a relation in strategy between the raised-fist media intervention of the U.S. athletes at the 1968 Mexico Olympics (discussed in Chapter Three) and the RAF's 1977 Schleyer video kidnap. Both succeed in their piratical intent of dramatically seizing the airwaves.

During the 1960s and 1970s, the increasing bounty in strategies of comandeering the media and also the influencing power of television both grew in parallel. This can be witnessed by the huge wave of media-oriented airplane hijacks and hostage crises across the globe.

A significant cipher connecting the Olympic Mexican media stunt and RAF Schleyer Video occurs in the strategic live television bank heist by the California-based Symbionese Liberation Army (SLA) in 1974.

Three years prior to the RAF's hostage video, "urban guerrillas" the SLA made headline news by kidnapping newspaper heiress Patricia Hearst. This group then had Hearst and themselves filmed robbing a Los Angeles bank at gunpoint, the heist having been recorded on the bank's closed-circuit security cameras. This video footage was utilized on prime-time American news to show that incredibly, but indisputably, a kidnapped newspaper heiress had now switched sides and was now an armed member of a guerilla cell. SLA strategy deliberately subverted "the Man's" video high-technology for the group's own "anti-capitalist" means. A cheeky twist to this tactic is that the only identifiable (non-masked) armed bank robber is the daughter of the owner of the Hearst Corporation, the SLA story's biggest disseminator.

This innovative use of video in a media-oriented terror strategy clearly preceded and influenced the RAF Schleyer Video. The success of SLA media tactics undoubtedly inform the strategy of the RAF, and as McAlister points out, the fast developing technological possibilities of the period allowed new media-oriented strategies to develop international currency.

In 1976, a Hollywood movie *Network* satirized and sanitized the media's complicity with such tactics. In the film, a caricature seemingly based on Angela Davis, called Laureen Hobbs a verbose young black Communist leader shouts at a television producer "You can blow the seminal prisoner class infrastructure out your ass. I'm not knockin' down my goddamn distribution charges."[6] As the film implies, terrorist groups and the media were developing a mutually-advantageous relationship, trading advertising space for their ideologies in exchange for edge-of-the-seat newsfeed

Returning to Scribner's suggestion concerning the supposed groundbreaking strategy of the RAF video, clearly the visual styling of the 1977 Schleyer video with its group logo backdrop was influential on the look of the Italian Brigate Rosse's imagery of kidnapped industrialist Aldo Moro one year later. [7] Although, media-oriented hijack dramas continue to this day, crucial to the broader success of these tactics during the 1970s was that, in that particular era, the media gave terrorists direct screen-time visibility plug-in.

British Prime Minister Margaret Thatcher questioned levels of coverage of terror attacks by the Irish Republican Army (I.R.A) in the media in the early Eighties when she famously argued that terror strategies rely on "the oxygen of publicity."[8] Press coverage helped draw attention to the I.R.A's aims.

Similar to the I.R.A blanket coverage on British television during this period, in West Germany, the press' extensive coverage of media-oriented terror tactics hyped the RAF's attacks, projecting their ideals to a huge national audience. As noted, the RAF explicitly aimed from their start to instrumentalize media and to challenge the state. But against this "hypodermic" model of injecting their own presence into the body media, the West German media also enthusiastically participated in *spectacularizing* terror as newsfeed stimulus to grab their audience's attention and accelerate ratings—and, in Springer press's case, to smear the entire New Left. The RAF terror debacle was a media-centric campaign, in the war of *terror-images*, state agents or terrorists often ended as victims, while the press always won in terms of ratings and of the level of public engagement.

In Western Europe at this time, against Thatcher's conception of terrorism, it could be said that by the end of the 1970s a "theater of terror," the hostage drama, had become a familiar feature in the news media, but, as McAlister[9] notes, this terror tactic developed in a bio-sphere that worked with a pre-established, sophisticated visual and verbal palettes. Terror group hijack videos entered a huge solid-state closed-circuit communications system where all *information* is presented within particular discursive structurations. The news media's framing of any terrorist *identity* was already predetermined. Within this parapolitical system, the RAF *identity* is itself instrumentalized and magnified as part of the larger agenda of Springer, the largest media Cold War conglomerate in Europe. In such a context, this conservative media group had the ability to subjectify any discourse that appeared to challenge or threaten its masternarrative.[10]

Contrary to Thatcher's call to deny the oxygen of publicity, it seems the RAF terror "wave" was enthusiastically covered by the media perhaps for the state and media's own political ends. It should be noted in this regard that during the entire RAF period of activity from 1970 to 1993, thirty-six people died—mainly group members. Compared to state violence worldwide during the same period, this number is relatively minute. Despite this, the RAF news story was blown up into a huge ongoing national drama throughout the Seventies due to the extensive media coverage of the group's hijacks, bombings and assassinations.

Germany's hyper-media coverage of the RAF "melodrama" adds to an escalating theatrical series of events that ultimately led to the plane hijack hostage *crisis* in 1977 at Mogadishu, a "sensational" news event which reached huge global audiences. Springer's invocation of the imminent threat of Leftist urban guerilla revolution—promoted through its witch-hunts for Leftist leaders in the Sixties—seemed to have come true by the late 1970s.

As S.I. member Guy Debord noted in 1977 in regard to this dynamic: "The story of terrorism is written by the state. The citizens (spectators) always have a partial grasp of terrorism and militancy. They know just enough to be convinced that "compared with terrorism," everything else must be "more rational and democratic."[11] So did the widely-held public perception of a crisis situation in West Germany create the social permissions for a draconian clampdown on civil liberties and the installation of huge new police surveillance regimes, closing down all oppositional voices on certain topics, creating a state of democratic exception.

Complex historical realities post-World-War-Two and the preceeding Cold War climate fed contexts where terror acts, such as those of the RAF, were presented in a specific manner within the media arena. Through increasingly visually-horrific acts, the terrorists and the state staged symbolic spectacles of visual violence. This conflict developed an unusually high visual presence during this period as the state, media and the RAF attempted to "dominate the discourse," invoke the mythic and *produce* a culture of hysteria. The RAF's *imagined* threat appeared in retrospect much bigger than it in fact was. It provoked a national wave of paranoia of fantastical proportions. It was, to borrow Marx's term, a "heilige Jagd" (a holy witch hunt). [12]

One year after Meinhof's death, Springer news stories returned to the theme of motherhood in their *reporting* of the 1977 Mogadishu airplane hijack crisis, as freed Lufthansa passengers arrived back in West Germany. One *BILD* news story prominently displayed a photograph of a ten-year-old boy waiting at the airport holding a hand-written placard that proclaims "Ich will meine Mutti wiederhaben" (I want my mommy back). In this tabloid saga, similar to the rhetoric of the 1950s *Heimatfilme* genre, Springer's closing narrative to this hijack drama adds a telling postscript. The plaintive words on the child's placard are not kidnap demands, they present instead an opportunity for *BILD* to install a subtext, a reminder of the "naturalness" of parental (i.e. state) order and the call for all women to return to the traditional familial matrix.

138

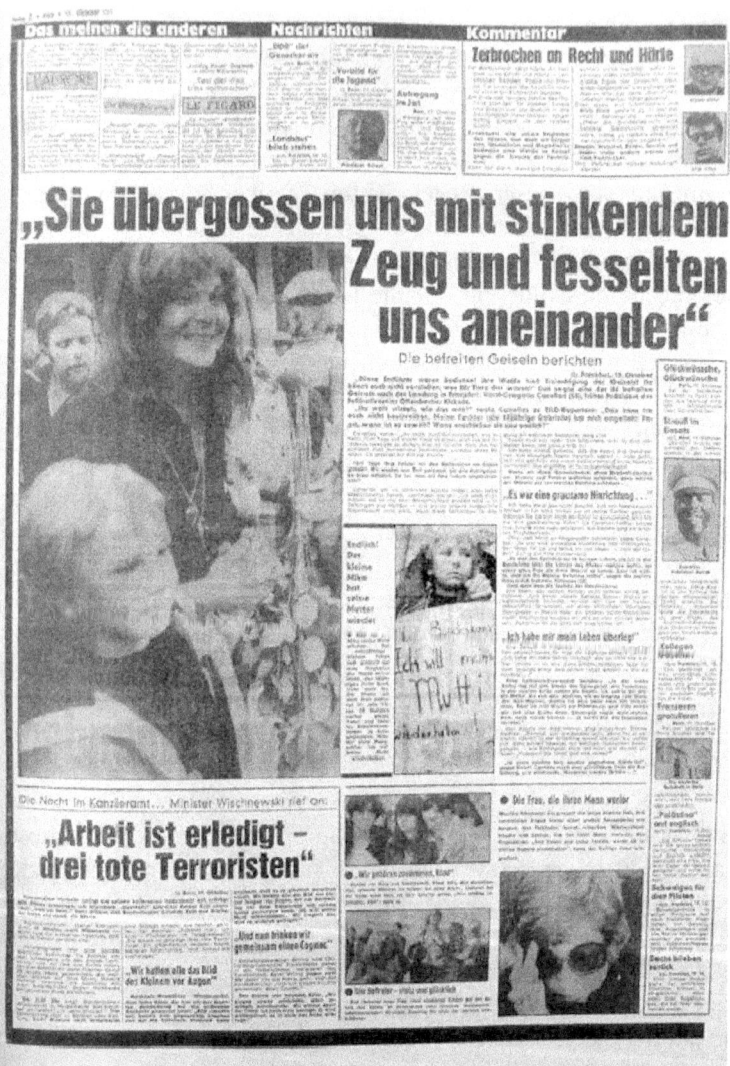

Fig. 40. Page Two of BILD, October 19th, 1977. A child holding a placard waits for his mother's return from Mogadishu. It reads "Ich will meine Mutti wiederhaben" (I want my Mommy back).

The impact of terror on the media

      This chapter *reads* four moments in the history of the RAF in relation to the West German media in the 1970s. It dissects intersections demonstrating media ability during the Cold War to shape public opinion and to show innovations in the media-oriented terror strategies by the RAF themselves during this era.

      It analyzes ways in which mythos constructs around the RAF's identity. It shows Springer's theatrical presentation of the RAF, and how this media debacle is marked in particular ways by the emerging technologies of the era—as demonstrated by the RAF's strategy of the hijack video.

      My central thesis is that the *location* on which the RAF debacle began and most fully took place was the media, and *framing* of the RAF—the visio-verbal language born in this arena by both media and terror group—shape later understandings of *identity*. Although over a longer period, media *construction* of the RAF was contested by counternarrative representations, throughout this initial 1970s period, as shown in this chapter, the RAF public identity was predominantly formed by the media's lens.

      As we have witnessed, new stereotypes of *outrageous* terror language develop due to the specific formats and contexts discussed, as "Spectacular New Media" forms during this era cluster around the subject of terror. In the early 1980s, the kind of coverage terrorists had earlier received became much more controlled, much less sensational. Global news reporting on terrorism had shifted in significant ways. The era when the RAF 's opportunity to create "the revolution through headlines" was seemingly over.

      Statistical studies cited by Chomsky and Herman show how *framing* of terror news changes in key ways between the 1970s and 1980s,.[13] The overloading of this type of "news item" in many countries in the West during the late 1970s led to the emergence of tighter, more explicit state and media controls as well as mandates on the type of coverage and level of visibility that was to be given to the subject of terror. It also appears that this form of news-byte featuring sensational terror tactics appeared to have become exhausted, simply due to its saturation coverage.

However in the wake of 1970s terrorism, during the early Eighties a new wave of media production operatives learn from, adopt and adapt a visual and verbal lingua-franca which had developed in the news presentation and media-oriented strategies of terrorists.[14] In the coverage of all news there developed in the 1980s a more intentionally spectacular, aestheticized, *immersive* wide-screen look to news coverage, using the new bleeding-edge techno-logical language from that around the terror dramas of the Seventies. We can witness the new slanguage in the *accelerated* speed of news coverage during the early Eighties, in the hyper-accelerating speed of the sound-byte, flashed news, and the almost forensic study of high-profiled celebrity/criminal specimen-ed life.

Running parallel to this trope of the media adopting *sensational* new visceral techniques of reportage, due to state mandates the RAF at this point slips out of coverage in the mainstream news. It re-emerges instead as a virulent strain of cultural/cultured *production*. The RAF now shifts from the newspaper "headlines" into the culture and entertainment sections.

[1] For a fuller study of this technique during the Chinese Cultural Revolution, see Li Zhensheng's *Red-Color New Soldier*. New York: Phaidon, 2003.

[2] Conjuring up Barthes' *punctum*, as discussed in Chapter One.

[3] Barthes, *Camera Lucida*, p.59.

[4] From Slocum, Melani McAlister, "Iran, Islam, and the Terrorist Threat, 1979-1989." p.155.

[5] Scribner, "Buildings on Fire: The Situationist International and the Red Army Faction." *Grey Room* 26, Winter 2007. MIT, p.32.

[6] From the movie *Network* (1976), directed by Sidney Lumet, written by Paddy Chayefsky.

[7] One gruesome example is the recent 2007 Virginia Tech serial killer's suicide video.

[8] Cited in the following article: http://www.findarticles.com/p/articles/mi_m1571/is_25_18/ai_89389343

[9] As McAlister notes, as cited on p.138, coverage of hijackings and bombings offered a "magnifying effect," similar to "a form of political advertising."

[10] In this context the term "subjectify" suggests to present a discourse or an image-text as a subject used within a larger culture's discursive construction. This term is adopted from Hall and Hebdige in "Subculture: The Meaning of Style" 1977. Another framing might use the term "objectify" rather than "subjectify". Here I use it to imply that any terror image or its discussion is framed, literally "subjectified" by the dominant mainstream culture, which suggests a loss of agency.

[11] Guy Debord *Comments on the Society of the Spectacle*, trans. Malcolm Imrie (London: Verso, 1990) p.24.

[12] This is a reference to the opening lines of Marx and Engels' *Communist Manifesto*.

[13] Chomsky, p.176.

[14] This argument based on discussion in Chomsky and O'Sullivan's study of shifts in news coverage after the 1970s terrorism wave.

140b

Chapter VII

PUNK AND TERROR STYLE

What has happened to Seventies-era RAF-related imagery since that time, that is to say, after its initial media presence? The following three chapters look at re-use of RAF imagery in cultural settings, and the ways popular culture, the music industry and the fine art market have interacted with these images—and how the conjunctant interspecial breeding and détourning of RAF imagery in these enclaves has destabilized this identity and shaped public perception of the group.

Since the media coverage of the RAF subject during the 1970s, seeded from signs created by the group and from media coverage in the West German press, a hybrid RAF visual identity has grown. This hybridized RAF/MEDIA identity has been increasingly evacuaté of meaning through its de-connotated use. How do such patterns occur?

A study of RAF cultural production allows an exploration of several crucial questions concerning terror imagery and the power of culture. As Chapter One noted, specific RAF images such as their graphics and particular media photographs associated with the group have later become associated with commodity culture. What role does this imagery play in these later contracts?

The following chapters will consider how this imagery has been *re*-used and abused, and discuss whether this process renders powerful and provocative signs of alterity neutralized. Are RAF images simply "hot signs"[1] from one era that are cherry-picked as commercial sigils for exploitation in another? What is the relation between political alterity, visuality, and commerce? What role might Gerhard Richter's "infamous" 1988 cycle of paintings, *October 18th 1977,* play in the contained currency of RAF imagery in the fine art *contract*? What makes terror "consumable," and what happens as a result of its commodification and consumption, also what defines ethical appropriate-ness around the use and re-use of terror-related imagery.

Over the past thirty years, in the re-use of RAF imagery, this visual *identity* has become a loose signifier invoked by competing discourses—state, main-stream, and counternarrative —competing to assign or redefine association with the group.

Cultural production around RAF continues unabated to this day. Its edgy, underground, political connotation still makes it a potent/portential sub-object for fine art, pop culture, arthouse and now even mainstream cinema. (Contemporary well-known feature films which reference the RAF include Spielberg's *Munich* (2006),[2] and in Germany, Uli Edel's *Der Baader-Meinhof Komplex* (2008)[3]).

However, as noted in Chapter One, despite these shockwaves of cultural production, in public discussion in West Germany the subject of the RAF is still marked as awkward and unresolved territory. This *state* of affairs is illustrated in the 2005 Berlin Kunst Werke art museum exhibition *Zur Vorstellung des Terrors: Die RAF* which was mired in controversy when its curators attempted to use state funding for an institutional fine art show that dwelt on RAF-related artworks. Riots ensued at the opening and predominantly negative press from both Left and Right. The response still shows that the *imagery* remains taboo in Germany even thirty years after the deaths of their first leaders, and fourteen years since the group's last attack.

Added to these issues circling around the re-cycling of RAF imagery, in some symbolic appropriations, they are used with ironic intent. Because of this *irreverent* usage, the RAF-related visual identity increasingly develops as a superficial signifier promiscuously traded across cultural economic zones —by rock bands, in the fashion industry, and ironic-pop art references.

In post-détente cultural contexts, transnational markets have emerged for images previously deployed as propaganda which are regurgitated for their nostalgic appeal and camp value —sometimes glamorized and valorized like a brand logo and used on T-shirts, pins, bedding and other pop cultsch items. In the mutually-assured destructive (MAD) context of the Cold War, Leftist icons such as Che Guevara held an esteemed place in Western counterculture, where such imagery soon develops a less politicized value—signaling a very loosely-defined outlaw identity.

With the fall of the Wall, deactivated signs of terror, including the RAF logo, have flooded into the canon of pop culture. Why should these images that defined an era now enter the sights of cultural play? Imagery that was once demonized in the public sphere develops next level aestheticization through its collusion/inclusion in fine art and pop culture. What dynamics develop the cultural currency of such imagery?

In addressing these questions, this chapter will analyse the use of RAF signifiers/sigils in the music industry, focusing on 1970s London Punk and Punk's cut-and-paste appropriation of terror's visual style, discussing this stealth of semiotics, juxtaposing theories on subcultural signage from the work of Malcolm Gladwell, Stuart Hall, Fredric Jameson, Dick Hebdige, and Heath and Potter.

As noted, the manufacture of "bodies" of RAF-related over-the-counter-cultural produce begins in the late 1970s, an early example of RAF re-usage occured in Britain in 1978, when musicians the Clash appropriated the RAF logo as a Punk T-shirt slogan. This particular type of appropriation of RAF imagery has had a curious, unexpected, long-ranging, reflective impact. Understanding the particular social and political contexts in which the RAF visual *identity* re-surfaces is crucial to getting a grasp of its afterlife and its *nature*.

To understand the reasons for the *Punk* adoption of terror imagery, it is useful to conside the gestalt from which Punk emerged.

Pop and Terror Style: 1977 London Punk and the Use of RAF Imagery

Punk in its most coherent socio-cultural form and musical and visual style developed in London in 1976-77.[4] The "Punk Aesthetic" is typified by economies of means and a piratical view of other cultures, their sacred symbols, and icons. With somewhat similar strategics to the RAF, 1977 Punks deliberately engaged in an "image war" that was played out in the media—albeit for different ends. Part-agitational art prank, part-commodity, part-capitalist-masked-as-anarchist, with the politics of gesture, this frankenstinian aesthetic creates a charged visual impact with the Punk shocktrooper's use of taboo imagery in public.

1977 Punk fashion featured clothing suggesting institutional settings or supposedly taboo behavior, featuring straight-jackets and bondage trousers—implying either escape from a mental asylum, or a taste in sado-masochistic sex. Punk T-shirts provocatively featured images of swastikas, rapists, bondage, or gay porn. Punk used such signs to intentionally shock, and they courted controversy and arrest by blatantly wearing such imagery on the street in 1970s Britain.

Prime movers in the construction of the "originary London Punk" during the era were the clothing designer Vivienne "Let It Rock/SEX/Seditionaries" Westwood and graphic designer Jamie "Sex Pistols" Reid.

The work of both Westwood and Reid sourced its subversive intent from the confrontational aesthetics and stance of Sixties Paris, its political underground and avant-garde, the earlier Lettrists and Situationist International (S.I.)—groups whose work intentionally hijacked and destabilized the meanings of Establishment signs, through strategies of rendering the "unviewable" publicly visible, and through antagonistic strategies they termed "détournements."

Like the RAF, inspired by the Situationist International,[5] Punk deliberately employed *tabooed signage* to outrage conservative elements in British post-World-War-Two society, targeting among others, the 1970s tabloid media.[6]

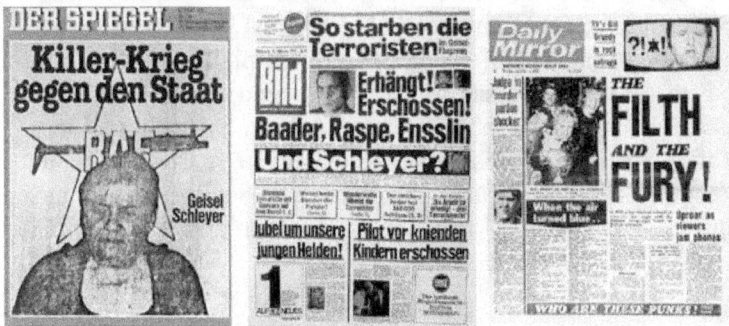

Fig. 41. West German and British newspapers from Fall 1977. (left-right) Schleyer kidnap; Baader, Raspe and Ensslin found dead; The Sex Pistols hit the British headlines: "The Filth and the Fury."

Punk emerges amid the real-life political violence of late 1970s Western Europe. In the scrapbook of shocking signs that Punk drew from, are those related to terrorism. No bombs were thrown in the name of Punk, but the rhetoric of outrage and visual styles associated with terror were deliberately invoked. The *visuality* of violent political revolt was used as part of Punk 's aesthetic lexicon to provoke and shock. What is the relation between the *identity* of London "Punk" and the RAF terror *identity* in the European news? Similar language is used by the West German press in their portrayal of the RAF, and the vigilante tabloid rhetoric aimed at nascent Punk in 1976-77. Both the German and British media adopt similar extreme verbal and visual styles in their representation of these social phenomena.

Punk clearly borrows some of its shocking *look* from media re-presentations of the "terror group identity" from this era. Comparing Punk and terror visuals, this is apparent in a number of ways. There are similarities in a tabloid image of the sneering face of an arrested RAF member and the front-page framing of early British Punk stars. Both terrorist and Punk *display* their resistance to pose correctly for the camera. In their 1972 arrest, RAF members Holger Meins and Jan-Carl Raspe notoriously affected menacing grimaces for their police mugshots. In their media war, aware these photographs will be used to sell newspapers marketed around their scandalous status, Meins and Raspe contemptuously and gruesomely ape for the camera. Likewise, in 1976 in the first British tabloid photographs of the Punk phenomenon, Sex Pistol Johnny Rotten contemptuously leers at the camera in a very similar manner.[7]

Other points of reference include the way that Punk shock-troopers' affected the alienated stare of the prisoner, cropped and/or the *obviously* dyed hair of the fugitive, or the stocking mask of the bank robber. In press photographs Punks pose in calculated spastic gestures similar to those of captured terrorists. Both terror groups and punk groups use ransom note lettering and assumed identities. Always aware of the tabloid villainization of high-profiled criminals, Punk deliberately subverted the simplistic language of tabloid infamy in using obviously faked names such as Johnny Rotten, Sid Vicious, or Gaye Advert, which knowingly mock the subjectification of media scandal. There are also *connections* between the deliberate awkwardness of Punk lout-couture and the brutal puritanical look of jail garb. In Punk Aesthetics, the fragmented body expressed the body dysmorphic and an asexuality curiously similar to the look of imprisoned terrorists of the era.

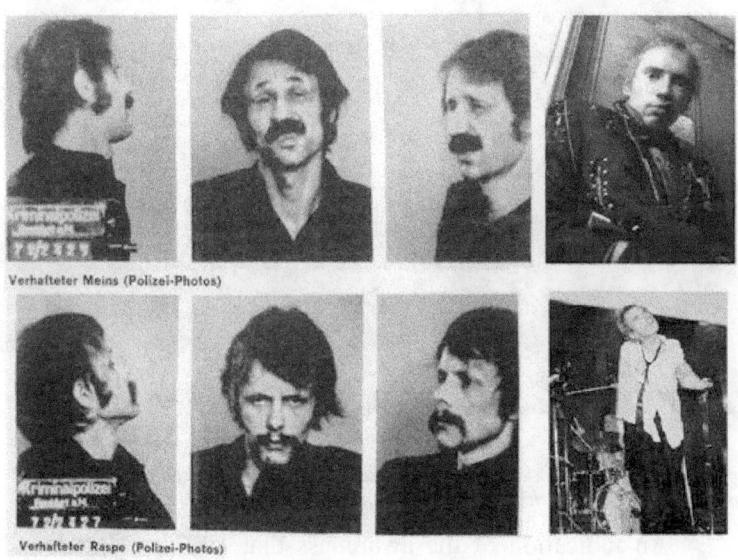

Fig. 42. The tabloid grimace: Arrest photographs of Holger Meins and Jan-Carl Raspe from 1972, widely circulated in the West German media during the mid-1970s; Johnny Rotten, London, 1976 as featured on various British newspaper front-pages in 1976-7.

Not long after the RAF and other 1970s terrorists hit the headlines, many of their terror-related signs became established as part of the anti-fashion style of early London Punk. But how aware were British Punks of West German terror iconography?

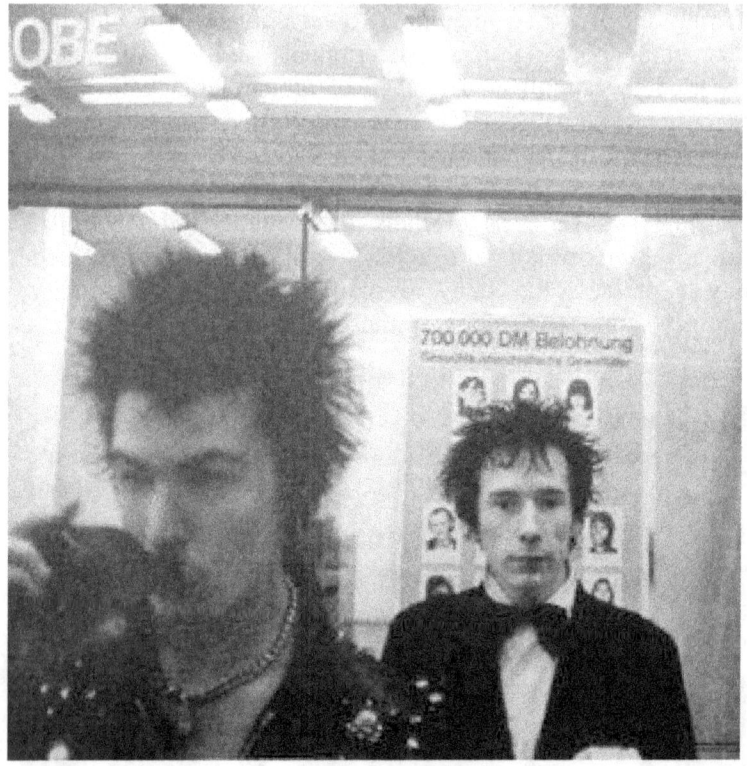

Fig. 43. The Sex Pistols and the RAF: Sid Vicious and Johnny Rotten pose under a RAF Wanted poster in West Berlin, 1977. Photograph by Bob Gruen.

An indication of the awareness that 1977-era London punks had of the ongoing West German terror wave is an image by rock journalist photographer Bob Gruen of Sex Pistols Johnny Rotten and Sid Vicious on tour in Berlin in 1977 posing beneath a RAF Wanted poster. The poster headline describes the RAF as "Anarchistische Gewalttäter" (violent anarchists). The joke of the Sex Pistols posing in this context is that their banned single "Anarchy in the UK" was a major hit in the British pop charts around this time.

But beyond showing the familiarity of some Punks with West German terror, what does such verbal interplay reveal? Arguably the acts that terrorists such as the RAF introduced into West European media canons created a new type of outrageous social outlaw identity which Punk across the world then deliberately played upon—as surrogate symbions of fear.[8] But is there a claim that Punk aestheticized the identity of the RAF? Initially, it seems a dubious connection to make.

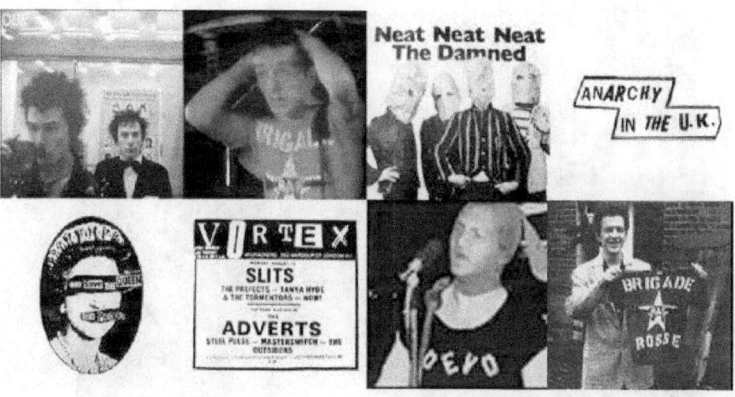

Fig. 44. Punk and terror style in 1977 (l-r, from top to bottom): The Sex Pistols pose in front of a Wanted poster for the RAF in 1978 in West Berlin. The text reads "Anarchistische Gewalttäter"; Strummer performing on stage in 1978 in a RAF/Brigate Rosse T-shirt, later used as footage in the feature film "Rude Boy", 1980; The Damned's first single cover, 1977; Logo from Sex Pistols' first single, 1976; Logo from Sex Pistols' second single "God Save the Queen", 1977; Vortex Punk club advertisement, London, 1978; U.S. band DEVO performing in bank-robber-type masks c.1978; Joe Strummer London 1978, with his RAF/Brigate Rosse T-shirt.

An explicit example of Punk's *deliberate* co-optation of RAF imagery is clear in photographs of Joe Strummer, lead singer of the Clash. Pictured on stage in England at the 1978 "Rock Against Racism" festival. He wears a mutant red T-shirt emblazoned with the RAF logo and Brigate Rosse lettering.[9] This *image* was immortalized in celluloid when footage from the gig was included in the film on the Clash, *Rude Boy* (1980).[10] This viral sigilization of the RAF sign by a musician surprisingly had a much longer impact as the Clash's fame spread globally.

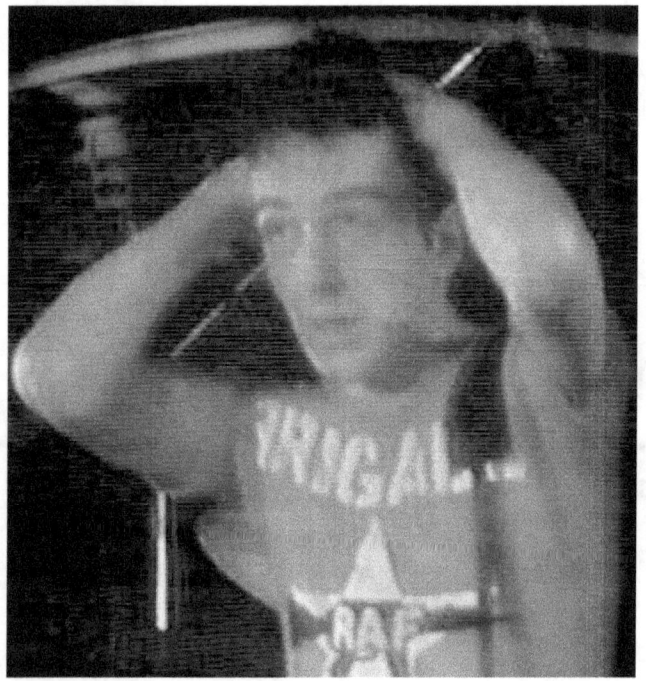

Fig.45. Strummer on film, in his RAF T-shirt. On stage at the Rock against Racism festival, London, 1978. From the movie "Rude Boy."

How did this *borrowing* of the RAF logo in a British radical musical context affect its meaning? Is Strummer claiming solidarity with the RAF by using their logo, or is the connotative shock value of a "terror sign" something he just borrows for its potent cultural currency and its ability to outrage?[11] Is Strummer's *gesture* a hommage to the terror ethos or is he simply wearing a "hot," politically-contentious sign? Does his adoption of the RAF logo as a badge of honor really differ from Sid Vicious wearing a swastika T-shirt? Joe's re-usage of the RAF logo is interesting to track as verbal inarticulacy was one of the deliberate provocations of 1977-era

London Punk stars. Clearly part of the affect of Punk was an attempt to function on a number of levels, both extremely puerile, yet extremely articulate and aware. Both Strummer and Vicious were figures who were clearly extremely intelligent, yet often deliberately affected a verbal inarticulacy in press interviews.

At the time, Strummer received much criticism in the British music press for wearing this T-shirt,[12] he was neither German, nor Italian, nor terrorist. He was a young, fashionable, provocative British musician on the edge of world fame. The Clash had become stars, signing a major recording contract with the multinational music/media corporation CBS. The inclusion of this terror group logo T-shirt in footage of the concert in "Rude Boy," a semi-mainstream feature film on the Clash, rendered more complex issues.

How does the use of a terror-related sign outside its original context affect its meaning? If London Punk in its initial 1976-77 phase (before its enfolding into the mainstream music industry) intended to shock and provoke in a quasi-political fashion, how did its appropriation of outlaw political signs then affect reflexively these referents? In 1978, Strummer's symbolic use of the RAF logo on a T-shirt did not appear to significantly impact the RAF's public identity. But over a longer period, this changes. Strummer's growing fame not only gave the RAF logo a hip identity, it also decontextualized this sign. Its usage in a pop cultural context develops a pirate discourse that outruns its original association for many.

Still thirty years after Strummer popularized the RAF logo in a music industry context, copies of his RAF/Brigate Rosse logo T-shirt are now on sale on St. Mark's Place in New York. They are priced around $30. This newly-printed T-shirt on sale in 2007 at a location popular for street fashion and rock memorabilia indicates that a visual slippage has occurred.

How did appropriation affect perception of the RAF's public identity? Strummer made the RAF logo iconic in international youth culture in the 1970s, but in the process of borrowing, the logo's meaning is destabilized. Further than just co-opting this sign, the marketing of the RAF logo on St.Mark's Place indicates that its association with rock music has overtaken its original associations. But who does the "Strummer/RAF T-shirt" now commemorate to its buyer—the RAF? Or Strummer, who died in 2002 and whose career has been the subject of much posthumous mythologizing? Here again is the ebb and flow noted in Chapter Three concerning the "evacuation" of Che's image. When a hip connotation is established around an underground, uncopyrighted, radical or terrorist signifier, a critical mass develops around it and markets emerge for the trappings of radicalism.

Radical Chic, Co-opted Commodity, and Post-modernism

What happens to underground political signage due to emergence of phenomena such as Punk? Punk developed in the late 1970s as a short-lived, but influential cultural mass, marketed globally through teen fashion and album sales. Punk destabilized many of the outlaw signs it co-opted. British cultural writer Michael Bracewell notes that the late 1970s was an era during which there was a fusing of mainstream and independent cultures.[13] British Punk's sampling of underground political signage mirrored wider patterns prevalent during the late 1970s of destabilizing and integrating imagery associated with alterity *through their inclusion* within larger imaging systems. Much imagery and style formerly marked as forbidden, outlawed, or unsuitable for the public suddenly enters the mainstream during this era. Was Punk the only possible discursive forum where this migration could occur?

By loosening powerful political signs (such as the RAF logo) from their referents, Punk sampling was a key transitional intersection in what Fredric Jameson termed the postmodernist turn. Strummer's adoption of a terror group logo sets a precedent for the co-optation of other politically-disturbing signs as Punk style, for their momentary shock value, rather than for any ideological agenda. Another example of this template is Vivienne Westwood who marketed her infamous "Cambridge Rapist" T-shirt (which appeared to glorify his crimes) as fashion wear during the period. Punk sought in using such shock imagery to satirize capitalism's commodification of even the most publicly unacceptable subjects. But the piratical patterns established in Punk actually themselves created a precedent for waves of wider co-optation of catalogs of socially outlawed, deviant, political and sexual imagery into wider discursive settings.

Jameson's argument is that any effort to contest dominant ideology threatens to be reabsorbed by capital, so that "even overtly political interventions like those of *The Clash* are all somehow secretly disarmed and reabsorbed by a system of which they themselves might well be considered a part, since they can achieve no distance from it."[14] Jameson provides an interesting analysis with which to unpack these dynamics in pop music, but it is important to realize that these patterns of absorption and oscillation remain in play. Regenade discourses, despite absorption into dominant ideology, retain some valence of resistance, and this linguistic ebb and flow is part of an ongoing pattern that continually impacts culture.

Tropes similar to the Clash/RAF T-shirt can be detected in the usage of another Leftist sign by the music industry. In his study of the history of Che Guevara's image, historian David Kunzle cites that the 1990s million-selling Los Angeles agitprop rock group Rage Against the Machine (signed to the Sony label) used the Korda Che image for an CD cover and on promotional T-shirts featuring the band's name.

Kunzle states that in a poll taken during the mid-1990s on the streets of L.A, respondents were asked to identify the Korda Che image. Several replied "Isn't he the singer of *Rage Against the Machine*?"[15] People recognized the face of the legendary Argentinean Leftist guerilla, but this rock band's appropriation confused his local identity and significance. This kind of visual slippage around popular icons from earlier eras becomes increasingly commonplace for next generations in the media-saturated Information Age.

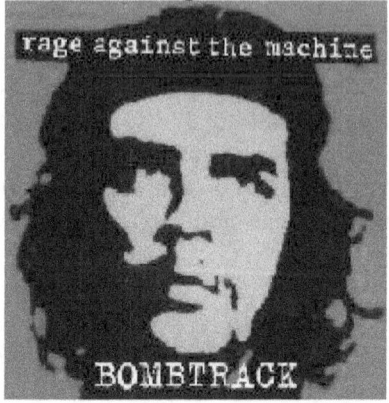

Fig. 46. CD cover from 1994 by rock band Rage against the Machine (Sony) "Bombtrack."

But for how long can a symbol of alterity retain its "political" resonance in commercial settings? Malcolm Gladwell's study *The Tipping Point: How Little Things Make a Big Difference* (2000) discusses the *ways* innovative ideas achieve critical mass and move into the mainstream, becoming well-known concepts and products. Writing about marketing aimed at youth and the commodifying of hip culture, Gladwell observes the currency of certain sneaker brands for teenage groups during the 1990s.[16] He discusses a group of teen skateboard style innovators who developed a particular style of dress that then virally spread amongst their peer groups. Markets then emerged around their style, which were noticed and then targeted by cutting-edge fashion companies such as the skate sneaker company, *AirWalk* to supply a *need*.

Gladwell notes that the relationship between hipster and fashion entrepreneur is based on temporary and sometimes tricky equations. The currency of an edgy style relies on its elite, "avant-gardist" status. The fashion producer first caters for the taste makers, then later begins to mass-market these products to a much wider public as cutting edge cultural *accessories*. But the producer does this at the expense of trading their original innovator group for a faster, larger pay-off. Gladwell argues that in the case of *AirWalk*, the speed of the mass-marketing of the brand soon led to the disenfranchisement of the company's original hip core buyer market. The velocity of this market-crossing, he claims, ultimately led to the company folding.

What Gladwell's example around teen style illustrates is that when an underground aesthetic reaches critical mass, different magnetic fields and economic forces cluster, which begin to fracture this style's earlier resonance as a hip or "avant-garde" signifier. The marketing of Punk fashion illustrates similar patterns, where shocking subcultural signs (such as the RAF logo) become included in wider economic systems which, over time, erase these signs of their contextual meaning and cultural currency.

With Punk the "turning point" of capitalist logic leads to the refiguring of underground political signs into commodity culture—through absorption and de-connotated use in mass-marketed teen fashion, slowly dissolves and re-casts these signs in public understanding. The "countercultural sign" can still hold its earlier resonance for a period of time, the shift is not immediate, and a grace period exists where this type of outlaw sign floats across a broad semantic field, seeming to interrupt the linguistic order, creating a cognitive dissonance. But, as time passes, the earlier political understanding of this sign diminishes due to its increased conception in commercial terms. The sign of a revolt turns into a style.[17]

Jameson sees a parallel paradigm in the shifting conceptions of fine art into commercial rather than political terms after the "cultural turn" of the late 1970s.[18] Jameson notes developments in the post-World-War-II era towards a more economically fluid society, where all cultural production becomes more flexible in its social valence. As to why such a pattern should occur, Jameson suggests that the posthumous canonization of earlier, shocking art waves such as Dada reduces their shock factor, and refigures public conceptions of shocking as a geographic or temporal, rather than a universal or historical construct.[19]

Jameson argues that contemporary cultural production is received with different criteria than earlier models, and oppositionality is now no longer really a genuine or discrete category, but instead a marketing ploy, a gesture, a pastiche of a politically alternative positionality, aimed to shock, often marketed at the provocative.

In this longish quote, Jameson formulates the contemporary cultural power relation in these terms:

> there is very little in either the form or the content of contemporary art that contemporary society finds intolerable and scandalous. The most offensive forms of this art - punk rock, say, or what is called sexually explicit material - are all taken in stride by society, and they are commercially successful, unlike the productions of the older high modernism. But this means that even if contemporary art has all the same formal features as the older modernism, it has still shifted its position fundamentally within our culture. ..older modernism functioned against its society in ways which are variously described as critical, negative, contestatory, subversive, oppositional and the like...(However) we have seen that there is a way in which postmodernism replicates or reproduces – reinforces - the logic of consumer capitalism;[20]

Similar to Jameson's analysis of fine art, Punk's adoption of RAF imagery and similar symbols indicates that a similar shift occurred in 1970s popular culture. Punk's cross-over commercially carried within it many key underground and taboo signs, but this tropiary migration greatly fragmented understanding. Subversive imagery is re-enfolded into the mainstream purely for its ability to shock. Such a patchwork mosiac indicates a broad cultural change during this era towards a more *distanced*, often ironicized set of social relations.

Despite the plausibility of Jameson's explanation of a shift in the conception of most cultural production as "no longer shocking," I argue that this pattern is due also to a larger logic, a more essential societal shift.

Geography theorist David Harvey would discus this move in different terms. As the twentieth century gave way to the twenty-first, a huge shift occurred because analog media has surrendered to digital communication technologies,[21] making it possible for the transmission of information much faster across huge new ranges of infrastructures. This has led to both to an increased deregulation of all information and greater market-based, laissez-faire freedom. In this new model of de-regulated dissemination, subcultural signs flow more easily across much wider discursive fields, perhaps more due to the shift in the space-time continuum of the digital era. The shifts of postmodernism can be attributed as much to the wind of technological progress as to the expedience of capitalist logic.

Another analysis is offered by Toronto sociologists Heath and Potter, who locate a key period for this cultural shift before the late 1970s, and instead in the 1960s due to the twisted economic logics of hippie culture. Heath and Potter argue that contrary to popular conceptions:

> There was never any tension between the countercultural ideas that informed the '60s rebellion and the ideological requirements of the capitalist system. While there is no doubt a *cultural* conflict developed between members of the counterculture and the

> defenders of the establishment, there was
> never any tension between the *values* of the
> counterculture and the functional
> requirements of the capitalist economic
> system.[22]

In Heath and Potter's analysis, the entrepreneurial values of the 1960s counterculture actually mirrored those of the mainstream. The *integrity* of ideological anti-capitalist signifiers in countercultural settings is compromised due to their existence within the logic of the "capitalist economic system." By the late 1970s, these conceptions of "alterity" spread across broader cultural milieus. Punk marketing mines this awkward intersect, in the con-fluence of "counterculture-anti-market" ideology and its commercial entrepreneurial spirit.

The phenomenon of Punk also brought with it new strategics for young radicals in the late 1970s, moving from the direct engagement with social justice of violent confrontation with the state such as terrorism, to the body politics of performing a shocking visual identity. In Punk/Rhetoric, the individual's own body is conceived as a site for political and social struggle.[23] The "personal was political."

The eccentric personal grooming and eclectro-shock visual of Punk intended to outrage and confront bourgeois values. Parallel, as Punk develops currency as cutting-edge style, broader economic markets emerged and a shift occured. The *subversive intent* of Punk was soon established as a fashion, as a teenage niche market where shocking visuality is styled, employed in *glamor*izing "excessive" behavior and narcissistic ennui.[24]

As earlier noted, cultural commentators Gladwell and Jameson gave concise analyses that explain the evacuation of meaning around outlaw signs in relation to market forces, Heath and Potter offer a differing warrant for the socio-anthropological shift in the conception of outlaw signs during the 1970s. However, none of these analyses fully explain societal trends of the carrying-forward of politically troublesome signs into later cycles of cultural production as nostalgic, sentimental, ameliorative tokens.

The short-lived, but visually-dramatic media-implosions of Punk and Terrorism in the 1970s led to both becoming cultural markers, part of the retrospective cultural periodization of the 1970s. Both these two supposedly countercultural movements produce a visually memorable graphic aesthetic—a fractured, traumatized, printed gestalt. These two styles over time have become somewhat interwoven into public imagination—due to stylistic crossovers like those of Strummer and the Clash.

As a vicarious halo is sainted on the young "tragic" deaths of iconic rebel figures such as Che, Ulrike Meinhof, and Sid Vicious, a discussion of Punk's sampling of RAF imagery in the late 1970s provides a useful and important specimen. It shows the *nature* and impacts of this imagery's initial re-use, highlighting an unusual early chapter in the history of recycling of trope RAF. It also allows for discussion of the trope's role in changing societal and cultural relationships. However what really brought the RAF into a wider field of public discussion during the late 1970s was a body of literature and cinema (unrelated to Punk) that propagated a fuller understanding of the story of the RAF. These works refigure the RAF as figures of historical record and as cultural *import-ants*, rather than objects of tabloid scandal or underground icons.

[1] To borrow Marshall McLuhan's term.

[2] Spielberg's film focuses on the murder of the Israeli athletes at the Munich Olympic in 1972, but also features a related group based on the RAF, and in one scene, uses the RAF logo in the background mise-en-scene.

[3] The feature film *Der Baader-Meinhof Komplex* (released in 2008), based on Stefan Aust's groundbreaking 1981 book on the RAF, was directed by Uli Edel, and produced by Bernd Eichinger, two high-profile figures in the German film industry, with a new screenplay by Aust. It features the much-respected actors Moritz Bleibtreu, Alexandra Maria Lara, and Bruno Ganz. This film was heavily funded by both the German Film Fund and the Berlin Film Fund. Unlike the controversy surrounding the attempted use of state funds for the Kunst-Werke exhibition, no outcry has surrounded the film's government funding for allegedly ten million Euros. Further details on this film are available at http://www.imdb.com/title/tt0765432/

[4] Recent scholarship on Punk concur that while Punk's seeds lay in an earlier US musical movement, it emerged in its most visible and coherent socio-cultural form as a musical and visual style in London in the late 1970s. Noted historians of Punk and its cultural antecedents include Greil Marcus, Clinton Heylin, and Jon Savage.

[5] A connection between the RAF and the S.I. is mentioned by Scribner and Peters.

[6] This connection between Punk and the S.I. is well-documented by Marcus, Savage, and others.

[7] If the imprisoned terrorist prisoner's alienated, confrontational expression was due to police beatings and/or hunger strikes, the facial sneer which became a signature in tabloid images of punks was more likely due to recreational abuse of cheap amphetamines.

[8] Why should this occur with the RAF? Arguably a terror group sign is "sexy" because they are conceived as a group defined by their acts rather than words.

[9] We should note here that Strummer's T-shirt features the typo "Brigade," not "Brigate."

[10] The film *Rude Boy* part fiction, part-"rockumentary" was directed by Jack Hazan and David Mingay. It was filmed in 1978-9 and released in 1980. Although not considered a critical success, it was nominated at the Berlin Film Festival 1980.

[11] Strummer and a friend (most likely Clash manager Bernie Rhodes) designed the RAF logo shirt, part of the DIY fashion aesthetic of the era.

[12] Notably, imagery related to the much-closer-to-home Northern Ireland terrorists were never used by high-visibility Punk bands in this period, despite the fact that many of the central figures of this London Punk scene were Irish by descent.

[13] Bracewell, p.22.

159b

Jameson, *Postmodernism,* p.49.

[15] Kunzle, p.105.

[16] In relation to the construction of hip and youth markets, it was notable that, simultaneously with adopting "radical" causes in the late 1970s, *The Clash,* Strummer's group, was the first high-profile London Punk band to employ professional stylists for newspaper photo-shoots. This move was key to the Clash's success internationally as teen icons of another register to the originary but more shambolic Sex Pistols.

[17] This term draws from *Revolt into Style: The Pop Arts in Britain,* the title of George Melly's study of the marketing of 1950s and 1960s British pop music.

[18] Jameson writes in *Postmodernism* "The older or classical modernism was an oppositional art; it emerged within the business society of the gilded age as scandalous and offensive to the middle-class public - ugly, dissonant, bohemian, sexually shocking. It was something to make fun of (when the police were not called in to seize the books or close the exhibitions): an offense to good taste and to common sense, ...whatever the explicit political content of the great high modernisms, the latter were always in some mostly implicit ways dangerous and explosive, subversive within the established order." http://evans-experientialism.freewebspace.com/jameson_postmodernism_consumer.htm

[19] In this regard, Jameson writes in *Postmodernism* "the classics of high modernism are now part of the so-called canon and are taught in schools and universities - which at once empties them of any of their older subversive power. Indeed, one way of marking the break between the periods and of dating the emergence of postmodernism is precisely to be found there: in the moment (the early 1960s, one would think) in which the position of high modernism and its dominant aesthetics become established in the academy and are henceforth felt to be academic by a whole new generation of poets, painters and musicians." http://evans-experientialism.freewebspace.com/jameson_postmodernism_consumer.htm

[20] Jameson, Ibid.

[21] This framing draws from Hargreaves, p.32.

[22] Heath and Potter, p.5. They add that "The counterculture was from its inception, intensely entrepreneurial."

[23] A parallel to this argument can be found in *The Rebel Sell* on p.96-7.

[24] Jameson writes in this regard, "the frantic economic urgency of producing fresh waves of ever more novel-seeming goods (from clothing to airplanes), at ever greater rates of turnover, now assigns an increasingly essential structural function and position to aesthetic innovation and experimentation." *Postmodernism,* p.5. Varon, Heath and Potter, and others have pointed out the relationship between "counterculture" and commerce. Against this, Marcuse proposes that technology has created the possibility to both monitor and

pacify a society and that the media creates the illusion of a pluralistic society, of multiple and opposing views, but that the media is in itself only part of one dominant totalitarian ideology. Does the RAF imagery lose or retain its political power, or is Marcuse's assessment more accurate, that the possibility of an independent, "outside" voice (or sign) is itself an illusion? The plurality of choice within it could be compared to the choice between Coke and Pepsi. As Marcuse puts it, there is: a flattening out of the contrast (or conflict) between the given and the possible." (*One-Dimensional Man,* p.8). The presentation of opinions offered as different are an illusion. They are both equally part to the same dominant power structure. This is no choice; a monopoly in the culture exists. No genuine outside voice is included. The state's system of control and communication is hermetically sealed. In Marcuse's analysis the powerful and elite keeps the great bulk of the population "manipulated and indoctrinated" so that they "parrot, as their own, the opinions of their masters" from Marcuse. *Repressive Tolerance. An Essay.* Boston: Beacon Press, 1965, p.57.

Chapter VIII

PANIC SHOPPING/CONSUMING TERROR:

THE RAF AS OBJECT OF CULTURAL PRODUCTION

Over the twenty-nine years since the deaths of the RAF's first leaders in 1977, this "terror" cell has been dissected under lenses of social history,[1] feature films,[2] museum exhibitions,[3] and university conferences.[4] In academic studies, the RAF has been analyzed in relation to the Frankfurt School,[5] Freud, [6] Feminism,[7] Semiotics,[8] Poststructuralism,[9] Cinema Studies,[10] and art history.[11] Given the extents of pre-existing texts around the RAF, my study has focused specifically on the history of imagery relating to the group and its relation to broader visio-cultural systems.

There are important aspects of the RAF story that have not been explored. Understanding the ways that RAF imagery moves through a much wider community reveals a great deal about the way mainstream culture deals with imagery that is deeply problematic due to its prior associations.

Although a communiqué in 1998 announced that the RAF had disbanded, the RAF story is not over, as so many historical studies have (conveniently) attempted to posit,[12] the ghosts of the RAF visual phenomenon continue to haunt us. Added to this, as I write, RAF group members continue to be released from Stammheim prison and make their voices heard by publishing books and appearing in documentary films.

This chapter considers the roles of academic and artistic discourse in developing and relocating the RAF as historical subjects within the realm of culture. It traces the waves of cultural production around the RAF subject since the 1970s, looking at the "histories" of RAF studies and directly at Gerhard Richter's 1988 paintings of the group. It discusses the enfolding of this subject into mainstream discourse, and considers who now owns or stands in control of the RAF's histories and legacies. It looks at pop culture's co-option of this kind of alterity, and also theoretical models for unpacking the "Terrorkultur" phenomenon. Further, I consider "ethical dilemmas" of using RAF imagery within a fine art setting.

In order to discuss these issues a key question is, what was it initially about the RAF that cultured a context for such continued interest in this subject? Writer Heinrich Böll points out that in the early 1970s the West German state tried to shut down any voices that challenged the media-state's overwhelmingly negative representation of the RAF.[13] By 1977, West German terror was a national crisis. A reaction to the complete embargo around open discussion of the RAF subject was that a particular type of cultural production emerged that countered the dominant presentations of this subject. But due to state pressure, this sympathetic counternarrative [14] could only emerge in *marginalized* cultural settings, novels and arthouse cinema.

Sociologist George Lipsitz uses the term "counter-memory" in reference to "the local...the personal. Counter-memory starts with the particular and the specific and then builds outward toward a total story. Counter-memory looks to the past for the hidden histories excluded from dominant narratives." "Counter-memory" and "counternarrative" indicate a distanced, apart relational position to an established or dominant discourse. What occurs due to the continued counternarrative use of subjects like the RAF is that these *presentations* later develop as the only dominant narrative source of the topic.

I trace here the history of successive schools of academic and cultural production around the RAF, because these waves contribute directly to the "re-coding" of the RAF subject. As RAF discourse begins to shift away from the newspaper front-page into cultured settings such as academia and arthouse cinema, these works let the RAF story emerge as a subject of cultural and historical relevance.

As noted, Böll attests that due to increased governmental pressure in the 1970s, the only real arena for "uncensored" discussions of the complexity of the RAF web was forced to emerge outside mainstream channels—in more marginal space. [15] And ironically the state's forbidding generates a lot of RAF cultural production.

Initially, in both cinematic works and academic studies on the RAF created in the 1970s, there is a focus on biography —pinpointing the human, psychological aspects of the RAF drama—rather than its social or idealistic dimensions.[16] In addressing the human dynamic in the RAF story rather than the societal one, writers and filmmakers attempted to sub-navigate the complex political mandates and state controls surrounding coverage of the RAF. They cater to an audience interested to know more about the personal lives of RAF members and their families.[17]

The first written studies of the RAF emerged in the late 1970s, this literature often focused on examining the psychological motivations behind the members of the group. Some studies sought to explore connections with Vietnam[18] or with Germany's Nazi past[19] to explain the members' actions. During this period some commentators used psychoanalysis[20] or feminist theory[21] to analyze the cell.

In a parallel world, the RAF's rewound last days were *dramatically re-enacted* in a contemporary cinema. Within a few months of the real events, films on the group were being made by the emergants of the New Wave of West German cinema, including Fassbinder, Böll, Schlöndorff and von Trotta.[22]

In Phase One of RAF cultural production there was a tendency to fictionalize the members in docu-drama-simulacrae, rather than outline their aims.[23] Simultaneously with these works, another genre of writing emerged relating to the study of terrorism. Media theorists Herman,[24] Zulaika,[25] and Puar and Rai[26] flag the emergence in the late 1970s of a writing genre based on the "terrorist personality." The development of this genre has been related to the emergence of a "terror industry" within the media, blurring journalistic "expertise" with psychological supposition on the criminal mind. Herman and O'Sullivan noted the development during the 1970s of what they termed "terror experts." They claim that "institutions and individuals somewhat involved with the government" during this period began to be "engaged in the production and sale of informational-perspectival output"—often promoting the "state"'s agenda. [27] [28]

This genre is exemplified by Gillian Becker's *Hitler's Children* (1976), remarkable for being the first well-known study on the RAF, and also because Becker equates the violence of the RAF with that of National Socialism.[29] The book did not age well. Written shortly before the death of RAF leaders in jail, Becker positioned *universalizing* theories around the terrorist mindset. Compared with the insights of many later works on the nature and phenomenon of terror,[30] many such checkbook-journalistic studies on "terror group" psychology now seem breathtakingly misleading, and were clearly Cold War *placed* anti-Leftist propaganda.[31]

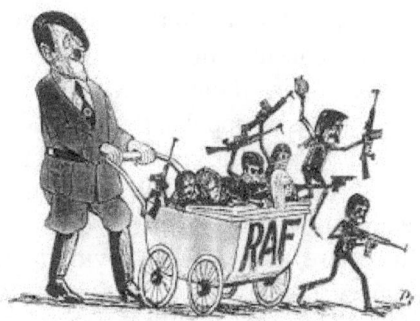

Fig. 47. A newspaper cartoon lampooning the RAF as "Hitler's children," shortly after the release of Becker's book with the same title in 1977.

Instead of some of the dubious existent studies of the group's psychology such as Becker's, a cleaner, more productive vector for engagement is to consider the public dynamics of mass hysteria generated in the media around the RAF phenomenon. My study considers the "psychological" aspects of terror, but unlike Becker, focusing instead on the *abilities* of both media and terrorists to psychologically terrorize a society within the Cold War context by invoking a mythic figure of "terrorism"

The first phase of cultural production related to the RAF is followed by a second wave in the mid-1980s, sourcing Marx rather than Freud, switching from a focus on the group's biographical narratives or on psycho-babble hypotheses on their acts. This work considered the RAF's broader relation to West German society.

Discourse analyses of the RAF during the 1980s center on particular *artifacts* pertaining to the group, such as their communiqués and the linguistic aspects of RAF-related texts,[32] some *framed* in relation to Semiotics and Poststructuralism,[33] others made synchronous studies of RAF ideology relating it to different terror groups of the Vietnam era.[34] Further works compared the RAF history with the re-enactment of their acts in cinema and literature.[35]

The modes of research made in this second wave of RAF study offer a deeper consideration not only of the RAF phenomenon itself, but their whole milieu and context of the group. Critical Theory was a popular (and holistic) model of engagement—a way in which to consider the broader socio-political context of the post-war West German student movement and the aims of the 1968 generation.

These second-phase RAF works provide more rigorous, less sensation-hungry analytical research, considering contemporary figures adjacent to the RAF who were influential on the group, such as Rudi Dutschke, writer Bernward Vesper,[36] Herbert Marcuse and the Frankfurt School—the culture and theories which intellectually the RAF drew from. An interesting holistic circularity arises in discussing the RAF in relation to the Frankfurt School. How can we now re-consider the role of Marxist discourse and the language of radicality in academia during the 1960s? Did the emphasis of theory over praxis in German Leftist academic circles trigger the RAF's recidivist move, when they dropped their studies for direct action rather than rhetoric in the shadow of Vietnam? These questions were central for the West German New Left movement in the late 1960s.

The second phase of RAF study exposed the deeper tentacles of the 1970s West German terror debacle. Although these works on the RAF did not profoundly shift discussion of the group, at a grass roots level, they crucially changed perceptions of the RAF for a younger generation of researchers, refiguring understandings of the group, developing them from subjects of scandal to objects of historical study. This second wave switched from psychoanalytic supposition to, at last, earnest engagement with their political intent.

Media Terror as Fine Art: Gerhard Richter's *October 18th 1977*

A paradigm shift in studies of the RAF was rendered by the 1989 exhibition of fifteen figurative paintings, *October 18th 1977* (1988) by one of Germany's best-known artists, Gerhard Richter. This groundbreaking series of paintings marked a crucial change in direction of discussions of the RAF. Richter's *intervention* into the existing discourse on the RAF was to return the focus to the visual, the media-related aspects of the drama. Challenging earlier widely accepted preconceptions of the RAF as either perpetrators or victims, Richter focused instead on visual trauma and its impact on public memory, bringing RAF imagery into a wider cultural debate on national mourning and its representabily, or lack of representability.

In his painting, Richter reproduces mass-media images of the group in life and death. He paints large-format figurative oils on canvas of well-known media images of the group. He presents the RAF in a new way, reframing these newsprint *images* in a didactic manner, jamming these once-powerful images of the group into a fine art setting. His first exhibiting of the *October 18th 1977* series in 1989 in a small museum in Krefeld, and the critical response it generated, introduced a qualitatively different element into the discussion of the RAF, engaging the *re-consideration* of the debacle.

Richter establishes a new "cultural ontology" through his paintings by the isolation of one distinct type of RAF imagery as his object matter—media images related to the RAF leaders' arrests and deaths, avoiding some of the most *remembered* RAF-associated images, such as logo or photos of their bombings or victims.

This issue of representability remains a key faultline in discourse on the RAF. It has been argued that representation is itself a privileged position in the framing of history. There is no small irony in the fact that Richter—the uncontested master of figurative "realism" in contemporary German art—makes this work, and that Richter chose to focus entirely on the personal images related to the group's leaders.

In nine of his fifteen paintings Richter reproduces several images of RAF leaders Baader, Ensslin and Meinhof lying dead in their cells. These works are titled *Erhängte (Hanged), Erschossener (Shot)*, and *Tote (Dead)*. He also paints a portrait based on a high school photograph of the teenage Meinhof, *Jugendbildnisn (Youth Portrait)*, and three images of Ensslin posing in front of her jail warders, *Gegenüberstellung (Confrontation)*. Besides these portraits of the RAF leaders in life and death, Richter painted two still-lifes, using specific well-known media photographs—clues from the mise-en-scène of Baader's prison cell after his death. One painting, *Plattenspieler (Record Player)*, is a close-up of Baader's record player, where he supposedly kept his suicide gun. Another, *Zelle (Cell)*, is an image of Baader's prison cell and his bookcase.

The only further subjects Richter includes are two outdoor images, *Festnahme (Arrest)*, a picture of the empty parking lot where the police spectacularly arrested Baader, Meins and Raspe in June 1972—the use of this image being a reference to the sensational media surrounding the whole RAF subject. A final, larger-scale blurred canvas, *Beerdigung (Burial)*, is based on a photograph of the crowd at the 1977 funeral of Baader, Ensslin, and Raspe at Dornhalden cemetery in Stuttgart, alluding to the anonymity surrounding the RAF leaders' deaths and funeral. Blurring of an image seems to make it appear a "meditation" on the increased "erasure of history" of the RAF from public encountered memory.

All Richter's paintings here are based on famous photographs from the media saturation coverage of the October 1977 drama eleven years before. With strategies reminiscent of the RAF, does Richter sidestep and purposefully ignore images of bombings because they have wider possibilities of interpretation or a more explicitly political, or didactic association? He presents the RAF leaders dead in their cells as

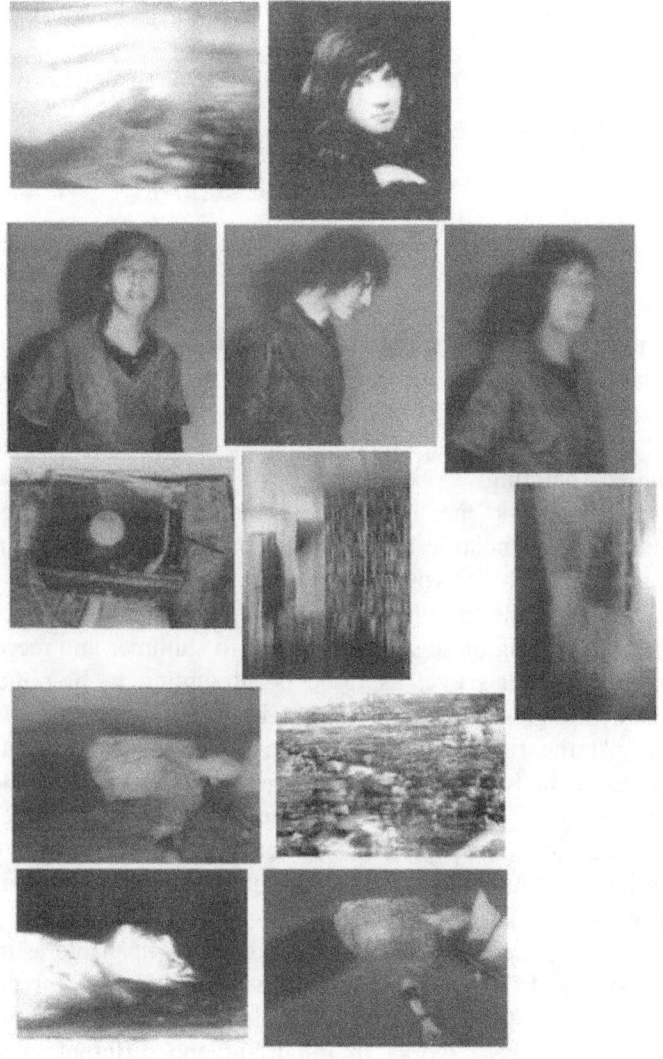

Fig. 48. Gerhard Richter, "October 18th 1977." (left-right, top-bottom)"Festnahme 2," 1988. Oil on Canvas, 92 cm X 126.5 cm; "Jugendbildnis," 1988. Oil on Canvas, 72.4 cm X 62 cm; "Gegenüberstellung 2," 1988. Oil on Canvas, 112 cm X 102 cm; "Gegenüberstellung 3," 1988. Oil on Canvas, 112 cm X 102 cm; "Gegenüberstellung 1,"1988. Oil on Canvas, 112 cm X 102 cm; "Plattenspieler," 1988. Oil on Canvas, 62 cm X 83 cm; "Zelle," 1988. Oil on Canvas, 201 cm X 140 cm; "Erhängte," 1988. Oil on Canvas, 201 cm X 140 cm; " Erschossener 2," 1988. Oil on Canvas, 100.5 cm X 140.5 cm; "Beerdigung," 1988. Oil on Canvas, 200 cm X 320 cm; "Tote 1," 1988. Oil on Canvas, 62 cm X 73 cm; "Erschossener 1," 1988. Oil on Canvas, 100.5 cm X140 cm.

tragic, misguided youth. Does the way that Richter frames these images permit the viewer the *possibility* of sympathizing with the group? Notably not one RAF victim appears in any of his paintings. By painting some and conspicuously avoiding other subjects, Richter sets up the potential for the audience to valorize the RAF.

Unlike Joe Strummer's RAF "solidarity" T-shirt, Richter's paintings evince easy or clear readings, he *deliberately* blurs the image. His subjects fade to grey, unfocussed, melancholic haze. They seem to obscure meaning through grisaille brushwork effects. Gerhard Richter's choice of elusive images and the physical handling of his paint produces ambiguity, making these subjects appear to shimmer and recede before the viewer's eye, as if he is attempting to blur their memory through sweeping, mechanical brushstrokes.

At the first exhibition of these paintings at Museum Haus Esters in Krefeld in West Germany, the subject matter generated huge controversy, but these works were widely interpreted by the press as "Trauerarbeiten"[37] (works of mourning)—poetic eulogies to a particularly dark time in recent national history.

This series of paintings stirred up interesting interpretations from noted art historians Benjamin Buchloh and Robert Storr. Both of these Richter scholars contextualize and institutionalize these works in important and different ways. Writing in 1994, Buchloh discusses this body of work within a larger survey of Richter's oeuvre, he considers de-tails like the settings of their original exhibition (in a Mies van der Rohe-designed building) and their relation to his notion of "polit-kitsch."[38]

Storr devoted a monograph to the series of paintings published by MOMA in 2000. He discusses how the series interfaced with existing genres of painting related to revolution, outlining the ideological context of the RAF for a non-German audience. Storr notes Richter's *daring* to tackle this subject in 1988 at a time in Germany when mention of the RAF was still taboo and extremely problematic, as some cells were still active. (In October 1986, three years before Richter's works were exhibited, the RAF assassinated a high-ranking state official, Gerold von Braunmühl, and in the same year as the paintings' first exhibition, 1989, the RAF blew up Alfred Herrhausen, head of Deutsche Bank. These cold-blooded attacks provoked much public outrage).

Storr and Buchloh in their respective texts center discussions on the RAF's significance to Richter. Both writers address aspects of the social history of the RAF and the critical controversy that Richter's paintings provoked. But the main focus of the work of both writers is to attempt to locate these paintings within the artist's canon. Both historians discuss the RAF, but neither focuses extensively on the broader social shockwaves of the whole debacle, the history of his photographic sources, nor the impact of Richter's works.[39]

It is important to now explore these issues and consider what has occurred in reactive response to the wide public exhibition of Richter's paintings. The works could not possibly address the entire complexity of the history of the RAF. And while Storr and Buchloh's works on Richter add important insights into discussion of the RAF, other histories remain to be told. The continual re-emergence of the RAF subject in a wide range of public settings over time cannot be ascribed to Richter's paintings alone, but the later canonization of this series through its acquisition by New York's MOMA in 1996 for allegedly $3 million and its later public prominence, contribute to the re-framing this terror group as historic specimens. [40]

Conceptions of the RAF have shifted since the exhibition of Richter's work for a variety of reasons. One important effect of museum canonization of paintings is that there is a level of discursive closure around the RAF's visuality. How does this occur?

The West German government's efforts to dominate all and any perception of the RAF in the 1970s were always challenged by counternarratives. But from the first exhibition of Richter's paintings until their museum acquisition in 1996, these paintings seem to be part of a counternarrative history documenting the RAF. They brought back to light and memorialized an extremely uncomfortable moment in recent time, perhaps the darkest chapter of West German history. The paintings existed as an awkward narrative thread, a delinquent symbol, that re-framed the RAF leaders as human beings and victims, rather than their previous *existence* as monstrous tabloid villains.[41] How does the affect of the acquisition of Richter's cycle of paintings by New York's MOMA then fracture this conception of his work? I argue that through museum canonization, Richter's paintings have now been *installed* as the official masternarrative on the whole topic.

As noted in Chapter One, the reproduction of imagery using the connotative charge of left-wing radicalism in an art museum context creates a strange dichotomy. Imagery promoting violent anti-capitalism becomes re-contextualized in artworks in a high-end capitalist cultural marketplace. As Aust and Storr note, high on the RAF Wanted list were many top captains of industry like Hans-Martin Schleyer. The irony is that that many of the MOMA board members, responsible for the $3 million acquisition of the Richter work, also come from the same strata of business society that the RAF despised.

Secreted Otherness: Assimilating the Opposite

Museum acquisition of Richter's work in 1996 privileged his specific choice of RAF images, and this was to arguably shape all later conceptions of the RAF.[42] But how did this procedure now impact the RAF´s public identity?

Gerhard Richter is not the only highly visible contemporary artist to work with "difficult" subject matter. Over the last forty years, a number of museum-level American and European fine artists have used media images related to violent Leftist political struggle with a range of intentions and strategies. Artists working with such themes include Andy Warhol (images of Mao, of race riots, or the FBI's Ten Most Wanted Men),[43] Cady Noland (images of the SLA and Charles Manson), and Johan Grimonprez (images relating to the RAF and Middle Eastern terrorists). What happens to this type of imagery due to mainstream settings and when a museum acquires a series of paintings of dead Leftist terrorists? Does it aestheticize terror as an object?

French sociologist Pierre Bourdieu wrote extensively on patterns of aestheticization, cultural legitimation and the importance of the appearance of institutional acceptance in shaping public opinions. In *Distinction: A Social Critique of the Judgement of Taste* (1979), Bourdieu argues that:

> the effect of the hierarchies of legitimacy, (the hierarchy of the arts, of genres, etc.) can be described as a particular case of the 'labeling' effect well known to social psychologists. Just as people see a face differently depending on the ethnic label it is given, so the value of the arts, genres, works and authors depends on the social marks attached to them at any given moment (e.g. place of publication).[44]

Bourdieu argues that public legitimation impacts on the value and conception of cultural production. Related to this idea, in another work, *The Field of Cultural Production* (1993) he notes the limitations implicit in this hierarchical hegemony:

> Fields of cultural production propose to those who are involved in them a space of possibilities that tends to orient their research, even without their knowing it, by defining the universe of problems, references, intellectual benchmarks (often constituted by the names of its leading figures)[45]

In Bourdieu's framing, the museum *fame* of Richter's work make these paintings anchors within the flow of RAF visuality —and I argue, the sine-qua-non masternarrative[46] marker on this subject, as if declaring the subject now famous, defined, and closed.

Conceptually relevant is the term "masternarrative," as outlined by Slavoj Zizek: "*discourse* is in its fundamental structure authoritarian. ...out of the free-floating dispersion of signifiers (slippage) a consistent field of meaning emerges through the intervention of a master signifier." What Zizek highlights here is that a masternarrative grows in a play between discourses and the range of signifiers in which a masternarrative develops. In this framing, Richter's work emerges as a masternarrative on the RAF due its ability to inspire and stand above other work on the RAF theme.

Bourdieu's analysis offers a challenging assessment of cultural hierarchies. But as noted, the dominant culture's attempts since the 1970s to control all and any perception. Even after the museum acquisition of this subject matter, there remain two tendencies in play—both never complete. Richter's work still retains a counternarrative trace.

Sociologists Heath and Potter challenge any reading of stable benchmarks, elites and public taste in regard to the effects of "museum-ification." Noting that taste is intrinsically grounded in a sense of distinction, they argue that "not everyone can have good taste because cultural artifacts exist within and are contingent on a wider social framing. Mass good taste for all is a conceptual impossibility."[47] In other words, taste is intrinsically linked to social status and shifting elites. Heath and Potter suggest instead that:

> Through public art galleries and subsidies to producers, modern governments have invested significant resources in promoting the aesthetic education of the public. Yet has this improved the overall caliber of popular taste? Of course not. When an artistic style becomes popular, (as with [ ]...Salvador Dali in the United States), it is simply demoted in the canons of aesthetic judgement. Precisely because of their popularity, an appreciation of these styles no longer serves as a source of distinction. Thus "good taste" shifts toward more inaccessible, less familiar styles.[48]

Heath and Potter's argument brings home the importance of the role of context, framing, and cultural drift in the public conception of a work. They claim that once critical mass is reached around an artwork, other discursive formations around it are reflectively shifted. The "charge" of the avant-garde working with edgy subject matter (such as imagery of terrorists like the RAF) is diminished in an artwork's museum canonization.

Theorists from Marx, to Gramsci, Adorno, and Hall argue around issues of cultural play and hegemony.[49] All analyze culture in terms of dominant societal relations and culture's role in the maintenance of the hierarchy of social order. Contrary to this "top-down" Marxist reading, I argue that since the 1996 MOMA acquisition of Richter's "high culture" objects, a different emotional and discursive climate has developed around all RAF imagery. In the case of Richter's paintings of terror subjects, elite cultural acceptance also floats RAF imagery into other milieus, varying the valence of the subject as a whole. Richter's "museum-ification" limits meaning and discussion around RAF imagery, and the entire subject starts to lose its rhetorical power due to its level of institutionalization.

The *aestheticizing* of a taboo subject reduces whatever earlier, awkward, rhetorical charge it once held, re-coding images and encoding new social permissions that permit the subject entry into middle-brow popularity and therefore consumability. Museum acceptance thus leads RAF imagery to develop a level of aestheticization and "neutralization" politically. Similar in patterns discussed in Chapter Two around images of Che Guevara and Angela Davis, when certain kinds of "politically-charged" public imagery reach a high degree of visual saturation in public dominion, meaning around such signs starts to evacuate.

This pattern is detectable in the RAF's case by the increase in *ironic use* of RAF-related imagery in a variety of settings since Richter's "museum-ification." Works of this type often play precisely on the new institutional and commodified status of RAF imagery. Due to the range of cultural and intellectual production around the RAF in the wake of Richter, conceptions of the group (and all imagery associated with them) expanded to their hip aura.

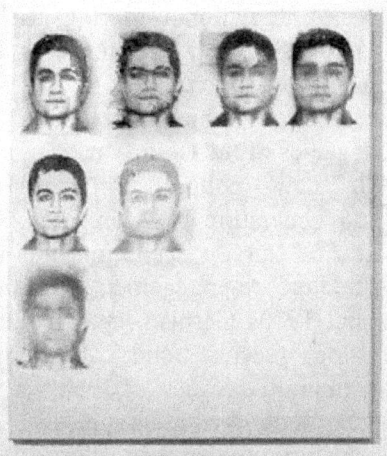

Fig. 49. Mohammed Atta as Fine Art Subject:
Andreas Diefenbach, "Untitled," 2006, multilayer print, dispersion,
frottage on canvas, 90x80cms. Courtesy Galerie Christian Nagel, Berlin.
As shown at the Armory Art Fair in New York, 2006.

The institutional stature of Richter's paintings brings up further questions: What is the connection fused (or acknowledged) in acquisition of these types of works, between cultural hipness and 1970s terror icons? What does the acquisition of this imagery allow? What tacit acknowledgements? Do "difficult" political images vicariously fulfill base needs and functions (as graven images) as they enter the arcade? Does Richter provide a model for succeeding waves of aspiring avant-garde artists, curators and graphic designers, and how is their later use of terror imagery different to Richter's? And what happens to this taboo as a result of the tectonic shifts that occured because of Richter and MOMA's handywork?

Phase Three: Post-Discourse
With the fall of the Wall, and in response to these shifts in the cultural climate around the RAF subject, a third wave of cultural production around the RAF emerged around 2000—

concurrently with an international touring Richter museum retrospective. Much of the renewed interest in the RAF has figured in or around Berlin, where, after the fall of the Wall, a new gestalt culture emerged which has focused on exploring and exploiting the legacies of the Cold War.

Since 2000, new cultural production prototypes concerning the 1968 generation have emerged. One genre is typified by the historical survey exhibition, this type of study offers a more "abstracted" re-engagement with this era. Work concerning 1960s and 1970s German history often falls under this rubrik, i.e. the recent trend of German-language publications that examine the legacy of 1968 via a "Where are they now?" montage of individual biographies.[50]

Many social history studies made thirty-five years after Vietnam utilise a temporal or geographical axis in parallel-profiling the experiences of the 1968 generation geo-politically.[51]

A work of this genre that received much attention is Jeremy Varon's book *Bringing the War Home* (2004), which compared the history of the RAF and the U.S's Weather Underground. Varon parallels the formation of both terror groups in response to Vietnam, tracking moves towards violent confrontation with their governments. Grounding his discussion in relation to critical theory and psychoanalysis, Varon's work adds significantly to Cold War study by comparing two anti-Vietnam movements on different continents and their motivations for violence.

The RAF story works well as a counterbalance for Varon to explore the history of the Weathermen, an arguably lesser known U.S. terror group. But this vector of comparability is unstable in a number of ways. Varon's central thesis is that that the difference between the RAF and the Weather Underground was between a group who "acted out" rather than one that "worked through" their issues. I argue that the post-war West German cultural context cannot be easily equated with the U.S. during Vietnam era.

I suggest that as a terror phenomenon—in terms of actual media presence—a more resonant point of comparison for the RAF during this era were the media-centric strategies of the Symbionese Liberation Army (SLA) or even Charles Manson.[52] [53] In terms of tabloid coverage, (as discussed in Chapter Five) the RAF and SLA both pinpointed at the media. The Weather "Underground" targeted state buildings and never used much explicitly media-oriented strategies. Similar to the RAF, the SLA become the subject of much projection as "folk devils" of the media and they also were to die spectacularly.[54]

Varon does not foreground the significance of visuality in terror strategies (an aspect central to RAF tactics). However, the visual rhetoric of Western 1970s terror groups drew significantly from an international urban guerrilla style earlier established around Che, the Latin American struggle and the PLO. This aspect of Western terrorism can clearly be witnessed in documentaries on the RAF and the Weather Underground, such as Verlag der Autoren's *Deutschland im Herbst*, or Sam Green's *Weather Underground* or Johan Grimonprez's *Dial H.I.S.T.O.R.Y.*

In terms of visual studies of the Cold War, two recent art exhibitions are of particular note. In a style reminiscent of earlier museum surveys on the visuality of 1960s politically movements (such as the legacy of the Situationist International,[55] or posters of the Vietnam era),[56] [57] Trisha Ziff's *Che! Revolution and Commerce* [58] (at New York's International Center for Photography) in 2006 gathered photographs, fine art, pop cultural ephemera and websites that have used Korda's Che image over the past forty years.[59]

Another recent exhibition, *Zur Vorstellung des Terrors: Die RAF* (at Kunst-Werke, Berlin in 2005) curated by Biesenbach, Sonnenblum and Felix Ensslin (son of deceased RAF leader Gudrun Ensslin), was the first museum exhibition which gathered RAF-inspired artworks by a range of mid-level and famous fine artists and filmmakers, some 1968-related memorabilia and timeline on the RAF from the 1970s to 2000.

The result, witnessed by a long-running public furore around this exhibition, was a sense of a missed opportunity of re-opening this whole subject to wider debate in an open-handed manner—rather than simply gathering a range of museum-level fine artists and academics who have made work related to this terror group. *Zur Vorstellung des Terrors: Die RAF left* in its wake an increased sense of false closure and of the mainstreaming and marketing of the hip, cult-like halo around the RAF subject ©. Frustratingly, this exhibition added little new per se to the discussion of the deeper significance and trauma of the RAF phenomenon—and conspicuously sidestepped addressing the three-million-dollar [60] question of the *ethic* of a fine artist appropriating a terror image and selling it to a museum.

An important addition to the study of radical Cold War imagery is the book *Vorwärts bis zum nieder mit* (2001), produced by Assoziation A, which gathers street posters, graphics, and flyers from the German Leftist movements of the late 1960s up to 2001, including a range of international RAF solidarity posters. This catalog provides good documentation of the iconography of these social movements and the visual grammar of "radical" style from counterculture over a forty-year period. As opposed to the salon-society of the Kunst-Werke show, *Vorwärts bis zum nieder mit* seemed more respectful of the liberatory spirit of 1970s radicalism by including a free CD, which contained JPEG's of all posters in the book—presumably for their further dissemination.

Notably, despite these hostings of Cold War-related images, no in-depth academic research in the emergent field of (what Scribner has termed) "Terror Kultur" has studied reasons for the patterns of aestheticization and commodification around imagery of Cold War Leftist terrorists.

Consuming Terror: Fine Art, Pop Culture, and the Chic of Terror

Another new tendency clustering around Cold War subjects is the de-contextualized quotation of signs. Recent works related to the RAF have adopted a less reverential attitude. Post-2000, a detectable trend in re-engagement with the RAF subject has been the "name-check"—used either ironically or as a historical marker.

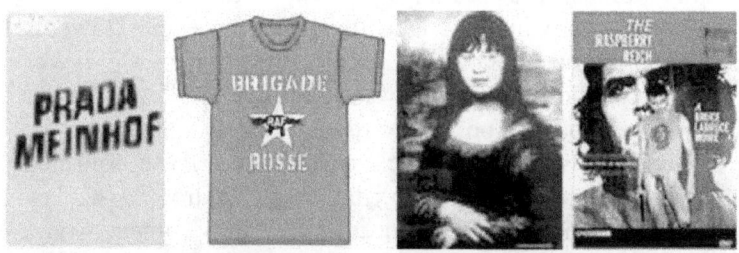

Fig. 50. "Terror chic" accessories:(left-right): Scott King/Crash magazine, "Prada Meinhof" issue, 1999; RAF T-shirt for sale in 2000. "Meinhof Monalisa"screenprint by Scott King. "The Raspberry Reich" film, directed by Bruce LaBruce, 2004.

Since then, many "textes"[61] that reference the RAF manifest in cinema, on the Web or fine art. Under current cultural settings, RAF images are visual "textes" which have become malleable through continued de-contextualized overloading. In many cases, the "name-check" often take the RAF's status as icons in the popular canon for granted, simply "quoting" RAF imagery or their *name*, often referring to them somewhat erroneously as the "Baader-Meinhof." The citation, like Bonnie and Clyde, is used to allude to the (now-retrospectively-ascribed) glamour of the mythos of the 1970s urban guerrilla.

These traits are a prime illustration of what Tom Wolfe described as "Radical Chic" and Benjamin Buchloh defines as "polit-kitsch"[62]

In relation to this "name-dropping" tendency around the RAF, once a particular framing of a subject becomes established as a style, that style then starts to inflect and infect its understanding.

An example is "Che T-shirt" or "RAF T-shirt" being worn as a fashion statement in 2008. The regurgitation of such a signifier develops new understandings around these *identities* of 1960s and 1970s political violence. The "actual" *intention* of the contemporary RAF "name-check" is often indistinct, partially because the meanings "attached" to this "outlawed" subject-matter are in flux. Due to recent tendencies towards sentimental souvenir, nostalgic commodification of Cold War era countercultural signs, what was once part of a "pure" visual grammar denoting political revolt, starts to fade in understanding over time. In such surroundings, these orphaned signs often mature instead as edgy, stylistic tropes. As key witnessed earlier cited concerning Che's image, and Strummer's RAF T-shirt in pop cultural settings, any political charge associated with these subjects is slowly shunted into irony.

Whether the salvage of these signs is serious or irreverent, tasteless or ethical, one question is: How have the current waves of "Che chic" and "Ostalgie" (the nostalgic appreciation for the aesthetic style of East German products) become linked to RAF "terror-kultur"?

If it is clear (from the discussion in Chapter Two) why Che Guevara's Korda image became an icon of rebellion in the context of the Cold War era, can we now explain how a similar connection has developed around RAF iconography after the Cold War? What has forged a relationship lately between cultural hipness and 1970s Leftist terror? Why should such a pattern also occur around dead West German terrorists, and for what reasons might these images now have appeal as cultural commodity? Why are later generations in the West still unearthing these archetypes of historical signage, re-contextualizing and sometimes inadvertently decontextualizing them in cultural production? Does the presence of RAF imagery in contemporary visual discourse relate to Richter's museum canonization? Might this be a response to the co-optation of RAF imagery by the "cultured" establishment? What are the *intentions* of re-producers of later waves of radical imagery in fine art settings?

Tom Wolfe pinpointed the strange cultural pay-off of "radical chic," and white liberal intelligentsia's superficial embrace of 1960s black U.S. radical politics. Forty years after his landmark essay, radical chic has been superceded by 1970s "terror chic." [63] [64]

Writing in 2006, *New York Times* critic Holland Cotter noted some recent New York fine art exhibitions show a tendency towards featuring works, using radical imagery, which often exhibit "a bad-boyish theme that Andy Warhol more or less finessed with his *Most Wanted Men* paintings forty years ago." [65] Cotter argues that the self-congratulatory tone of some of this work "feels like tired old news. It's strictly an insider operation, limited to mildly tweaking the conventions and protocols of the art world while supporting business-as-usual. No wonder the (art) industry thinks it's just the cleverest thing and gives it full approval." Cotter sees this work as "prominent and powerful" as well as "trifling."

Discussing these themes in contemporary fine art, Fabrice Stroun argues that "our present longing for "subversive" cultural production remains mired in a double-bind: namely, a flawed dialectic oscillating between a rejection of (an) authorative subject and a simultaneous attempt to reinvest it with (nostalgic, cynical, even "critical," etc.) meaning." [66]

Stroun spots a major crack in contemporary cultural production. Art production influenced by critical theory is often concerned with deflating the political valence of its subject's referent. This frequently results in work that is hip but seems ideologically emptied and vacant. The use of terror imagery as "fine art work" acts as faux political dressing. As artist Barbara

184

Kruger sardonically noted in a late 1980s artwork "When I hear the word culture, I get out my checkbook."

If this is true of work that appropriates imagery relating to 1970s terror, how does this "flawed dialectic" function? What is at the core of the dynamic that Stroun alludes to? In order to consider the roles of "the taboo subject" in cultural production, two conceptual terms are useful to consider.

Regarding the chemistry of successful farce, British playwright Joe Orton wrote that "a combination of crudity and elegance is always ridiculous."[67] Polymath Arthur Koestler used the term "bisociation" to define a clash between two mutually exclusive "rule codes," "two self-consistent but incompatible frames of reference at the same time; this clash makes us function simultaneously on two different wavelengths."[68] Koestler argued that *tension* caused by bisociation is purged through either sexuality, scientific fusion, artistic confrontation, or laughter.

Koestler's analysis relates to Stroun's framing. Contemporary artists often adopt edgy political subjects for their oppositional, confrontational, Other, apart, qualities, simultaneously co-opting anti-capitalist" symbols with ironic intent as commodity—producing an object that intentionally plays on binary inconsistency.

A different framing of this dynamic is offered by Klein's book *No Logo* (2000). In Klein's bestselling study of branding in the 1990s, she discusses combining two opposing narratives with combustible intent. Klein champions "culture jamming"—an adbusting street activist strategy, "the practice of parodying advertisements and hijacking billboards in order to drastically alter their messages."[69]

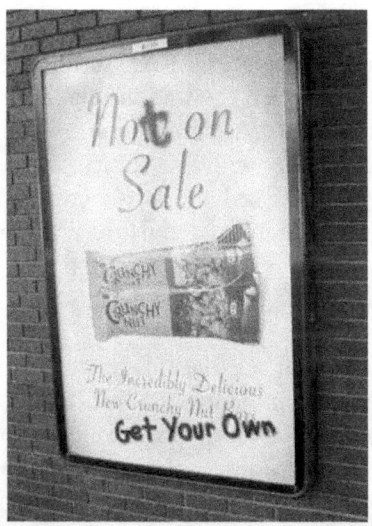

Fig.51. Culture jamming recycled: Advertising campaign for Kellogg's Crunchy Nut bar, Limerick, Ireland, 2007

Klein sees this "act" as a counter-hegemonic tactic for the corporate age, satirizing the colonializing tendencies of globalized franchised marketeering.

However, (as displayed in Fig.49) one can also witness how swiftly the once-radical rhetoric of culture jamming is absorbed (co-opted) into advertising's visual slanguage—slashed and re-cycled in "edgy" graphics aimed at youth's (market) desire to adopt (live) rebel style.

These terms "culture jamming" and "bisociation" elucidate some of the dynamics at play in contemporary graphic design. But we also need to consider how the intentions of the fine artist adopting of "political" imagery have shifted since Richter's era. What are the contemporary ethics surrounding the use of this subject in fine art contexts?

The Fine Art of the RAF

Rather that trying to unpack the whole controversy surrounding the Kunst-Werke exhibition, one issue to consider here is what might "constitute" constructive and respectful use of imagery related to public trauma within a fine art setting.

A comparison of Richter's RAF series with the work of three other artists of a later generation who use RAF imagery (all featured in the Kunst-Werke show) provides a perspective of the current states of play with this subject in fine art.

Chapter Two discussed the ways copyright law enacts around Leftist images that exist outside clear legal status or ownership rights. The re-use of certain images becomes problematic when they are taken into a high-visibility commercial setting.[70]

After the Cold War, Leftist imagery becomes chic'd and decidedly less threatening. Since the mid-1990s, Korda's Che image has become embroiled in several high-profile breach of copyright cases. The Smirnoff Vodka company appropriated the Korda Che image in 1997 for a British subway advertising campaign. They did this without Korda's approval or clearance, and were forced to pay his estate $50,000.[71] Ironically, control of this "anti-capitalist" sign is now policed by the decidedly capitalist Berne Convention (as cited in Chapter Two).[72]

In a similar case in 2004, Bruce LaBruce, a Canadian filmmaker, was sued for a similar amount by the Korda estate for LaBruce's use of Che's image as a backdrop in some scenes of his low-budget, independently-released, gay soft-core art film *The Raspberry Reich* (2004). Since the 1990s, the Korda estate has become increasingly vigilant about what they consider illegitimate or non-acceptable appropriation of Che's image, due to the increasing commercial use of this iconic Leftist image.[73]

Regarding the Smirnoff court ruling, Korda himself stated in 2004: "As a supporter of the ideals for which Che Guevara died, I am not averse to its reproduction by those who wish to propagate his memory and the cause of social justice throughout the world, but I am categorically against the exploitation of Che's image for the promotion of products such as alcohol, or for any purpose that denigrates the reputation of Che."

Korda's attitude seems to reflect a general consensus about re-usage of 1960s and 1970s Leftist signs. The exploitation of the icon in commercial settings disrespects his *memory* and presents an ethical and legal dicotomy. But should Korda have equated the use of a multinational distillery and that of a low-budget gay independent filmmaker?

Notably no one sued LaBruce for also prominently using the RAF logo in his film. Within these issues of authorship and ethics, what makes the sale of Richter's RAF paintings to the Museum of Modern Art for three million dollars in 1996 different? What constitutes socially responsible re-engagement with the RAF's likeness within an elite cultural fine art market? Are Richter's blurred photo-based paintings of the RAF a socially acceptable use of this imagery because they were intended as a valedictory meditation on the abiding tragedy of violence? Was the museum acquisition of Richter's work *an attempt* to bring closure to troublesome, unresolved, hidden history? Or did it set the permissions for a broader re-engagement with RAF-related subjects in fine art contexts? How does a museum's "re-framing" of the RAF subject through Richter, legitimate the further use of public imagery relating to terror in the cultural arena? All these questions are thrown into relief by the Smirnoff-LaBruce-Che-RAF-Richter nexus.

The controversy surrounding the 2005 Kunst-Werke exhibition highlights some of these tendencies, issues that illustrate the way some fine artists feel themselves exempt from wider legal or social obligations, and that as part of an "avant-garde" artistic tradition. Some artists feel they are entitled to appropriate taboo subject matter without recourse. (This is a pattern earlier alluded to by Cotter).

We can address some of these questions in relation to works by some of the artists in the Kunst-Werke show who exhumed the RAF subject for their work in a later era. What might constitute resonant re-use of terror imagery in a fine art setting? Can there in fact be any such thing in our sensation-oriented contemporary art culture?

The video *Dial H.I.S.T.O.R.Y* (1997) by Belgian artist Johan Grimonprez (which was featured both at Kunst-Werke, and also Dokumenta X in Kassel in 1997) documents the history of airplane hijacking from the 1960s to the 1990s. Grimonprez's video includes RAF-related news footage from the Mogadishu hostage crisis. His work seems a more acceptable use of imagery related to political violence because Grimonprez attempts to elucidate on the deeper social and political dynamics of terror, rather than just using these images for their sensationalistic charges.

Two other works also featured in the Kunst-Werke exhibition make less referential use of RAF subjects. Bruce LaBruce's *The Raspberry Reich*, and the video installation *Hans und Grete* (2003), by a younger American artist Sue de Beer. De Beer's work, a narrative about U.S. youth culture, loosely sites RAF signifiers. Like LaBruce, de Beer "name-checks" the RAF. But her engagement with the RAF subject appears less resonant, because it uses the RAF *identity* primarily for shock—as "terror chic." LaBruce or De Beer's works name-check the RAF as hip signifier, as gestured fashionable, contrary, urban ennui. These works do not add insight into the RAF story or the realities of 1970s terrorism.

The works of LaBruce and de Beer rely on the RAF's cultural charge, and arguably, on some level, on Richter's work, as master-marker and supra-signifier, to position and contextualize their work as "socially-engaged" fine art production.

A semiotic analysis of cultural production featuring the RAF subject would divide its use along two particular axes. Historically-specific documentary works such as Grimonprez's film or Richter's paintings, "go to great lengths to establish the denotive links between the historic signifiers used in their narratives and their empirical referent, in an effort to legitimize their narrative vis-à-vis history."[74]

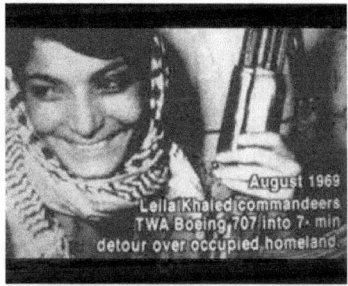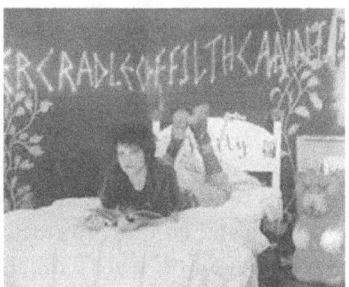

Fig.52 .Post-Cold-War RAF-related Fine Art: Johan Grimonprez "Dial H.I.S.T.O.R.Y." video, 1997; Sue de Beer, "Hans und Grete," 2002, video installation.

Dehistoricized texts like LaBruce or de Beer's actually "downplay the links between signifier and empirical referent so as to draw out the connotative charge of the signifier without raising the issue of historical accuracy."[75] In dehistoricized texts, RAF iconography is *borrowed* as a trope, a floating, nomadic signifier of danger and the thrill of the illicit. According to German history scholar Christopher Clark, such a dynamic's "lack of attention to history results in a flattening out of the past, which allows for a number of questionable displacements."[76]

At this point in the discussion, has all imagery relating to the RAF, Che, and other icons now undergone a surgical shifting and lifting due to frequent de-connotated ab-use by pop culture or fine art contexts? After the Cold War context, has all use of 1970s terror imagery past or present now become dehistoricized?

Analytical models from the field of sociology provide other perspectives on the dynamics playing here. In his 1977 study *Subculture: The Meaning of Style,* Dick Hebdige uses a Gramscian model to analyze patterns of fashion transculturation between immigrant Jamaican groups and white working-class British teenagers during the 1970s. Hebdige studied the ways these two groups interacted through specific visual signifiers, and how the meanings of these signs altered according to their context.

Hebdige cites theorist Stuart Hall who argued that hegemony can only be maintained as long as the dominant class "succeed in framing all competing definitions within their range."[77] Hall argues that in order to stay in power, those controlling the culture frame any threat to their dominance in a deliberately subordinate manner that neutralizes any ideological challenge. Hall states that "subordinate groups are, if not controlled, then contained within an ideological space that does not seem at all "ideological," appearing instead to be permanent and 'natural,' to lie outside history."[78]

In Hall's framing, the adoption of RAF imagery illustrates similar patterns of cultural reassignment. Like the migration of Jamaican style that Hebdige discusses, in this study, RAF signs have been given a place in culture—but through art history (via Richter's paintings), where they have been assigned an association as subjects of art, documents of history.

While Gramscian analysis of hegemonic social relations provides a good perspective on shifting sociological sands, it also leaves some issues less adequately accounted for, such as supply and demand. Does the subcultural theory model analysis of Cultural Studies remain valid over transhistorical contexts— between the 1970s and 2007, the accelerated Age of Anxiety? Reassignments around the RAF can be explained as side-processing of the twisted cultural logic of our era, where all popular icons, good or bad, are conceived commercially.

Despite the usefulness of the British Cultural Studies model in addressing some aspects of this subject, parapolitical issues remain undressed.

Hebdige's angle brings to light other questions: What might constitute valid re-use of politically-charged images in a fine art setting? Can there in fact be any such a thing in the highly commercialized stakes of the contemporary art world? Doesn't this pattern of aestheticization often occur around an interstitial and uncopyrighted subject? These questions of ethics in the fine art markets hark back to issues pointed out earlier by Bourdieu and Cotter. Often contemporary art strategies that use "radical" subject matter seem similar to Punk Strategy, unchaining signs, using them only for their shock value.

The issue of profit around the RAF images' re-use presents a further conundrum. Should the RAF's victims' relatives decide what constitutes acceptable usage and commodification around residues of this subject matter? Who are entitled to be the arbiters of what are legitimate or ethical re-uses of terror-related imagery? Does the endless pattern of détournings of the RAF into an object for art projects and studies in academia render it irrelevant for cultural re-engagement? Or might it now be more appropriate to focus on *engaged* projects, such as establishing "Truth and Reconciliation Committees" as in South Africa?

This returns to questions to which Viett had earlier referred, concerning the intent and result of cultural production. One of the problems of discussing the valence of the re-use of RAF imagery in fine art settings is the potential to establish binary framing, contrasting constructive and responsible use with trivia. On such a terrain, it seems more productive to attempt to establish a taxonomy of Terror Kultur.

"The "Political" gets Personal": Richter and de Beer

Often of the generation of fine artists who emerge in the 1960s and 1970s, it has been said that the credo to their work was "the personal was political",[79] suggesting the resonance of a personal perspective—often based on a marginalized social experience—in the discussion of larger social and cultural formations. How was that notion represented for Richter's generation? And can such an identification remain an intellectually-valid mode of engagement for contemporary art practice?

The notion of "the personal being political" gained currency in the late 1960s as cultural producers sought to collapse the traditional division between private and public identity. This dichotomy was sustained by traditional, patriarchal ideologies that relegated certain aspects of the subjects' identities to the private sphere—thus placing them outside political discourse and perpetuating oppression by not accounting for them.

For an artist of Richter's generation, to claim that the personal was political was a way of rejecting that division: an attempt to force a recognition of hitherto marginalized identities and experiences within a public sphere and to open up discursive spaces within the political arena.[80] In the 1970s, issues relating to personal identity (such as those pertaining to women, gay people, or people of color) were not given much currency in the public sphere and certainly not discussed as having political implications. The women's rights movements in Europe and North America during the 1970s, as well as the corresponding gay and civil rights movements, focused precisely on this false separation of the personal and the political, and sought to articulate the personal in the public sphere.[81]

But conceptions of the term "personal" have shifted a great deal in the thirty years since this tactic came into effect. The cultural climate in the West has moved from periods where a personal perspective seemed radical, revelatory, and daring, to an era where the "politicism" of artistic strategy has been superceded by the cult of personality, now most widely associated with exhibitionism, commercial exploitation, and celebrity crucifixion. It is difficult to speak of the personal in the same terms in the current cultural context of America when the Patriot Act allows the U.S. government unprecedented access into our personal lives and when copies of Paris Hilton's "private" porn videos flood the Internet.

"The personal" and "the political" have few of the *associations* that they had in earlier eras when this phrase tagged personal empowerment and activism.[82]

Gay U.S. writer Jack Malebranche discusses this reductivist shift from political to commercial terms in relation to the gay community. He argues that the term "gay" no longer refers so much to same-sex love or sex, but now to a "subculture, a slur, a set of gestures, a slang, a look, a posture, a parade, a rainbow flag, a film genre, a taste in music, a hairstyle, a marketing demographic, a bumper sticker, a political agenda and philosophical viewpoint." The social valence of a political identity based around sexual orientation has shifted to become less "politicized," and more conceived in terms of niche consumer markets. Malebranche claims that after the 1990s, "Gay is a pre-packaged, superficial persona—a lifestyle."[83] This shift is mirrored across a range of formerly-marginalized socio-political groups.

Part of the problem of discussing Richter's series from 1988 now is the difficulty in tracking the cultural shifts in time and mapping a *place*. In West Germany at the time they were made and exhibited, these works were widely considered challenging and didactic—a personal engagement with a subject "outside" the paradigm of public discourse, partially because the RAF were still active in this period. Contemporary art works from 2008 that address 1970s European terror can be conceived of in different terms—as a retrospective aestheticization, a mythologizing and romanticization of this *identity*.

Discussing contemporary Feminist art practices, British theorist Katy Deepwell points out that "the personal is political — that very important slogan of Feminism — does not mean the personal is always or automatically political."[84] Deepwell argues that although the personal can be a starting point for political reflection, it only becomes "consequent" when developed as an engagement with the broader questions and shared collective experience that "political" artwork has sought to address.

Contemporary works often put the formal tropes or subject matters of earlier eras to different uses. This pattern is evident in a trend since the early-1990s of recycling of 1970s art strategies, to produce new works that borrow heavily from the visual language of 1970s Conceptualism. The British artist and theorist Victor Burgin has remarked on the 1990s trend of artists plagiarizing the formal aspects or ideas of an earlier generation. Discussing 1970s-era Conceptualism, he writes: "[Conceptualism expressed a] desire to resist commodification and assimilation...the 'new' conceptualism is a mirror image of the old – *nothing but commodity, nothing but style.*"[85]

But it is hard to agree wholeheartedly with Burgin, for as art historian Hal Foster has pointed out, Conceptualism and performance-related works themselves drew much from earlier work such as that of Duchamp and Dadaism.[86] Art by its nature is never reverential. It has always been influenced by earlier movements and disparate viewpoints, and has often used appropriation, changed context and intent.

It is interesting to consider these issues of intent and understanding by comparing Richter's 1988 work with another artist of a later generation who has used RAF-related themes in their work—in this case, Sue de Beer, an American artist from a different generation.

In Richter's paintings, he appears to ask whether it was possible to engage with the enormity of a terror phenomenon and its toll of human lives.

In a review of *Hans und Grete*, art critic Stephen Hilger writes, concerning the RAF's role for de Beer, "their widespread influence elevated many figures in the group to the status of counter-culture legends." Hilger points out that "de Beer's video incorporates elements of the Baader-Meinhof (RAF) story in the tortured psychological dramas of its characters. Media images of Meinhof, alongside rock and goth posters, appear in the work as a visual anthem for the teen characters' fatalistic credos and dark obsessions."[87]

Working with the tropes of Poststructuralist style, De Beer "samples" the RAF in her work as a "texte" (as Hilger puts it, as a "visual anthem") relating to her main theme, contemporary U.S. teenage mores. But this quotation appears to only *play the sample* of the RAF's status as figures of media scandal. De Beer conflates the RAF identity into the pantheons of countercultural signifiers, casually equating their identity with rock stars.

Through referencing the RAF, de Beer's work has a similarity with Richter's, but compared to his more proactive engagement with terrorism and *subjectivity*, her piece seems a cynical drive-by past the subject; *Hans und Grete* adds little new insight on the "Baader-Meinhof" complex—a, by now, well-covered topic.

At this point in the cultural dialogue, few would argue that a work such as de Beer's, which name-checks the RAF (and was originally exhibited in a high-end commercial New York gallery) really has the transgressive frisson of Richter's work in the context when it was first exhibited in West Germany.

Ironically, despite this, the work by de Beer is categorized as related to political art. Art writer Michael Glover argues that it is a mistake to see much post-1990s, so-called personal "identity politics" works such as that of de Beer's, as having genuine engagement with any political perspectives. Instead Glover sees this type of work as often an unmediated, self-referential monologue, more closely related to an "exhausted Romantic narcissism."[88] De Beer's piece illustrates this more self-absorbed vector of engagement with the "personal" in relation to youth culture.

In an earlier context, Richter's work genuinely appeared to challenge the parameters of acceptable subject matter for the fine art medium, bringing his own ambivalent perspective to the ongoing West German terror debacle into the arena of cultural debate. His work was a sincere and polemical engagement with the subject of national trauma, and a meditation on the role of visuality in the terror debacle. As noted, Richter exhibited this work publicly at a time when the RAF subject was still a very sore wound.

The specific type of involvement with the RAF subject that de Beer's work illustrates, shows one way that personal engagement as *strategy* mutates away from its earlier challenge and resonance. Works such as De Beer's *Hans and Grete* highlight dichotomies in the contemporary art market, one that feeds on edgy, sensationalistic matter. As Stroun notes, "our present longing for 'subversive' cultural production remains mired in a double-bind," "oscillating between a rejection of (an) authorative subject and a simultaneous attempt to reinvest it with meaning."[89] De Beer's work suggests problems in the prevailing cultural modes of career cynicism and subject piracy —appearing to quote 1970s European terrorism solely for the RAF's transcontinental "hip" factor—as scandal trope— renegade "retro" signifier and media outlaws. This reference is made in a cultural context where the concept of Communist terror has lost any imminent sense of threat. How many of de Beer's generation in the U.S. have a clear knowledge of the RAF's history?

De Beer's use of the subject in a fine art setting is for its bisociative play (to use Koestler's term), as an eso-teric artworld referent. Clearly any prior subversive ideological valence around this sign is displaced in context. De Beer's target in *using* RAF imagery relates to the twist in Punk Logic of inserting signs of taboo into public space. But, as critic Cotter had earlier pointed out in the New York Times, in these types of work, within this fine art context, the *real* horror of RAF terror is airbrushed, replacing it, by its aestheticization and use as a subcultural currency. As Jameson argues, in Postmodernism, nothing is shocking. Even the subject of terror is wide open for cultural and therefore economic play.

But a question remains: Would Richter's series be received in the same way if it were shown for the first time today? The *climate* of West Germany in the 1980s was an *environment* where this work existed in different contexts. However, due to the end of the Cold War, Richter's work's museum acquisition, the mid-1990s art boom, and the birth of the Internet, the conception both of Richter's work and the entire RAF subject have altered dramatically.

In conclusion, returning to the original issue in question: Is the "political" still "personal," as it was for an earlier generation? In the 1970s and 1980s, artists often thought of using the subjective in a political manner, but there has been a major cultural quake. Radical critique of society using the resonance of personal experience is still possible, and the "same but different" political issues persist, however it is hard to imagine the sincerity of such a strategy as Richter's being received in the same way in the contemporary, post-everything, *ironic* domination of our era.

As illustrated in the discussion of Grimonprez's work, there still *remains* relevant engagement with the terror topic of the 1970s. Many contemporary artists still engage in exploration along the interface of dominant narratives and personal agency. However, the accumulation of later associations related to the subject of "the political" requires an acknowledgement of changing cultural contexts. Can an artwork can only ever be viewed as political if it succeeds in challenging the dominant views that are specific in that era? Only then can it provoke and engage its audience. Works that seemed politically challenging in their original context often lose their impact for later generations as their historical setting shifts or the work's levels of familiarity reach saturation points. These two "aspects" should not be underestimated. Museum-ed Richter shows how context changes work's perception.

There are two reasons for the change. In the case of the Richter series, a different era's dominant cultural mode shape-shifts later perceptions. Added to this, works such as that of De Beer exemplify a type of artistic transculturation—a tendency of more market-oriented, sensation-hungry art practices that co-opt innovative stylistic devices and subjects associated with the more marginal, such as the political— *faking* their "political" intent. This tendency towards a surface imitation of earlier political work reflexively effects how these earlier works are later perceived. Although the personal can remain political in fine art praxis, these contextual shifts make the discursive "personal-political" dynamic operate amid a much more complex set of matrices.

Studying the ways that "RAF imagery" moves through walls of cultural community reveals a great deal about the incestuous relationships between the outlaw and the mainstream. Massed culture feeds on the forbidden and taboo, which it routinely defangs to enhance its normative regime. Within such a context, whatever counternarrative charge Richter's works once had now seems somewhat *erased* in integration.

Although the RAF officially disbanded in 1998, the RAF story is not over because the ghosts of this debacle continue to haunt us, through news stories, cinema, museums, rock music, magazines and books, and more recently the Web. Like harpies, the popular press and contemporary artists still suck on the RAF subject, relentlessly attempting to milk this subject one more time. Thirty years on, RAF members are still being released from jail, and each time this occurs, the tabloid media start another flurry of retrospective RAF coverage. It is as if this awkward chapter of German history refuses to end.

[1] Böll and others.
[2] Such as the films of von Trotta, Schlöndorff and Fassbinder.
[3] Biesenbach.
[4] In Cardiff, 2005.
[5] For example von Dirke, Varon, Juschler.
[6] Pearlstein.
[7] MacDonald, Edschmid, White.
[8] For example Miller, B.H.
[9] For example Plowman.
[10] For example Elsaesser, Hoerschelmann.
[11] Examples include Richter, Buchloh, or Biesenbach.
[12] Peters ends his book with this conception, using the official disbanding of the group to frame this claim (p.715-26).
[13] Boll in Baumann, p.ii.
[14] Lipsitz, p.231, cited by Hoerschelmann, p.87.
[15] Böll in Baumann, p.i.
[16] As many have noted, Böll's 1974 novel appears to set the paradigm for this genre. Well-known "biographical" works include the films of von Trotta, Schlöndorff and Fassbinder.
[17] As Böll attests in the first page of the introduction of Baumann's book, during the 1970s any published work that appeared to represent the terrorists in any way outside the state's presentation was subject to immediate censorship and legal action against the publisher.
[18] Varon, Storr, Peters.
[19] Becker.
[20] Pearlstein.
[21] MacDonald, Edschmid, White.
[22] Such as Fassbinder's *Deutschland im Herbst* (1978) and various films by von Trotta and Schlöndorff.
[23] Examples include the films of von Trotta, Fassbinder and Böll.
[24] Herman, p.11.
[25] Zulaika p.165-6.
[26] Puar and Rai, p.121-4.
[27] Herman, p.7-11.
[28] Ibid.
[29] Storr notes the fallaciousness of Becker's work, Storr, p.31.
[30] Such as the work of Varon, Storr and Peters.
[31] Also notable in this genre of Cold War anti-Leftist propaganda and the "terrorist personality" is the work of Claire Sterling.
[32] Miller, B.H, Teraoka.
[33] Van Dirke, Stout, B.H. Miller.
[34] MacDonald.
[35] White.
[36] Plowman.

[37] Storr discusses reviews from initial Richter 1989 exhibition.

[38] Buchloh has outlined the term "polit-kitsch" in his discussion of the work of Anselm Kiefer. Buchloh writes, "Kiefer is only the most prominent of the German artists who have modeled themselves on concepts that Habermas has defined as "traditional identity." In the course of their restoration of these concepts, these artists have produced a type of work—widely disseminated in the 1980s and have produced its own kind of fall-out in North Americas as well—that could be best-identified as polit-kitsch. Its attraction seems not only to be its reconstitution of traditional identity for the generation of West German who wish to abandon the long and difficult reflection upon a post-traditional identity. The attraction of polit-kitsch—and herein lies its international appeal—its reconstruction of the artistic privilege associated with traditional identity, i.e., the claim to have privileged access to "seeing" and "representing" history." (Cited in Buchloh's dissertation, footnote 4, on p.112). Buchloh implies here that Kiefer's own relation to a "political" subject (in this case here, World War Two) is not explicitly addressed in the piece. Instead, Richter argues, Kiefer exploits the subject's resonance as a charged public signifier that a "great artist" has a privileged way of both seeing and publicly representing. Buchloh sees the "polit-kitsch" artwork as one where the artist's engagement with a political subject is non-dialectical. The artist does not interrogate his own privileged location nor the contextual use of his subject.

[39] Due to the art history contributions on Richter and the RAF paintings by Storr and Buchloh the entire visual RAF's socio-historical context can now be more ably discussed.

[40] Storr suggests that MOMA may have paid circa $3 million to buy the works in 1996 (p.55).

[41] The Hilton Kramer article cited is one of many outraged responses both in the U.S. and Germany to the works' acquisition.

[42] An indication of this is New York Museum of Modern Art and German museums' competition to buy Richter's paintings. Storr (p.55).

[43] Also relevant to note is Warhol's "Ten Wanted Men" piece for the 1964 World's Fair, a work based on FBI mugshots of notorious criminals. The history of this mural is discussed at greater length in Richard Meyer's *Outlaw Representations*.

[44] From Bourdieu, *Distinction,* p.86.

[45] From Bourdieu, *The Field of Cultural Production*, p.176.

[46] Zizek, Slavoj. *Enjoy Your Symptom*. 1992, 2001. New York: Routledge (Zizek. p.102).

[47] Heath and Potter, *The Rebel Sell*, p.127.

[48] Ibid.

[49] Examples of this type of theorizing around the role of cultural production occur in Marx's "The Commodity Fetish," Gramsci's *Prison Notebooks* and

in Adorno's "The Culture Industry: Enlightenment as Mass Deception" in *Dialectic of Enlightenment*.

[50] This framing draws from Peifer, p.12. Examples cited therein.

[51] Notable examples of this genre include the work of Varon, Mark Kurlansky, and Carole Fink, Philipp Gassert, and Detlef Junker.

[52] As can be noted in Patty Hearst's autobiography concerning the SLA's history and relation to the media.

[53] Even a figure such as Charles Manson bears relevance here in terms of media villainization.

[54] I here reference Stanley Cohen's term "folk devils" from his book *Folk Devils and Moral Panics* on media hysteria around the British Mods and Rockers youth phenomenon.

[55] Such as Boston Institute for Contemporary Art's 1989 survey exhibition on the Situationist International, "A Brief Passage of Time".

[56] Such as the exhibition "Decade of Protest: Political Posters from the United States Vietnam Cuba 1965-1975" (1996), catalog by Smart Art, which featured essays by David Kunzle, Susan Martin, and Carlo McCormac.

[57] Such as Kunzle's UCLA Fowler Museum exhibition *Che Guevara: Icon, Myth and Message*.

[58] Ziff's work owes a debt to Kunzle's earlier study, *Che Guevara: Icon, Myth and Message*. Los Angeles: UCLA Fowler Museum of Cultural History in collaboration with the Center for the Study of Political Graphics, c1997.

[59] Ziff's exhibition toured and was developed as a book of the same name.

[60] The reported sum that MOMA paid Richter.

[61] My use of the word "texte" here is inspired by Barthes' conception of the term in his seminal essay "From work to text." In it, he argues that semantic production is not closed, with a finite meaning, but open-ended, and subject to shifts, additions, and quotation. Barthes' *Image, Music, Text*, p.51.

[62] Buchloh. *Gerhard Richter, p.111*.

[63] This question is addressed at further length in my 2005 interview with Bruce LaBruce in *Kultureflash* magazine. Also of relevance on this topic is Bourdieu's 1969 *The Love of Art* which discusses the demographics of the art museum audience.

[64] In a vacuous culture, market forces slowly co-opt any resistant subculture, often superficially adopting its most superficial trappings, turning "bohemian" style into a broader consumer culture. The history of the Long Island town of East Hampton exemplifies this cultural shift, from the "avant-garde" art scene of Jackson Pollock and Willem de Kooning in the 1950s, to the current middlebrow haut-bourgeois "success culture," where fine art now functions as a dressing in a community where the mass-marketed, "faux-bohemian lifestyle" design of Ralph Lauren, seem more indicative of the contemporary cultural climate. In this dynamic, the influx of New York avant-garde artists in the 1950s and the press coverage of their careers in association with this area

developed a romantic myth around the Hamptons that actually makes them retrospectively appear to have acted as the shock troops of gentrification in one small Long Island community. In the same way, the visual history of 1970s terrorism becomes a site around which to market cultural production, using the awkward social charge of terror.

[65] Cotter. See Works Cited.

[66] Stroun from Guyton/Walker catalog, p.15.

[67] From: *Crude vs. Elegant -Thoughts on a marketing technique*, Rupert Goldsworthy, *Collected Essays,* 1999. Regarding cognitive dissonance, "Orton's quote regarding the ridiculous from his diaries of the mid-Sixties also rings very true. It defines what one particular marketing technique might be -the product title that combines these formulas and the dynamics of sex and power. The first element, the "elegant" might be defined as the high, the sedate, prim, the conservatory, the academy, the sacred (i.e. marriage, the family, the monarchy, the state, or Nature) and also the holy cow or the "serious. " This element is combined with the low, the obscene, the vulgar, the comedic, the tacky, the synthetic, the unacceptable, the filthy, the unnatural, the sexual, the perverse, or disaster, or murder. These two elements are then combined into one impossible, surreal, almost anthropomorphic whole. A recent example of this cognitive dissonance is the combination of the names of popular icons, Marilyn Monroe and Charlie Manson to create the rock band name Marilyn Manson, or in another example, the spectacular and fatal Graf Zeppelin crash, which led to the rock band name Led Zeppelin). Joe Orton's quote hinges on the word "ridiculous." As a playwright he argues that farce deliberately builds its scenarios on such a balance. But what really constitutes "ridiculous"? The primal shock of suddenly seeing life and death, or beauty and ugliness, thrown together is transmuted into another sensation: humor or sexuality. Koestler in *Ghost in the Machine* links smiling and laughing with literally "baring the teeth" as a manifestation of fear—at the shock of suddenly glimpsing the cruel visceral realities of life and death. Ridicule is related to belittling. This "crude vs. elegant" dynamic often works as a subliminal technique in mass marketing. In an era where product identification is so hugely present and so often the name of a product is its most important feature, and in a culture where sex sells, there have to be specific equations that trigger that buying urge. As Marshall McLuhan presciently wrote in 1956: "This is the first age where the greatest minds of their time are concentrated on advertising and to get their audience in a state of continual rutting is their aim." (Citation from McLuhan's *The Mechanical Bride*, 1956, p.5).

[68] Koestler cited in Picart.

[69] Klein cites de Gerada, p.280.

[70] Even if that image was produced in a Communist country which does not acknowledge transnational copyright laws. From Ariana Hernandez-Reguant. *Copyrighting Che: Art and Authorship under Cuban Late Socialism* in *Public*

198e

Culture, Duke U P. Vol. 16. No.1. Winter 2004. p.9.

[71] Cited in Ziff, p.21-22.

[72] The "Berne Convention for the Protection of Literary and Artistic Works" in 1886 began protected ownership over scientific advances and artistic works beyond national borders, thus introducing the concept of transnational copyright. Notably during the twentieth century, communist states did not acknowledge or adopt the transnational laws of the Berne Convention. Further clarification on the convention can be found in Chapter Two, p.50

[73] Korda interview in *The Christian Science Monitor,* March 5th 2004.

[74] Geisler, p.178.

[75] Geisler, p.178. This framing also draws from Clark, p.46.

[76] Clark, p.45.

[77] Hebdige, p.16

[78] Ibid.

[79] This term is often attributed to Hannah Arendt.

[80] The phrasing in the first part of this paragraph draws closely from discussion with Wilson Neate.

[81] Ibid.

[82] Cited from Malebranche's book, *Androphilia, A Manifesto: Rejecting the Gay Identity, Reclaiming Masculinity*. Baltimore: Scapegoat Press. Cited in *The Gay and Lesbian Review*, September 2007. Vol XIV, Number 5, p.42.

[83] Ibid, p.42.

[84] In this regard, Deepwell has compared the work of artists Tracey Emin and Suzanne Lacy. Deepwell, Katy. *Feminist Aesthetics in an International frame.* n.paradoxa. Vol.1. 1998. London: KT Press.p.25.

[85] Godfrey. P.386

[86] Godfrey. p.386

[87] From Stephen Hilger "A look at Hans und Grete" http://www.sevenseven.com/debeer/hilger2.html

[88] Glover. p.6

[89] Stroun, p.15.

198f

Chapter IX

GERMAN HISTORY AND THE "UNDEAD" BODY

Why do images of dead 1970s RAF terrorists continue to circulate so long after the group disbanded? One reason for their ghostly presence is the increased importance of information as power supply. New systems of communication refigure our preconceptions of history and of the world around us. An increased blurring has occurred between "real life," and "life" passed, fictionalized worlds of the cinematic eye, the lens of television and computer screens. Signs in these contexts such as those relating to the RAF, can continue to exist, but, in a more fractal space-time continuum.

Both Jacques Derrida and comp lit writer Charity Scribner[1] discuss the role of Leftist signs after the toppling of Soviet Communism, and ways that these signs seem to *exist* as signifiers oddly evacuated of meaning. A particular theme running through Derrida's *Specters of Marx* (1994) is the importance of these evacuated signs in "re-imagining the culture."

The continued fascination with dead 1970s Leftist terrorists can be related to a manifestation of electrical life in the era of film, television and the Internet. Many of the people we know and refer to every day are no longer living. Icons such as Marilyn Monroe, John Lennon, or Princess Diana are repeatedly dug up for use as tabloid signifiers in newspapers or to be projected onto screens for decades and decades after death.

Twenty years from now, at least half the on-screen entities that a child growing up in the West will be familiar with will never really have lived (such as Mickey Mouse or a Tamagotchi) or they will no longer be living (revivified rock stars and celebrities). These on-screen manifestations exist as the electrical specter of our era.

What totemic role might historical figures like Che or Ulrike Meinhof play in this game? Discourse around dead Leftist icons continues to manifest that figure's presence long after their death. This kind of second "life' (and the often unresolved history to which it alludes) drifts through cultural flow, often being invoked as an elemental figure in the re-conceptualization of past events, necrophiliacly unearthed, re-used, re-imagined and sold.

Perhaps this is the gathering that Derrida saw in *Specters of Marx* when he spoke of "a population of ghosts with or without a leader."[2]

Addressing the phenomenon of "Terror-kultur"

As illustrated by recent uses of Che's image or of logo RAF, the informational overload of today has accelerated the takeover of the very DNA of many key signifiers associated with 1960s and 1970s Leftist propaganda. The "Strummer RAF" logo T-shirt on sale in the New York of 2007 is proof of the way that this logo has become rock chic'd, a process that both erases and re-imagines this sign's association.

It is relevant in a discussion of the exhuming of imagery of dead terrorist bodies to note since World War Two the imagistic power of the historic dead.

Susan Sontag stated that the Holocaust has become the global masternarrative of human suffering for our era, around which all other dead historic bodies are relativized. She writes that:

> At the time of the first photographs of the Nazi camps, there was nothing banal about these images. After thirty years, a saturation point may have been reached. In these last decades, "concerned" photography has done at least as much to deaden conscience as to arouse it. [3]

Sontag claims that Holocaust imagery has become *normalized* due to the nature of its framing and in the extents of its viewing. This is a dynamic discussed in Chapter One, citing Friedlander on the extent of Holocaust studies. Overfamiliarity with a subject can breed contempt and contributes to its trivialization and sense of arting.

High visibility of images of dead RAF members across public settings (in magazines, books, cinema, the Web, or on museum walls) has similarly reduced their historical resonance and ability to shock.

Talking about dead German bodies, it is relevant to consider the Austrian tradition of a "schaulustig" (voyeurist) fascination with the viewing of the inanimate human body, both alive and as a corpse. Such obsessions are witnessed in the nineteenth-century popularity of stories about the "schöne Leiche" (the beautiful female corpse), such as the Viennese Volksmund tradition. These narratives also have a distinct necrophiliac aspect.[4] This pattern in recent German history has received public legitimation through the monolith-ing of the Holocaust, but it has a longer history. This is a tradition that not many other Western cultures share.

This edgy enjoyment in objectifying the body of the projected Other is exemplified by the "Volkerschauen," the anthropological project in pre-World War One German zoos where "live African natives" were displayed in cages alongside zoo animals, as bodies without agency.[5]

A recent trace of this unusual German fascination with the inanimate "foreign" body is exemplified by the macabre Frankenstinian "Körperwelten" (Body Worlds) exhibitions, which featured the nude, dissected, resin-impregnated (plastinated) cadavers of undocumented Chinese workers posed in playful postures.[6] The show being the creation of East German-born scientist Dr. Günter von Hagens, who after first exhibiting the cadavers within a German museum setting, has built "Körperwelten" into a hugely successful touring franchise worldwide.

Examples throughout German history suggest that their cultural traditions show undisguised and unsettling fascinations with the reanimating of the captured foreign corpse, and its display.[7]

Controversies around the *denial* of the burial of RAF leaders Baader, Ensslin, and Raspe in Stuttgart in 1977, or of the return and interment of the body of exiled movie star Marlene Dietrich to Berlin in 1992[8] (still perceived by some Germans as a national traitor) further illustrate these unusual German relationships with "the corpse of the Other."

Such a bizarre cultural context may explain a lively ongoing public interest in historic and unresolvable subjects such as the RAF dead. This subject intersects with larger narratives in German history.

These patterns occur in both Fascist and Communist narratives. Examples include the "homo sacer" (as Italian theorist Giorgio Agamden has recently discussed, the stateless citizen's body in ancient Rome), fascinations with photographs of *disgraced dead* Fascist leaders such as Goering or Mussolini, or the displaying of mounds of concentration camp victims. This projective fascination with the foreign corpse seems to suggest a deeper dis-ease. "The corpse of the Other" is eroticized, eulogized (in denial?), in an ameliorative, perhaps exorcist gesture.

Historically, awkward relationships with the dead body (politic) are not only found in Germany's fascist past, but are also mirrored in the history of the Left. Within this "Myth of the Left," the public enshrining of Lenin's embalmed body, and likewise, the displaying of Mao's cadaver to the masses in Beijing suggest a similar cryogenic, cryptonomic trace in Communist Culture. The recent disinterment of Che's body in Bolivia and its triumphant return to Cuba suggests that to the Left, the revolutionary can never be allowed to die.

Returning to Derrida on the "Gespenst" (ghosting) following the fall of the Soviet bloc, in *Specters of Marx* his concept of the "New International" suggests allowing the ghost of historical memory to mutate and interrupt our thinking rather than repress it. Derrida argues that if a discourse is prematurely or unjustifiably erased, it will come back in an *undead* state to haunt the culture until closure is achieved. Derrida quotes the opening lines of the *Communist Manifesto*: "Ein Gespenst geht um in Europa, das Gespenst des Kommunismus"[9] Derrida relates this to Shakespeare and the ghost of Hamlet's father. He uses the ghostliness of Marx's conception of Communism to point the way that a ghost can appear to live on after its reported death, and that any attempt to hunt it down is fruitless. He writes of the desire to:

magically chase away a specter, exorcise the
possible return of a power held to be baleful in
itself and whose demonic threat continues to
haunt the century. Since such a conjecture
today insists, in such a deafening consensus
that what is, it says, indeed dead, remain dead
indeed arouses a suspicion. It awakens us
where it would like to put us to sleep.

Derrida points out that this "ghost" cannot simply be
"located" and "eradicated," its spectrality making it something
that cannot so easily be erased. Again, quoting the opening of
the *Communist Manifesto*: "All the powers of Old Europe have
joined (*verbündet*) into a holy hunt (*zu einer heiligem Hetzjagd*)
against this specter (*gegen dies Gespenst*),[10] Derrida cautions
"Vigilance, therefore: the cadaver is perhaps not as dead, as
simply dead as the conjuration tries to delude us into believing.
The one who has disappeared appears still to be *there* and his
apparition is not nothing. It does not do nothing." The undead is
compelled to return what has not been resolved.

In Derrida's framing, even discourse can embody an
undead. He writes that "as in the work of mourning, after a
trauma, the conjuration has to make sure the dead will not come
back."[11] To achieve this, one needs to listen to and engage with
the messages the ghost has returned to impart in order to finally
reach closure on an unresolved history. He suggests a strategy
of hospitality, of welcoming ghosts to haunt our ideologies and
enable us to continue to "learn how to live."

The eternal return of the RAF subject to the post-Cold
War era can be seen as illustrating the pattern that Derrida
detects. Unresolved threads of recent German history *need* to
continually re-surface in the culture until better clearance is
achieved.

Conclusion

In this conclusion, after recapitulating the research, I further consider the role of culture in mediation of historic public events. I also discuss the significance of this research in relation to other work continuing both on terror and on the RAF's history. What further research is called for by these discoveries? What broader questions do these studies address? What theories/praxis does it bring into question or reinforce?

Chapters One and Eight note the extent of pre-existing academic discourse on histories of the RAF. Due to these strings, as well as my desires to include the visual aspects, this study focuses not on the group's motivations or story, but on visio-cultural patterns around the RAF, re-searching the ways the media and cultural producers have dealt with imagery that remains since its very inception deeply problematic in German society due to associations with violence (political) and the way that image tropes move through the veins of society. The RAF story is not now over (as some studies presume)[12] because the history around the group is still in play and their visuality continually haunts us.

Chapter Two, "Cloning Che," considers the RAF logo and explores how time and context impact upon reson-ance of Leftist signage. It considers flows of meaning that circulate around signs of this type in earlier historical settings and how the logo often changed associations of this signage in later periods. As noted, Paris and Russia were contexts in which Leftist signs first emerged, initially developing *outside* the legally-bound, capitalist, or institutional matrix, and raised in these contexts, they often signalled a transient identity. Leftist signs were also subjected to wild projection in the media. The locating of this process impacts the "understandings" of all Leftist signs (related) in later settings. Although, over time, associations shift, in later use of Leftist signage, instability is inherent to their public conception.

"The History of the RAF Logo" and "Cloning Che" (Chapters Two and Three), demonstrate the manner in which Leftist identity changed association through its *use* by a terror group like the RAF. The tag of primarily Leftist ideological connection is superceded by one related only to terror. The RAF adopted a key communist signifier—the Left Logo of the red star—but re-contextualized and *slashed*[13] it by the super-imposition of a machine-gun image. Logo RAF assumed the red star's pre-existing image-power and built on the foundations of its "association" in constructing an identity—"urban guerilla" (or as the media framed it, "terrorist"). This binary combining conjures up an identity that is both reassuringly familiar and yet disturbingly new, resulting in an engineered emblem with mythic power. The red star of revolution is familiar in the public imaginary, but is re-appeared in its latest incarnation as part of a terror group logo. Continued repetition of this terror logo within media settings accompanied by dramatic news rhetoric starts to establish a newer type of public identity, a new branding—that of the Leftist terrorist.

""Das ist Terror!": Villain in Post-War German Press," The RAF in the Media: The Crime Location. The Female Terrorist" and "The People's Court: Visual Hijacking, the Corpse, the Hostage" (Chapters Four, Five and Six), focused on the tabloid fascination with the RAF as *notorious* public criminals. The Leftist terrorist identity initially emerges as a newspaper fiction, an identity from which the real person or their acts have been evacuated, supplanted by the image of the criminal monster—a *fascinating* figure who needs no introduction (so complete is the information on their lives and violent deeds). Due to the endless tabloid taunting of the RAF subject, the audience knew far more about the lives of these figures than was really relevant. Media villains such as the RAF became in the 1970s larger-than-life projections through the endless saturation of their imagery in print and on the screen. Levels of objectification around such figures during the 1970s led to a much broader tolerance of media harassment.

"Punk and Terror Style" and "Panic Shopping/Consuming Terror: The RAF as Object of Cultural Production," and "German History and the "Undead" Body" (Chapters Seven, Eight and Nine), considered the conveyor belt of cultural production around the subject of the RAF. They discussed the reasons that specific types of RAF-related imagery, such as graphics and particular media photographs associated with the group, have entered the world of cultural production. The chapter also discusses what occurs around these images in the sphere of culture.

In exhuming (and recontextualizing key) images of the RAF, producers of culture continue to shift perceptions of the group. As noted, successive waves of cultural production process and re-process this cadaver. Chapter Seven considers what impact this has on conceptions of the group and on the imagery itself. It discusses the impact of music industry rinsing[14] (RAF) logos, and the piratical patterns that develop around an underground political sign when it is included in hip subcultures such as Punk. I argue that the RAF logo has been somehat taken over as part of the social history of 1970s rock music (due to it being *used* by the band The Clash).

As shown by contrasting examples of use of RAF imagery in the fields of rock, fashion and fine art, their intents have varied greatly over time. But what appears to unify these actions is the way that succeeding waves of cultural production have fed off one another. Cinematic works and academic studies on the RAF informed usage in fine art and pop cultural production. Why are specific types of RAF images deemed *worthy* of re-use and what results in the re-contextualization of this politically-charged imagery? Public interest in visual icons of the Cold War such as Che led to the broader mass appeal of further Leftist imagery of that era such as that of the RAF.

As noted, these chapters located fields of re-engagement with RAF visuality. What is it that makes terror hot and "consumable," and what happens as a result of its commodification? Richter's act of canonization of the RAF by his painting plays a significant role in the renewed currency of brand RAF. But also as we have seen, a result of repeated re-uses of the RAF imagery in fine art and popular culture is that their understanding and contextual resonances diminish as they move further from their era and geo-politics as contexts change and time passes, these images morph and like a hydra, growing new kinds of association.

MOMA's acquisition of Richter's famous paintings of the dead RAF leaders contributed to the "museumification" of the RAF subject. This turn of events brings up many questions about the ethics of commerce and the role of culture as societal fluid. What is the working of the command-and-control center process of elite culture in the cultural absorption of terrorist subject matter and in the mediating of public trauma?

Important questions must be asked in relation to Art History about the *interface* of an artwork and its subject (icons of Leftist terror). One key intervention to make in the art historical study of these works is to *include* but to not privilege discussion of the fine art canon above other media. By crashing discipline, it allows the reading of these artworks to expand beyond any formal relation to the art historical canon. Perhaps it is more interesting to consider the transit of these traits as cultural by-products floating/drowning in wider social and cultural systems, rather than viewing Richter's paintings as the central conundrum to which the study must always return.

This study required a wide industrialized, open-cast mining of the strata of the stasis of theory—a transgressive historical, psychic archaeology. Protocols occur around signs that interrupt an established order. Institutional frameworks try to legally control or to co-opt signs that are outlaws in the public domain. What occurs around and inside radical and terror tropes in these spheres of vision? And what channels in a society process, acculturate and de-fang imagery that is politically-problematic, and regurgitate it at the mainstream as hip or kitsch? While looking at Che Guevara and Angela Davis, through the endless pop cultural saturation of these two icons, their imagery loses its (rhetorical) power and its association (political). Angela Davis pointed out how this "dumbing-down" had occurred around her 1960s image. This image-war has occured around most high-profile Leftist political icons. But other terror celebrities like the RAF still maintain some level of oppositional power many decades after decay. Such a perspective on the RAF is based on geographical and temporal proximity. The recent Kunst-Werke museum debacle of RAF-related artworks showed that, (unlike their exhibition at MOMA in New York) even thirty years after the first leaders' deaths, the RAF still remain a taboo subject in Germany.

Internationalist intents of the 1960s and 1970s Leftist guerilla movements are curiously mirrored in the way transglobal pop cultural production later trades imagery of Leftist revolutionary icons like Che and even the RAF across borders—for their potential as Cold-War "polit-kitsch." As noted in the discussion of Italian publisher Feltrinelli's piracy of Korda's Che image in Chapter Three, a pattern of appropriation of Leftist signs often emerges at a grassroots level which then later spreads into wider spheres. Post-Détente, a Leftist icon once employed by the state (in the context of the Cold War) to signify ideological opposition to capitalism is sometimes later re-used as irony, as a riff to sell a commodity. The revolt against capitalism that the public display of imagery of Che or the RAF symbolized is now re-contextualized in fine art or fashion as a "postmodern" comment. (Such an aim is illustrated in the culture-jamming intent of 1990s graphics like "Che Cher" or "Prada Meinhof").

Rock band's *Rage Against the Machine*'s appropriation of Che's image exemplifies how when a symbol of integrity which has great levels of public familiarity, even its "scent of authenticity" can be used even outside its original context—in this case for music industry marketing. Similar tropes are shown in the case of the viewer who witnesses Strummer's RAF T-shirting appropriation of so-called Punk Integrity, or Gerhard Richter's blurring of the dead (prisoners). This voyeur may only be partially aware of deeper connections or historical allusions. But even the uninformed sense the importance of this imagery due to its location on an art museum wall, or display in New York tourist meccas like St.Mark's Place. This exhibitionism installs a halo of mystery around these images, leading to the understanding/reading of these signs as legendary or historic signifigance. This parapolitical, covert aspect of half-knowing—the signaling that there is insider-information-required—creates a quality of the mythic around particular types of imagery and prolongs the half-life of the trope.

What does this study add to further understandings of the RAF histories, and how does it relate to ongoing patterns of absorption by cultural canons? Chapter One and Seven noted that in the last ten years *all* discourse around the RAF (both non-visual and visual) has become increasingly foreclosed, mediated, determined, and therefore remotely controlled in the playpen of academics and curators—often under a rubric related to a "big name" cultural producer such as Richter. Has the RAF become a piece of cultural "real estate," around which the discursive territory is increasingly determined? My book attempts to track the processing in the foreclosing, "institutionalizing" tendency that emerged around a subject that evinces easy or complete closure.

Re-packaging the RAF is a central locus of this study. It aims to unpack the ideologies which a range of interested forces have attempted to establish around the discourse of the RAF through political intent, by chance, or due to economic incentive.

However, such a study provides by its very nature a further sense of hermeticism. As shown, the RAF is an object that has already been subjected to relentless commodification. I attempt instead to use the RAF subject to open new perspectives on larger struggles, using the cartography of the RAF debacle to print the shifting interrelationships between media, culture, science, and the personal, during and since the thaw of the Cold War.

What broad historical questions does this research foreground? And what general theories does it bring into question or reinforce? One important issue that this study pinpoints is the changing of relations between the mass media and public, how modes of visual presentation shift in Cold War settings. It is clear that 1945 was an important world historical moment. But the cultural periodization that places 1968 as *a key* moment of global import and change, and the only year of worldwide student revolution, needs to be challenged. Such a linear perspective suggests the mainstream media's role in retro-framing public conceptions of recent history. As my study shows, it is obvious the 1970s saw a much more serious wave of anti-state political activism and violence.

The collapse of the Soviet bloc provides a new context from which to discuss the growth of Western mass media since the 1950s, and the manipulation and stereotyping of particular imagery by state and media forces to shape public opinion in the Cold War context. Also in this period, the increasing influence of the media needs to be analyzed in relation to the "framing" of history. And rather than only to focus on the media's *role* in the portrayal of events, I argue that the media's own growth and its dependence on the state's funding during this period also need close examination.

Another question that emerges during this study is the *impact* of technology on society as a whole, and how new mediums profoundly change personal relations. In the move into digital culture, the boundaries and power relations between people, machines, the state, media, and cultural production have all shifted dramatically. Our contemporary patterns of communication provide interesting perspectives on the functions of media/state in the '70s. As noted, the RAF story would have manifested in society as an entirely different being in the age of the Internet.[15][16]

What remains to be studied concerning the 1970s West German terror phenomenon? What other aspects of the RAF debacle still need to be viewed? As Appendix A notes, broader discussion is required on all ideas and entities defined as terrorist or radical; the current study is only a close reading of imagery related to one particular 1970s terror group. It also addressed the visual relation between the RAF, Che, the Black Panthers, Patty Hearst and Angela Davis because their "presences" in the media are relevant to tropes that concurrently emerged around the RAF. A further study might *consider* the depiction of Leftist, radical, and terrorist identities crossing ranges of geo-political terrains.

Another perspective yet to be considered is the "economic" history of the RAF, how 1970s terror interacts with commercial systems. What might such an exploration discover? Herman and O'Sullivan argued that a "terror industry" emerged in the Western media during the 1970s that intentionally developed and then exploited the myth of the urban terrorist. Over time, "the terror story" became a key component for contemporary news production worldwide—part of a constructed, serial, endless "war on terror." Forty years after U.S. screenings of Vietnam first brought "war into the people's homes" during the first golden era of television, a global news industry emerged around the marketing of the "live" *domestic* terror story (often parallel to the conspicuous lack of in-depth information on and ignoring of unreported, ongoing, international, official state wars). "Terror" developed as a huge news genre and economic hotspot. A study of the monetary growth in this branch of the news industry over the past forty years would provide fascinating research.

Beyond the growth of a new news category in the media, another important intersection between economics and terror also demands study. The emergence of Western radical and terror movements in the 1970s is possibly linked to the increase in university education after World War Two. During the Cold War, higher-education sectors swelled enormously in Western Europe and America due to state initiatives and the enormous wealth generated by national industries during the post-war boom. Statistics concerning the G.I. Bill in the U.S.

demonstrate similar patterns across other countries in the West during this time. By 1965, close to 1.2 million Korean War veterans had used G.I. Bill funding to enter higher education, over 860,000 for other education purposes, and 318,000 for occupational training. These numbers suggests that the 1960s was a period when a huge generation of university-educated adults came of age and this generation was economically and socially empowered (and unified) in a way that no generation before had been. This power, social and economic, sowed the intellectual and political seeds of the New Left's "progressive" agenda. Due to the Vietnam draft, the G.I. Bill, new media forums, and an emergent drug culture, this ferment led to revolt by some against the state and the preceeding generation. To better understand terror and its growth in the post-World-War-Two era, one needs to closely track the interrelation between media, technology, and the growing public influence of further education during this period.

One final thought occurs. The study of the history of 1970s West German terror imagery located contexts where the public came across this subject after its "news era," and with what various kinds of understandings. A question that surfaces in this regard is how future history and cultural production will memorialize imagery related to now-current terror waves, such as "9/11" and Al Qaeda. What factors will shape later re-presentations of these events?

It has been said that history is always written by the victors and that history itself is the struggle between competing narratives. This challenges the very idea of how to write an inclusive history of "terrorism"—a struggle that, by its very nature, aims to erase all opposing views.

[1] In Derrida's *Specters of Marx* and in Scribner's *Requiem for Communism.*

[2] Derrida. *Specters of Marx*, p.1.

[3] From Sontag, *On Photography.* p.20-2.

[4] A noted English-language writer on the subject of the "Volksmund" tradition is Bronfen. Also related and of note is the recent controversy concerning the "African village" which featured in a German zoo.

[5] See Bronfen on this subject.

[6] A subject discussed in much further depth in Thomas-Vander-Lugt in his 2006 dissertation, *Return of the Living Dead: Reading The Revenant Body in Post-1968 German-language Literary and Visual Culture.*

[7] In a recent catalog essay *Atlantic Postcards*, Mirzoeff cites Barthes' argument in *Camera Lucida* that photography is "about nothing other than death and how the photograph as automatically coded as historic—that "this has been."" Its opening of the shutter insists that "this was there" but also that it is not so any longer. A moment is seized out of time and recalls insistently nothing other than the passing of time, the approach of death." Discussing Barthes' concept of *punctum*, Mirzoeff states, "So much of photography has dealt with death for its modernity has been that of mass-produced slaughter. There is a debate to be had as to whether a Western viewer could experience the *punctum* in confronting African experience." From *Atlantic Postcards* catalog, 2006. NYU Steinhardt.
For a further discussion on Germany's "special relation" to the corpse, see Thomas-Vander-Lugt's work.

[8] Concerning the mixed public sentiments re. the Dietrich burial.
http://query.nytimes.com/gst/fullpage.html?
res=9E0CEFDE173FF934A25756C0A964958260

[9] Derrida. p.99

[10] Derrida. p.100

[11] Derrida, *Specters of Marx,* p.97.

[12] Peters ends his book with this conception, using the official disbanding of the group in 1998 to frame this assessment (p.715-26).

[13] Drawing from the language of design, "slash" in this sense means to violently render an image identity new or hybridized.

[14] Drawing from the language of contemporary dance music production, the term "rinsing" here means to remove something from its original context, often to take the last energies out of a well-used beat.

[15] Related to this shift, as can be witnessed, any media coverage of the RAF in 2007 immediately and prominently displays their logo and photographs to quickly re-conjure the whole debacle and its ideological setting.

[16] And as Chapter Seven discussed, websites have re-invigorated interest in the RAF subject and helped re-frame popular understandings of the group.

BIBLIOGRAPHY

Adorno, Theodor W. *Minima Moralia: Reflections from Damaged Life*. New York: Verso, 1993.

---. *The Culture Industry*. London: Routledge, 1991.

Adorno, Theodor W. and Horkheimer, Max. *Dialectic of Enlightenment*. London: Verso, 1944.

Anderson, Benedict. *Imagined Communities: Reflections on the origin and spread of nationalism*. London : Verso, 1983.

Anderson, Jon Lee. *Che, A Revolutionary Life*. New York: Grove Press, 1997.

Alexander, Yonah. "Terrorism, the Media and the Police" in *Terrorism: Threat, Reality, Response* (edited by R.H. Kupperman and D.M. Trent), Stanford, California: Hoover Institution Press, 1979.

Apter, Emily. "Weaponized Thought: Ethical Militance and the
    Group-Subject." *Grey Room* 14. Boston: MIT, 2004.

Aust, Stefan. *The Baader-Meinhof Group.* London: Bodley
    Head, 1987.

Azzociation A. *Vorwärts bis zum nieder mit.* Berlin: HKS 13,
    2001.

Baetens, Jan. "Cultural Studies after the Cultural Studies
    Paradigm." *Cultural Studies.* Vol, 19. No.1. January
    2005.

Barthes, Roland. *Camera Lucida.* New York: Hill and Wang,
    1981.

---. *Mythologies.* New York: Hill and Wang, 1972.

---. *The Rustle of Language.* Berkeley: U.C, 1986.

Bathrick, David. "Cultural Studies." Introduction to
    Scholarship on Modern Languages and Literature. Ed.
    Joseph Gibaldi. New York: MLA, 1992.

Baumann, Michael. *Terror or Love.* New York: Grove Press,

1977.

Becker, Jillian. *Hitler's Children.* New York: Lippincott, 1977.

Benjamin, Walter. Illuminations. New York: Schocken, 1969.

---. *Reflections: Essays, aphorisms, autobiographical*

writing. New York : Harcourt Brace Jovanovich, 1978.

Berger, John. *Ways of Seeing.* London: Penguin, 1980.

Biesenbach, Klaus ed. *Vorstellung des Terrors Die RAF.* Berlin:

Kunst-Werke, 2005.

Bogdan, R. C., & Biklen, S. K. *Qualitative Research for*

Education: An Introduction to Theory and Methods.

Boston: Allyn and Bacon, Inc. 1982.

Boll, Heinrich. *The Lost Honor of Katharina Blum.* London:

Vintage, 2000.

Boorstin, Daniel J. *The Image.* New York: Atheneum, 1962.

218

Bottomore, Tom. *The Frankfurt School and its Critics.* London:

    Routledge, 2003.

Bourdieu, Pierre. *Distinction: A Social Critique of the*

    Judgement Of Taste. Cambridge: Harvard University

    Press, 1984.

---. *The Field of Cultural Production.* New York :

    Columbia University Press, 1993.

Bourdieu, Pierre and Darbel, Alain. *The Love of Art.* Stanford:

    Stanford U, 1991.

Bracewell, Michael. *England is Mine: Pop life in Albion from*

    Wilde to Goldie. London : Flamingo, 1998.

Brown, Brian A. *Habermas and the Impure Image-Text: An*

    Inquiry into communicative potential of the Image.

    Masters Thesis. University of Windsor, Ontario. 2005.

Buchloh, Benjamin H. D. "A Note on Gerhard Richter's

    "October 18th 1977," *October,* vol.48, Spring 1989

---. *Gerhard Richter.* Doctoral dissertation. New York: CUNY, 1994.

Clark, Christopher. *Sexuality and Alterity in German Literature, Film and Performance, 1968-2000.* Doctoral dissertation. Cornell, 2003.

Cohen, Stanley. *Folk Devils and Moral Panics.* New York: St. Martins, 1980.

Corrado, Raymond with Evans, Rebecca. "Ethnic and Idealogical Terrorism in Western Europe" in Michael Stohl, ed., *The Politics of Terrorism.* New York: Marcel Dekker, 1998,

Cotter, Holland. "The Collective Conscious." *The New York Times,* (Arts and Leisure). March 5, 2006.

Conroy, Melissa S. *Theatron and Theoria: Vision, Visuality, and Religious Spectatorship.* Doctoral dissertation. Syracuse University, 2006.

Crary, Jonathan. *Techniques of the observer: On vision and modernity in the nineteenth century.* Cambridge: MIT Press, 1990.

D'Alviella, Count Eugene Goblet. *Symbols: Their Migration and Universality.* London: Dover Publications, 2000.

Dartnell, Michael York. *Mirror of Violence : The Revolutionary Terror of Action Directe as an Element in the Evolution of French Political Culture, 1979-1987.* Doctoral dissertation, York University, Ontario. 1993.

Dauber, Cori E. "The Shots Seen Round the World: The Impact of Images of Mogadishu on American Military Operations." In *Rhetoric and Public Affairs*, Vol.4, No.1. 1994.

Davis, Angela Y. "Afro Images: Politics, Fashion, and Nostalgia," *Critical Inquiry.* Vol. 21, No.1 (Autumn, 1994).

Davis, Melissa. *More than a Name: An Introduction to Branding.* Lausanne: AVA, 2006.

Debord, Guy. *The Society of the Spectacle.* Detroit: Black & Red, 1977.

---. *Comments on the Society of the Spectacle*, trans. Malcolm Imrie. London: Verso, 1990.

Deepwell, Katy. *Feminist Aesthetics in an International frame.* n.paradoxa. Vol1. 1998. London: KT Press.

---. *New feminist art criticism: critical strategies.* Manchester: Manchester University Press, 1995.

Derrida, Jacques. *Specters of Marx.* New York: Routledge, 1994.

Dyer, Richard. *Stars.* London: BFI, 1979.

Edschmid, Ulrike. *Frau mit Waffe.* Berlin: Suhrkamp, 2001.

Elsaesser, Thomas. *Antigone Agonistes: Urban Guerilla and Guerilla Urbanism. The RAF, "Germany in Autumn", "Death Game"*. Online article, 2002.

Ennslin, Gudrun. *Zieht den Trennungsstrich, jede Minute*. Hamburg: Konkret, 2005.

Feldman, Allen. *Formations of Violence*. Chicago: U.Chicago, 1991.

---. "Violence and Vision: The Prosthetics and Aesthetics of Terror" in Slocum, J. David, ed. *Terrorism, Media, Liberation*. New Brunswick: Rutgers, 2005.

Fink, Carole, Gassert, Philipp and Junker, Detlef. *1968: The World Transformed*. German Historical Institute, Cambridge. 1998.

Foster, Hal, ed. *Vision and Visuality*. Seattle: Bay, 1988.

Foucault, Michel. *Discipline and Punish*. New York: Pantheon, 1977.

---. *Madness and Civilization.* New York: Random House, 1988.

---. *The Birth of the Clinic.* New York: Random House, 1990.

---. *The History of Sexuality. Vol 1.* New York: Random House, 1990.

---. "What is an Author?" (1969). Trans. Donald F. Bouchard and Sherry Simon. In *Language, Counter-Memory, Practice.* Ed. Donald F. Bouchard. Ithaca, New York: Cornell University Press, 1977.

Friedlander, Saul. *Memory, History, and the Extermination of the Jews of Europe.* Bloomington: Indiana University Press, 1993.

Geisler, Michael E. *If the shoe fits.... Germans as Nazis on U.S. television* in *German Politics and Society,* 13.3, 1995.

Gitlin, Todd. *The whole world is watching: Mass Media in the Making & Unmaking of the New Left.* Berkeley: University of California Press, 1980.

Gladwell, Michael. *The Tipping Point: How Little Things Can Make a Big Difference.* Boston: Little, Brown, 2000.

Godfrey, Tony. *Conceptual Art.* London: Phaidon, 1998.

Goldsworthy, Rupert. *Crude vs Elegant: Collected Essays 1994-2002.* New York: CPF Publishers. 2002.

Goldsworthy, Rupert. *Interview with Bruce LaBruce.* Kulturflash magazine. http://www.kultureflash.net/archive/89/priview.html/ Online source. April 2004.

Glover, Michael. "The artist makes an exhibition of herself." London: *The Independent.* May 15th 2001. p.11.

Guins, R. and O.Z. Cruz, ed. *Popular Culture: A Reader.* London: Sage, 2005.

Hall, Rachel. *Danger and Desire: Instrumental Reason in the History of the Wanted Poster.* Doctoral dissertation. University of North Carolina, Chapel Hill. 2004.

Halperin, David Winkler, John J. and Zeitlin, Froma T. *Before Sexuality: The Construction of the Erotic Experience in the Ancient World.* Princeton: Princeton University Press, 1990.

Haraway, Donna. "The Persistence of Vision" in *Writing on the Body: Female embodiment and Feminist Theory*, ed. Katie Conboy,

Nadia, Medina, and Sarah Stanbury. New York: Columbia University Press, 1997.

Harvey, David. *The Condition of Postmodernity: An Enquiry into the Origins of Cultural Change.* New York: Blackwell, 1989.

Hearst, Patricia Campbell, with Moscow, Alvin. *Every Secret Thing.* Garden City, N.Y: Doubleday, 1982.

Heath, Joseph, and Potter, Andrew. *The Rebel Sell: How The Counter Culture Became Consumer Culture.* London: Capstone, 2006.

Hebdige, Dick. *Subculture: The Meaning of Style.* London: Routledge,

1977.

Herman, Edward S. and Chomsky, Noam. *Manufacturing Consent.* New York: Pantheon, 1988.

Herman, Edward S. and O'Sullivan, Gerry. *The Terrorism Industry.* New York: Pantheon, 1989.

Hernandez-Reguant, Ariana. "Copyrighting Che: Art and Authorship under late Cuban socialism." *Public Culture*, 16.1. New York. 2004.

Hocking, Jenny. "Orthodox Theories of "Terrorism": The

Power of Politicized Terminology." In *Politics: Journal*

of Australasian Political Studies Association, Vol. 19,

No.2, November, 1984, p.103.

Hoerschelmann, Olaf. "Memoria Dextera Est: Film and Public

Memory in Post-War Germany." 2001. New York:

Cinema Journal. 40.2.

Ian, Marcia. *Remembering the Phallic Mother: Psychoanalysis,*

Modernism and the Fetish. Ithaca: Cornell University

Press, 1996.

Jameson, Fredric. *The Geo-Political Aesthetic: Cinema and*

Space in the World System. London: BFI, 1992.

--*Postmodernism, or The Cultural Logic of Late Capitalism.*

Durham: Duke University Press, 1991.

Jay, Martin. *Downcast eyes: the denigration of vision in twentieth-century French thought.* Berkeley: University of California Press, 1993.

Jones, Steve and Jensen, Joli, eds. *Afterlife as Afterimage.* New York: Lang. 2005.

Juchler, Ingo. *Die Studentenbewegung in den Vereinigten Staaten und der Bundesrepublik Deutschland der sechziger Jahre.* Duncker u. H., Bln, 1996.

Karim, Karim H. *Constructions of the Islamic Peril in English-language Canadian Print Media: Discourses on Power and Violence.* McGill University, Montreal. Doctoral dissertation, 1996.

Khvostov, Mikhail. *The Russian Civil War (1) The Red Arm.y.* Oxford, UK: Osprey, 1996

Kim, Young Chan. *Advertising, Consumer Culture, Youth*

    Cultures, and Media Technologies: A Cultural-Historical

    Approach to MTV. University of Illinois at Urbana-

    Champaign. Doctoral dissertation, 2001.

Klein, Naomi. *No Logo.* New York: Picador, 2000.

Koestler, Arthur. *The Ghost in the Machine.* New York:

    Random House, 1982.

Kramer, Hilton. "MOMA helps Martyrdom of German

    Terrorists." *The New York Observer* (July 3-10, 1995).

Krauss, Rosalind. *The Optical Unconscious.* Cambridge: MIT,

    1993.

Kunzle, David. *Che Guevara:Icon, myth, and message.* Los

    Angeles: UCLA Fowler Museum of Cultural History in

    collaboration with the Center for the Study of Political

    Graphics, 1997.

Linker, Kate. "Representation and Sexuality." In *Art after Modernism: Rethinking Representation.* Ed. Brian Wallis. New York: New Museum. 1983.

Lipsitz, George. *Time Passages: Collective Memory and American Popular Culture.* Minneapolis: U.Minn, 1990.

Lotringer, Sylvere. *Semiotexte: The German Issue.* New York: Semiotexte, 1991.

MacDonald, Eileen. *Shoot the Women First.* London: Fourth Estate, 1991.

McBride, David. *On the Faultline of Mass Culture and Counterculture: A Social History of the Hippie Counterculture in 1960s Los Angeles.* Doctoral dissertation. UCLA, 1998.

McLellan, Vin and Avery, Paul. *The Voices of Guns.* New York: Putnams. 1977.

McLuhan, Marshall and Fiore, Quentin. *War and Peace in the Global Village*. New York: McGraw Hill, 1968.

Malebranche, Jack. *Androphilia, A Manifesto: Rejecting the Gay Identity, Reclaiming Masculinity*. Baltimore: Scapegoat Press. 2007.

Marcus, Greil. *Lipstick Traces*. Cambridge: Harvard, 1989.

Marcuse, Herbert. *Eros and Civilization*. Boston: Beacon, 1966.

---. *Repressive Tolerance. An essay*. Boston: Beacon Press, 1965.

---. *One-Dimensional Man*. London: Routledge, 1964.

Marshall, Jason C. *Demonizing the Counterculture: Los Angeles Newspapers and the Manson Murders, 1969-1971*. California State University, Long Beach. Doctoral dissertation, 2003.

Marx, Karl, and Engels, Friedrich. *The Communist Manifesto*. London: Penguin Books, 1985.

Melly, George. *Revolt into Style: The Pop Arts in Britain.*
Oxford, Oxford, 1989.

Meyer, Richard. *Outlaw Representation: Censorship &
Homosexuality in Twentieth-Century American Art.*
Oxford: OUP, 2002.

Miller, Bowman Howard. *The Language Component of
Terrorism Strategy: A Text-based, Linguistic study of
Contemporary Terrorism.* Doctoral dissertation,
Georgetown, 1983.

Miller, Henry K. "Fatal Attraction: Che Guevara, Carlos the
Jackal, Andreas Baader." *New Statesman.* October 2002.

Miller-Idriss, Cynthia. *Learning to Belong: Citizenship,
Schooling and National Identity in Contemporary
Germany.* Doctoral dissertation. U. Michigan, 2003.

Mirzoeff, Nicholas. *The Visual Culture Reader.* 2nd Ed.

New York: Routledge, 2002.

---. *Watching Babylon: The War in Iraq and Global Visual
Culture.* New York: Routledge, 2005.

Mitchell, W.J.T. *Picture Theory: Essays on Verbal and Visual
Representation.* Chicago : University of Chicago Press,
1994.

---. "What is an image?" *New Literary History*, Vol. 15, No. 3,
Spring,

Morgan, Robin. *The Demon Lover: The Roots of Terrorism.*
New York: Washington Square, 1989.

Morris, Rosalind C. "Theses on the Questions of War: History,
Media, Terror" in Slocum, J. David, ed. *Terrorism,
Media, Liberation.* New Brunswick: Rutgers, 2005,
p.297-319.

Mosse, George L. *Nationalism and Sexuality: Respectability and Abnormal Sexuality in Modern Europe.* New York : H. Fertig,1985.

Mulvey, Laura. *Visual and Other Pleasures.* Bloomington: Indiana University Press, 1989.

Murphy, Sheila Colleen. *Looking and Lurking: Media Technologies, Cultural Convergences of Spectatorship, Voyeurism and Surveillance.* Doctoral dissertation. University of California, Irvine, 2002.

Owens, Craig. *Beyond Recognition.* Berkeley: U.C. Press, 1992.

Pearlstein, Richard Merrill. *Lives of Quiet Desperation: An Inquiry into the mind of the political terrorist.* UNC Doctoral dissertation, 1986.

Peifer, Elizabeth L.B. *1968 in German Political Culture, 1967-1993: From Experience to Myth.* University of North Carolina, Chapel Hill. Doctoral dissertation. 1997.

Peters, Butz. *Todlicher Irrtum.* Berlin: Argon. 2004

Picart, Caroline Joan. *Humour and Horror in Science Fiction and Comedic Frankensteinian Films.* Scope, online magazine, 2004.

http://www.nottingham.ac.uk/film/journal/articles/ humour-and-horror.htm

Plowman, Andrew. "Bernward Vesper's "Die Reise": Politics and Autobiography between the Student Movement and the Act of Self-Invention." *German Studies Review,* vol.21, No.3 (October 1998), 507-524.

Postman, Neil. *Amusing Ourselves to Death.* New York: Viking, 1985.

Prinz, Alois. *Die Lebensgeschichte der Ulrike Meinhof.* Berlin: Suhrkamp, 2005.

Proll, Astrid. *Baader-Meinhof: Pictures on the Run.* New York: Scalo, 1998.

Puar, Jasbir K. and Rai, Amit S. "Monster, Terrorist, Fag: The war on terrorism and the production of docile citizens." *Social Text* 72 (20.3; Fall 2002)

Pultz, John. *The Body and the Lens.* New York: Abrams, 1995.

Rajgopal, Arvind. *Politics After Television: Religious Nationalism and the Retailing of Hinduness.* Cambridge: U. Cambridge, 2001.

Richter, Gerhard. *The Daily Practice of Painting.* Cambridge: MIT, 1995.

Rickels, Laurence R, ed. *Acting out in Groups.* Minneapolis: U.Minn, 1999.

Rizzo, Mary. *Consuming Culture, Buying Identity: Middle-Class Youth Culture, "Lower-Class" Style and Consumer Culture, 1945-2005.* Doctoral dissertation, 2005.

Ronell, Avital. "Trauma TV" from *Finitude's Score: Essays for the end of the millennium*. Lincoln: University of Nebraska Press, 1994.

Ross, Kristin. *Paris '68 and its Afterlives*. Chicago: Uni.Chicago, 2002.

Rote Armee Fraktion. *Communiques 1970-98*. Online source. http://www.baader-meinhof.com/students/resources/communique/index.htm http://www.germanguerilla.com/red-army-faction/documents   Online source.

Said, Edward. *Covering Islam*. New York: Pantheon, 1981.

Savage, Jon. *England's Dreaming*.

---. *Teenage*. 2007. New York: Viking, 2007.

Schowalter, Daniel F. *Images of Traumatic History: The Visual Rhetorics of Holocaust*. Doctoral dissertation. Indiana University, 2001.

Scribner, Charity. "Buildings on Fire: The Situationist
   International and the Red Army Faction." *Grey Room* 26.
   Boston: MIT, Fall 2007.

---. *Requiem for Communism.* Cambridge: MIT, 2003.

Seymour-Ure, Colin. *The British Press and Broadcasting since
   1945.* Cambridge: Basil Blackwell, 1991.

Shirato, Tony and Webb, Jennifer. "The Media as Spectacle:
   September 11 as Soap Opera." *Journal of Cultural
   Research*, Vol 8, No.4 (October 2004).

Sinclair, John. *Guitar Army.* 1972. New York; Douglas Book
   Corp; Rainbow Energies,1972.

Slater, Don. "Photography and Modern Vision: The Spectacle
   of Modern Vision." From Chris Jenks, ed. *Visual
   Culture.* New York: Routledge, 1995.

Slocum, J. David, ed. *Terrorism, Media, Liberation.* New
   Brunswick: Rutgers, 2005.

Solanas, Valerie (intro. Ronell, A). *S.C.U.M. Manifesto*. S.F:

AK Press, 1996.

Sontag, Susan. *On Photography*. New York: Dell, 1977.

---. *Regarding the Pain of Others*. New York : Farrar, Straus

and Giroux, 2003.

Springer Verlag, Axel."Chronik." Online source.

http://www.axelspringer.de/inhalte/unterneh/frame.htm

Sterling, Claire. *The Terror Network*. New York: Holt, 1981.

Storr, Robert /MOMA. *Gerhard Richter: October 18th 1977*.

New York: Museum of Modern Art, 1997.

Storr, Robert. *Gerhard Richter*. New York: Museum of Modern

Art, 1999.

Stout, Graeme Allen. *Arrest Images: Discourses on Terrorism

In Italy and Germany*. Doctoral dissertation. University

of Minnesota, 2006.

Stroun, Fabrice. "Dear Ketel One Reader" in Guyton/Walker

   The Failever of Judgement. Zurich: JRP/Ringier, 2005.

Tagg, John. 1993. *The Burden of Representation: Essays on*

   Photographies and Histories. Minneapolis: University of

   Minnesota Press, 1993.

Teraoka, Arlene. "The Essay as Weapon." From *The Politics of*

   the Essay. ed. R.E. Boetcher Joeves and Elizabeth

   Mittman. Indiana, 1993.

Thatcher, Margaret. *TV Interview for the BBC.* Margaret

   Thatcher Foundation.

   www.margaretthatcher.org/speeches/displaydocumen

   t.asp?docid=10559217th December, 1984. Online

   source.

Theweleit, Klaus. *Male Fantasies* Minneapolis: U.Minn, 1987.

Thomas-Vander-Lugt, Kristin E. *Return of the Living Dead: Reading the Revenant Body in Post-1968 German-language Literary and Visual Culture.* Doctoral dissertation. Indiana University, 2006.

Thompson, E.P. *Making History: Writings on History and Culture.* New York: New Press, 1994.

Thompson, John B. *Media and Modernity.* Polity.

Todd, Matthew Grant. *Critical Intellectuals and the New Media: Bernward Vesper, Ulrike Meinhof, the Frankfurt School and the Red Army Faction.* Doctoral dissertation. Cornell University, 1994.

Troyer, Lonnie Adam. *The Location of Terror: Counterterrorism, American Politics and the Docile Citizen.* Berkeley. Doctoral dissertation, 2000.

Usselmann, Rainer. "18th October 1977: Gerhard Richter's work of mourning and its new audience." *Art Journal.* 2002.

Varon, Jeremy. *Bringing the War Home.* Los Angeles: UC

Press, 2004.

Verlag der Authoren. *Deutschland in Herbst*, 1978.

Viett, Inge. "Lust auf Freiheit." *Junge Welt.* February 24th,

2007. Online source.

https://www.jungewelt.de/loginFailed.php?ref=/2007/02-

24/017.php?print=1

von Dirke, Sabine. *All Power to the Imagination.* Lincoln:

Nebraska, 1997.

Watson, James and Hill, Anne. *Dictionary of Media and*

Communications Studies. Sixth Edition. London: Arnold.

2003.

White, Christina Maria. *Gender and the German Autumn: The*

Representation of Terrorism and the Female Terrorist in

Social Discourses, Literature and Film. U. Minn.

Doctoral dissertation, 2001.

Williams, Raymond. *Television.* New York: Schocken, 1975.

Wills, Garry. *A Necessary Evil: A History of American Distrust of Government*, New York: Simon & Schuster, 1999.

Zhensheng, Li. *Red-Color New Soldier.* New York: Phaidon, 2003.

Ziff, Trisha, ed. *Che Guevara: Revolutionary and Icon.* New York: Adams, 2006.

Zizek, Slavoj. *Enjoy your Symptom.* New York: Routledge, 2001.

Zulaika, Joseba and Douglass, William A. *Terror and Taboo.* New York: Routledge, 1996.

APPENDIX A

Regarding the term "Terror"

No term adequately expresses the complex linguistic operations around this term. This is not a semantic positioning in solidarity with left-wing radicalism nor does it fail to recognize the state's attempts to develop a monopoly on violence.[1] Rather it can be argued that in the context of the Sixties and Seventies, black U.S. political activists the Black Panthers, Malcolm X, or Angela Davis were "radicals" because they never bombed. Whereas RAF leader Andreas Baader—tried and convicted of bombings in 1969 and 1977[2]—is more clearly definable as a terrorist. However Che Guevara—"symbol de rigeur" of radical liberation—is also alleged to have been responsible for mass prison executions during his control of the Cuban prison system in the early 1960s.[3] This kind of detail about Che makes it less easy to establish any politically-neutral terminology within this matrix.[4]

This issue of indefinability is a faultline in discussions on terrorism. Who is legitimized to name a terrorist as such? Which narratives attempt to detonate discourse on the legitimation of violence? [5]

In the recent climate of terror, the American government defines terrorism as "non-conventional use of violence for political gain." But, using this framing of the term, the U.S. was itself guilty of terrorism in Vietnam as U.S. citizens never constitutionally mandated the involvement of American troops in the war. To avoid this kind of linguistic problematic, and to differentiate from systemic terror, some theorists prefer the more neutral term "non-state actor." The RAF defined themselves in their communiqués in military terms—as urban guerillas (Stadtguerillas)—an elite "Kommando" at war with a government they felt to be ideologically bankrupt in its Vietnam policy.[6] [7] As Clausewitz famously noted: "War is the continuation of politics by other means."[8] Clearly, one man's freedom fighter is another media's terrorist.

Media theorist Jenny Hocking has pointed out that terrorism has a relational character that deters effective differentiation and explanation:

> Terrorism is not a neutral or purely descriptive term. In the sense that its understanding is based on perceptions of legitimacy structured according to a benchmark of political and social "normality," "terrorism" is an ideological construct. [9]

As many theorists have argued in this regard, the term "terrorist" is slippery and subject to free play. [10] The analytical value of the term is of limited use and not applicable to the huge range of phenomena termed under this rubric. A general explanation is not relevant to attempt here. Terror is never a finite entity but a label used to bracket a complex range of phenomena produced and defined by three interested parties— the media, urban guerillas and the state.[11] It is more useful in a discussion of the role of the media in the construction of terror to conceive of terror as more than a construct—rather as a location of rhetorical excess, of overload, an area publicly marked as beyond discourse. One might describe the specter of Internet child porn as having a similar place of absolute taboo and unspeakability in contemporary Western culture.

It is also important here to note the way that Anglo-

American discourses and theoretical frameworks guide contemporary understandings of terms like terror or radical. There is a tendency towards categorizing groups in relation to existing discourses from earlier periods and geo-political settings, using these terms without considering the role of context. It is necessary to note the different meanings Germany and the U.S. assign to specific cultural and social processors, and how a term like "radical" or "terrorist" becomes an signifier of changed meanings over time and space. As we shall see, the way the 1960s and 1970s German media classified acts and used terms fundamentally differs from contemporary American models. Furthermore, waves of American discourse interact with German culture, impacting on how some German social groups have understood and constructed their identities. This discursive shift is apparent in the influx of American culture during the Allied army's presence, and also due to the "Wirtschaftswunder" (the West German "economic miracle" during the post-war era, partially due to the U.S. Marshall Plan).

Parallel to these patterns, in the progress of Anglo-American study of global politics, traditional understandings of cultural geography have themselves also developed to become more "relativist"—more culturally-specific and less fixed. Thus, both frames of discourse continue to shift. By acknowledging the unconscious Anglo-American frame of reference at play here, it is important to provide a level of transparency in the use of the term terrorism.[12]

A discussion of images of radicals or terrorists should not elide press imagery of people with the actual people termed by the media or state as "radical" or "terrorist." It is debatable whether a photograph as an object is intrinsically capable of terrorizing. Although radical imagery is clearly not synonymous with terror imagery, even the linguistic formation around these two terms is contestable. In popular parlance, a poster in solidarity with the RAF is to some a radical poster suggesting liberation, to others an image endorsing terrorism. Less contestable as terror imagery is a newspaper photograph documenting a bomb attack.

Another way of framing this discussion is not to talk of terror as a finite entity but of a "media terror"—a series of violent visual spectacles played out in the media for the public. As theorist J. David Slocum has pointed out, terror requires a producer, a consumer, and a mediator.[13] This triangulated framing of terror highlights the key role of the news agency in the construction and delivery of the terror spectacle.

Image is Everything: Terror in the Media

Despite the contemporary cultural amnesia of American news media conceptions that posit 9/11 as "Year Zero" for terrorism on U.S. soil, the grammar of current terror discourse borrows heavily from a discursive model that first emerged in the Western news media during the 1970s. The rhetorics of terror employed in 1970s media and since September 2001 have much stylistic similarity. A particular type of rhetoric was established and deployed in the 1970s around the threat of left-wing terror, which was then reconstituted around the specter of religious terror in 2001. In both eras the media developed formal structurations in news coverage for coding an individual as "terroristic." Such protocols include the use of particular buzzwords, spectacular live news updates, endlessly circulating mugshots of fugitives, and photographs of suspects that are typically blurred or pixelated. Through such processes, media and state intentionally aim to *terrorize* their audience, deliberately promoting a climate of public hysteria around the mythic, spectral (Mabuse-like) figure of "the terrorist."

This sense of media fabrication is not a new phenomenon. Writing in 1963, Daniel Boorstin coined the term "pseudo-event"[14] to describe the American media's need to continually invent copy to fill broadsheets. It has been argued by a number of theorists that the "theater of terror" (and theater of cruelty) generated in the Western media in the Cold War context of the 1970s showed similar patterns.

In 1989, Herman and O'Sullivan claimed that during the 1970s there was a development in the media worldwide of what they term "the terrorism industry" and "terror experts." [15] They suggest that during this period "institutions and individuals somewhat involved with the government" began to be "engaged in the production and sale of informational-perspectival output"—that is to say, promoting the state's agenda.[16] Herman and O'Sullivan compare the amount of killings related to the RAF between 1970 and 1979 (thirty-one people, mainly the group themselves),[17] the disproportionate coverage they received in the West German press, and the media's refusal to apply the same evidential standards to worldwide state violence over the same period. As Grass noted, the RAF's actual danger to the country was relatively small.[18] The RAF's struggle was "the war of six against sixty million." The media's exaggeration of a terror threat directly served the West German government, and created the permissions for implementing new and higher levels of public control and surveillance.[19] An indication of this intent by the state is that RAF court transcripts from 1977 suggest that the West German secret police fomented the RAF's move toward armed violence—by covertly supplying weapons to the group in 1970.[20]

Parallel to the aims of the state or the conservative media, a key RAF intent was to instrumentalize media channels to provoke a nationwide climate of terror.[21] [22] The RAF stated on their formation in 1970 that "the revolution wouldn't be built through political work, but through headlines." [23] In the context of Vietnam, they deliberately aimed to create media-oriented spectacles through bombing attacks, in order to promote a sense of a doubt in the state's authority.

Due to the conjunction of all these competing media-oriented constructs, the West German terror wave developed an extremely high public visibility as a variety of elements attempted to increase the climate of hysteria. In any discussion of the history of the RAF, these details need to be closely considered—the intent of state, media, and terrorists to foment a climate of terror.

However, a distinction needs to be drawn here. It would be misrepresentative to suggest the entire post-war West German news media presented a unified voice. During this period, a plurality of opinions and issues were expressed, and a range of constituencies addressed. Rather than dismissing the entire West German media under one ideological rubric, Chapter Four focuses on the role of the "Boulevardpresse"—the conservative Springer Verlag print conglomerate, and its role during the 1960s and 1970s in promoting the threat of domestic terror.[24]

It is important to get a fuller understanding of the visual aspect of 1970s terror to see a better view on the present use of visuality in terror ism and its future. It is also important here to clarify the relevance of this book to the existing canon of RAF scholarship and to the study of subcultural style.

Similar to the extent of Holocaust literature, the plethora of RAF study has meant that perspectival clarity on the whole subject becomes increasingly muddied by endless retrospective media coverage and by pointless micro-study in academic works. Holocaust historian Saul Friedlander has pinpointed a problem in some recent historiographic research—a similar issue to one that Viett earlier alluded to—that the endless unearthing and unpacking of the minutiae of a pivotal historical moment neither adds crucial insights into its history, nor serves as enlightening study. Concerning Holocaust literature, Friedlander notes that: "the sheer multitude of specialized studies on the minutest aspects of this epoch tends to erase the sharp outlines of certain central issues, be they conceptual or ethical. Therefore, whether one wishes it or not, the very momentum of historiography may serve to neutralize the past."[25]

With this in mind, rather than hunting for yet further details in the RAF's history, I focus on the broader patterns and themes related to this subject. I consider the symbiotic relation between visuality and political violence and look at the ways that RAF images develop a currency in popular culture and fine art—how the look of terrorism feeds an aestheticized style of "terror chic." For these reasons, I am less interested in adding further detail to the history of the RAF than to elucidate shifts in public discourse which allow this imagery to become fashion-able and consumable in a variety of cultural settings.

But why focus on the 1970s and the RAF particularly? A variety of places—the U.S, Great Britain, Latin America and the Middle East—all experienced high levels of domestic terror during the Cold War period. In the context of contemporary Islamic Fundamentalist "terror," the phenomenon of Cold War left-wing terrorism can now be seen in a clearer light. In many of the aforementioned areas, images of particular icons—Che, Angela Davis, Patty Hearst, or the RAF—appeared repeatedly in the media as metonymic for terror.[26] The RAF are well-suited to be emblematic for 1970s terror because they had ideological connections to the Vietnam and Latin American struggles, and trained with terror groups in the Middle East. For these reasons —geographic and historical—the RAF are an ideal subject with which to investigate the role of visuality in 1970s terror.

Without wishing to circumscribe the intellectual challenge of a wider synchronic study, it is important to first clearly explain the complex dynamics at play around one distinct group. The study discusses the visuality of Che, the Black Panthers, Patty Hearst, and Angela Davis because their presence in the Western media bears relation to the representation of the RAF in West German press, and also because these figures provide an epistemologically congruent "control group" to reference. All these high-profile Left-wing figures appeared in the context of the Vietnam war to preach violent revolution in the West. Many of them became the poster children of campus rebellion across Europe and the Americas. A consideration of these figures and cultural tendencies around them provides the opportunity to consider the resonance of Leftist radical and terrorist identity across a range of geographies.

The 1970s in Western Europe was an era when the dominant narratives of television voices and the mainstream media were closely linked to state funding.[27] In West Germany in this period any representation of terror in the media was closely monitored by the state. To return to the initial question at hand: why focus on the 1970s and the RAF in particular? This set of historical circumstances and this body of information provide a feasible terrain with which to explore the particular dynamics in question. I bring into play three distinct bodies of knowledge: the study of Western Leftist signage, the history of recent media technologies, and "theories of resistance" in relation to consumer culture.

The first two chapters of this study focus on the 1800s to the late 1960s—eras that generated much Leftist iconography and a political identity that informs the RAF's visual style in the 1970s. The fourth and fifth chapters look at the years from 1970 to 1977— the period from the RAF's inception to the death of the group's first leaders in jail, the main era of their activity and presence in the West German media. The final three chapters study the late 1970s to 2008—eras when RAF-related imagery has developed cultural currency.

In order to trace the history of RAF imagery over these three periods, the central focus is on print imagery, concentrating largely on newsprint sources rather than television or radio. I do this for two reasons. First, because newspaper and print imagery in the 1970s offer a more diverse range of opinions than the state-funded television or radio broadcasts, and can thus often reveal more about popular opinions or biases prevalent during that era. And second, in West Germany during the 1970s, newspapers reached a broader segment of the population. This point is discussed at further length in Chapter Four.

I have focused on print media in an era when it was the dominant channel for news reportage in the visual medium. Clearly this is no longer the case. In the era of "YouTube," or the 1991 Rodney King camcorder footage,[28] the greater veracity of grainy live video or digital cellphone footage has made it the new "medium du jour." In light of this shift away from the dominance of print media, this moment provides an excellent juncture to consider its earlier role in news construction and its ability to shape public consensus.

In the competition over history and meaning, the three intervening decades have brought several shifts and turns. Contestation over narratives has resulted in syntheses, changes of direction and new emphases as recessive strains battle to overtake dominant ones. New political and social contexts have born new perspectives on the Cold War subject. The interplay between past and present continues to reshape and redefine public perceptions of the RAF and their history. Each time this subject has appeared to fade away, new resonance has been found and has carried RAF discourse forward. The real or imagined consequences of the RAF terror wave continue to provoke broad political debate in West Germany. This pattern can be witnessed in the 2005 Kunst-Werke debacle or the intense debate concerning the release of imprisoned RAF member Brigitte Mohnhaupt in 2007. (Mohnhaupt had served twenty-four years in jail for her involvement in the Schleyer kidnap and murder in 1977).

Although this study traces the history of RAF-related imagery, it also uses this subject to make a wider critique of socio-cultural shifts in recent time, and provides opportunities to reconsider theoretical conceptions of these patterns. It is inspired not only by pre-existing research on the RAF, but also by a genre of historiographic works associated with the field of Cultural Studies.[29] Whilst West German visual history remains central to this study, my methods and associative thinking draw from theorists and historians from a variety of disciplines, including E.P. Thompson, Michel Foucault, Stuart Hall, Pierre Bourdieu, Antonin Artaud, and Roland Barthes.[30]

This study is written in the style of an art historical inquiry, making a discourse analysis of the history of RAF media images. It works with what E.P. Thompson has called "the tripartite concerns of media scholars that involve processes of production, the text itself and consumption and interpretation of the text."[31] A guiding conviction central to this type of work is that not until we gather a collection of texts and read them against each other, "allowing them to vibrate against one another"[32] can we begin to get at the machinations of these discourses and their "structure of feeling."[33] Roland Barthes points out that "every text already contains a plurality of other texts" and each text "refers back differently to the infinite text of the already written."[34] He encourages the study of texts as "a deep, patient circuitous descent into the labyrinth of meaning."[35] In such a spirit, I trace the migration of RAF-related images from their earliest uses and contexts, through milieus where these images later re-appear.

This is not a comprehensive investigation into all imagery related to the RAF. My goal in this study is rather to reveal particular rhetorical constructions around RAF imagery that have been overlooked. As noted, social history studies of the RAF have traditionally downplayed the visual and media components to this complex.[36] Contrary to this perspective, I privilege the visual aspect because it enables a more complete understanding of the history of the RAF, and also explores why the visuality of this particular terror debacle retains much historical currency.

While some of the images discussed here are more familiar than others, all provide insights relevant to the ongoing discussion. Each intersection of visuality and the marking of terror reveals different functionings of the visual, and offers an opportunity to problematize and redefine theoretical understandings concerning the nature of terror imagery.

I pursue these investigations in relation to this marginal imagery not with the intent of challenging the cultural canon, but because the dynamics I wish to discuss are most palpably present in images that fall under the canonical radar.[37] I argue that the discursive procedures in the media during the 1970s are best exemplified by their portrayal of their most extreme and culturally-marginalized objects—objects such as images related to terror groups.

The unstable nature of the terror image makes it a subject that allows one to interrogate a wide network of meanings, providing the opportunity to consider the significance of terror imagery across a variety of contexts. These include terror's representation, its cultural and linguistic framing, and ethics concerning the consumption of terror-related cultural production.

To consider the interaction between the visual and "political," this study needs to explain its theoretical lens. To provide a level of transparency, I outline below its theoretical framing and its relation to other models in the fields of terror studies and visual culture.

Theoretical Models for the "Terror Visual"

My use of the term "political" in this context has a relation to the work of Michel Foucault.[38] Foucault refers to his methodology as an archaeology. For this transhistorical study, given that time is a central element, I mainly avoid ahistorical psychoanalytical frameworks, but work with a more flexible, more Foucauldian style of research. In his histories of medicine, incarceration and sexuality, he works with a variety of sources to reconstruct the dominant structure of thought of the historical period under consideration. Foucault's work has given rise to an understanding of an episteme as something historically specific and also multiple in its construction.

Halperin and Conroy note that the Foucauldian project of "examining past practices of the production of the self produces an historical distance that permits us to view earlier social conventions with particular sharpness." [39] It enables us to bring clearly into focus the purely conventional character of our own social experience. For example, no longer is an appeal to sexuality able to justify a supposedly universal sense of "human nature" or the "human body."[40] Likewise, studies of vision and the nature of visuality have attacked and attempted to dismantle the presumption that the "visual" is a natural or universal category.[41]

In Foucauldian analysis, the political has no finite location of power, rather there exist only a range of discourses shaping fields of knowledge and social identities which define the status quo. According to Foucault, the political has to do with the distribution of power. Anything that creates, maintains or perpetuates a particular power relation is political. That process is accomplished by discourse and, by extension, visual communication—given that the visual comprises a system of signification. [42] Seeing that visual communication is an important discursive form, the question at hand concerns the way in which various elements attempt to shape a subject's public identity through its framing.

For Foucault, the power of visuality is particularly manifest in the culture of surveillance. The visual operates as a spatially orchestrated system of control. In his studies of prison, being seen or "caught" by an entity which holds "the power to survey" is seen as something to be feared—especially by the occupants of an institutional structure.[43] Foucault argues contrary to Debord, that "Our society is one not of spectacle but of surveillance."[44]

Adjacent to Foucault's model, many theorists have discussed visuality in relation to control of vision. In Film Studies and Art History, the "gaze" has been used as an organizing term in relation to ideas of embodiment and projection. The gaze refers to the power of looking. It involves a complex set of relations between the gaze and its subject, between the act of seeing and the experience of being seen.[45] Such a framing acknowledges a two-way visual relation. Intersubjective models of the gaze include historian Martin Jay's argument that Modernity has had numerous "scoptic regimes"—that different ways of seeing have existed during the modern age.[46] Donna Haraway talks of an "optics of positioning."[47] Jonathan Crary, Allen Feldman, Rosalind Krauss and other contemporary theorists have cited figures from Descartes to Lacan in order to articulate their particular interpretations of the role of the visual.[48]

In my current study, Foucault's model provides a useful lens with which to consider the relation between terror and visuality.[49] I look at the role of vision and the importance of surveillance in the terror phenomenon. I aim to offer a better understanding of this type of visuality and the changing modes in its consumption. To do this, I discuss its relation to developments in technology, and consider the importance of surveillance both to contemporary social relations and to the representation of terror.[50]

The Relation between Image and Context

In a study of images of 1970s West German terrorists, it is important to lay out my understanding and use of the term "image," its parameters, and to consider some of the ways it has been used in recent discourse. It is important in an era of new media terror spectacles to look at the role of the image in the construction of a "myth of terror" and consider terror imagery's relation to its contextual framing.

It would be convenient to establish a clear and consistent conception of the term "image," but it is also necessary to resist the temptation to reify the term. An image is never "merely" an image. To regard it as a finite entity would be anathema to furthering our understanding of how it can function. Rather, we might begin by arguing that an image exists within a network of interpretative systems.

Discussing news media images of the Iraq war, Nicholas Mirzoeff proposes that there are three intersecting layers to be pried apart in images of such a "visual event." These layers are the locality of the viewer, the contents and contexts of the image, and the global imaginary within which the viewer attempts to make sense of the screen images.[51] We should consider each of these aspects separately. They depend on the viewer's habitus, the setting and subject matter of the image, and its wider interpretative milieu.

Susan Buck-Morss points out another aspect to the functioning of imagery in our current technological landscape. She writes, "The fact about images is that they do float in isolation; moving in and out of context, freed from their origins and the history of their provenance. The superficiality of the image, its transferability, its accessibility… all of these qualities render the provenance of the image ambiguous, if not irrelevant. An image is stumbled upon, found without being lost, arguably most at home when it knocks around the world. An image is promiscuous by nature."[52]

Buck-Morss notes that the fugitive nature of an image dislodges it from one fixed position, or any dogmatic assessment of its contextual meaning. We need to acknowledge the inherent fluidity of what the term "image" encompasses, and not continually attempt to ground any specific image in one historical setting,[53] but instead to consider framings as separate discursive procedures.

A further question emerges in this regard. What happens when people look and what sense-making patterns and capacities are engaged in that act?[54] Buck-Morss argues that the image as an object is "a detail in itself of a whole that is by definition only provisionally and strategically delimited."[55] But how we conceive imagery is dependent on its medium and context. We need to consider the significance of these settings and the differing interpretative contexts between the newspaper image, the moving television image, the cinematic image, and the Web. Our contemporary contextual framing differs dramatically from the 1970s.

Some theorists reformulate this question by arguing that the power of an image comes from its indeterminacy. [56] Sabine Hake highlights the relation between an image and its viewers. Hake points out that this has to do with the fact that the photographic image escapes meaning. An image is polysemous and indeterminate. It requires the presence of other images, or of language, in order for its elements to be deciphered and its meaning to be fixed; it also depends on interpretative communities to "assume its rightful place as representation and commentary."[57] Communities create consensus as to what meaning an image might have. As noted, in our current media-saturated environment the role of location has become much more significant in the interpretation of imagery. Framing has a sense-making capacity that informs a reader or viewer that some image "is" what it is—establishing what Barthes termed "that which goes without saying."[58] Barthes claims that an image imposes "meaning at one stroke,"[59] —as does, I would argue, its contextual setting. Barthes' argues in *Camera Lucida* that photography is "about nothing other than death and how the photograph is automatically coded as historic—that "this has been." Its opening of the shutter insists that "this was there" but also that it is not so any longer. A moment is seized out of time and recalls insistently nothing other than the passing of time, the approach of death."

Beyond the significance of context, it is also important to discuss how an image exists as a discrete entity, and to consider the ability of certain images—particularly those related to national trauma—to arrest the viewer's attention and deliver a very specific type of rhetorical punch. In *Camera Lucida*, Barthes uses the term *punctum* to describe the element in a photograph that intrigues the viewer. For Barthes, the *punctum* of an image is the aspect that produces its affective impact. It is the quality that interrupts broader, socially-informed interpretations of its meaning. To illustrate this concept, Barthes discusses the difference between an erotic and a pornographic image:

> (F)or me, there is no *punctum* in the pornographic image; at most it amuses me (and even then, boredom follows quickly). The erotic photograph on the contrary (and this is its very condition), does not make the sexual organs into a central object; it may very well not show them at all; it takes the spectator outside its frame, and it is there that I animate this photograph and that it animates me. The *punctum*, then, is a kind of subtle *beyond*. [60]

Barthes sees the *punctum* as the moment in which an individual is prompted beyond the frame of the image and drawn into its affective narrative. In discussing images of terrorism, it is important to note the way that the beyond of terror imagery (i.e. a photograph of a bomb attack) sutures into the myth of terror. Often what we look for in terror news coverage is not present, the actual terror event has passed and all that remains is its shadow an image of an evacuated crime scene.

Further to this point, and to Buck-Morss' conception of imagery's "promiscuous" nature, Roland Barthes notes that no photograph can be pure because our viewing of it is infected by what has "already been" in the field of the visual.[61] This is particularly true of an historic image associated with national trauma. We are "always already" involved in making associations related to earlier debacles. There is slippage in the public imagination between images of national trauma. This seepage needs to be explored, not ignored, if we are to get the fullest sense of understanding of this kind of imagery.

Our synaptic memory banks continually hyperlink between these other associative visual records of the visceral and sensational, the traumatic and horrific. Terror imagery from the 1970s is crowded by the ghosts of older narratives like National Socialism or Vietnam and by newer visual economies such as 9/11 or Abu Ghraib.

Barthes writes that rather than considering photographs as discrete entities he wants to develop a "history of looking."[62] Inspired by his work, in this study I investigate visual histories around the RAF phenomenon, considering intersections where an identity first emerges, how and where terror imagery breeds, and how understandings of such signs shift.

Our current perception of images relating to 1970s West German terrorism has been clouded and coded by the later lenses of cinema, television, textes, and the Internet. From our contemporary perspective, all RAF-related signs have become markers for the 1970s and the West European terror wave. Such a conception was initially generated by news stories in the West German media. Then in the decades since the 1970s, due to academic study and journalistic coverage, this imagery has continuously been employed and re-employed to signify certain events, "quoted" to support a narrative, or used to gloss over an argument's blindspots; as if to say, here is documentary proof, here is ocular forensic evidence, a fabricated facticity. But such a tendency to isolate geographies needs to be queried. It is necessary to avoid the closure inherent in presenting any particular image as evidentiary—particularly when discussing events in another country, in another era, in another language. It is important to interrogate the notion of RAF imagery as a discrete category. It is also more useful to explore the relation of these pictures to the broader history of Leftist imagery, and to position this identity existing in a continuing state of migratory flow.

[1] In the recent Western media coverage of Islamic Fundamentalist terror, there has been a tendency to use terms such as "terrorist," "radical" and "extremist" very loosely. Their meaning in such settings becomes almost interchangeable. But the wider meaning of such terms is difficult to define with any singular meaning or universal understanding. Given the complexity in defining what constitutes terrorism, as an operational definition for this study the term "terrorist" is used here to refer to those in the 1970s who perpetrated violent acts against the state, such as bombings. The term "radical" here refers to those in context in the 1970s who advocated violent means to achieve social justice—but were not convicted of physical violence.

[2] As cited in Aust. P.140-160.

[3] Anderson, p.69.

[4] In some conceptions, the "terrorist" is considered to be a political "radical" individual or group whose strategy appears to have moved beyond acts of "symbolic violence" to include acts of extreme violence such as murder (often appearing to have become provoked or enraged by covert government actions).

[5] Chomsky and Herman use the term the "real terrorist network." As Karim notes in this regard: "It is actually the violent world order which includes the powerful states that support for regimes of "National Security States" (NSS), that oppress their populations to keep an uninterrupted supply of raw materials flowing to Western multi-national companies, and the arming of regional powers to destabilize neighboring countries. -A key example being U.S. coverage of Iran during the Shah's reign. Dominant discourses construct terror as a public phenomenon and at the same time downplay the direct and structural violence of the state itself." Karim p.31.

[6] Rote Armee Fraktion, *Das Konzept Stadtguerilla*. Communique, 1971. http://www.baader-meinhof.com/students/resources/communique/deuconcept.html

[7] As noted, some of the West German media referred to the group derisively as a criminal "Bande" of gangsters, intent only on bank robbing. (Becker, p.5).

[8] Clausewitz cited in Morgan, p.331.

[9] Jenny Hocking, "Orthodox theories of "terrorism": The power of politicized terminology." In *Politics: Journal of Australasian Political Studies Association*, Vol. 19, No.2, November, 1984, p.103.

[10] Herman, p.7-11.

[11] Media theorists Herman and O'Sullivan argue the term terrorist is itself a construct and as such, slippery and subject to free play. Herman, p.7-11.

[12] The question of language and cultural differences between the US and Germany is at once a study in itself and also an element among many fluid elements which impact an individual's understanding of terminology.

[13] In the light of 9/11, J.David Slocum discusses this triangulation dynamic the terror phenomenon in his edited collection *Terrorism Media Liberation* (2005).

[14] Boorstin, p.9-12.

[15] Herman, p.7-11.

[16] Ibid.

[17] Herman and O'Sullivan, p.123.

[18] As Herman and O'Sullivan argue, p.7-11.

[19] An example of this provocation by the state (noted by Peters, Baumann, Varon and Aust) is that an undercover police informer, Peter Urbach, initially provided weapons to the RAF in 1970 and encouraged the group's move to violence. (Baumann, p.38, Peters, p.172, Varon, p.64). Further, the demonization and media overkill and state and media hunts for suspected leftists in West Germany during this period clearly served to shift the focus from the student movement's emerging inquiries into former Nazi war criminals still at large in West Germany (-a famous example was the Beate Klarsfeld-Kiesinger case).

[20] Aust, *Der Baader-Meinhof Komplex*. Court transcripts of interviews with Peter Urbach, undercover police agent. p.145-6.

[21] Baumann, *Wie Alles Anfing*, p.ii.

[22] Scribner notes that the RAF understood the rhetorical power of the terror image to fracture a sense of national security and instill "group-think"." Scribner discusses RAF terror image tactics in "Buildings on Fire," *Grey Room* 26, Fall 2007.

[23] Baumann, p.110. Also re. the group's use of the term "headlines" we also need to consider what this term constitutes. Does it also imply hijacking the front-page visual as well? It is easy to conceive of the RAF's Situationist-inspired détournement as an attempt to stage a "spectacle in the proximity of a wound "to bring home the "wound" of the ongoing genocide in Vietnam. As Scribner and others have pointed out, ideological and tactical links between the RAF and the SI existed through, among others, Berlin "Kommune-1" member and RAF associate Dieter Kunzelman, a former SI member.

[24] Also discussed in later chapters is the relevance of bracketing off the "the popular" (i.e. popular culture and mainstream cinema), the media, and the "cultural" (i.e. elite or high culture) as discrete fields over transhistorical contexts.

[25] Saul Friedlander, p.5-6, draws from Schowalter, p.16.

[26] Other profile terror icons from the early 1970s era repeatedly in the Western news media include PLO hijacker Leila Khaled, and Venezuelan terror-gun-for-hire Carlos the Jackal (Ilich Ramirez Sanchez), the latter responsible for the 1975 Vienna OPEC hostage crisis.

[27] Herman p.45.

[28] Of relevance here is Avital Ronell's discussion of the Rodney King incident in the essay "Trauma TV" in *Finitude's Score*.

[29] The term "Cultural Studies" can conjure a variety of meanings depending on its context. By citing Hebdige and Hall, I refer here to the group of theorists associated with British 1970s Birmingham Centre for Contemporary Cultural Studies program, known for using Marxist and Gramscian theory to study British working-class subcultures in relation to theories of reception and resistance. For a larger discussion on the differences between the U.S. and British models of Cultural Studies, see Bathrick and Baetens.

[30] Beyond the figures cited here, this type of cross-disciplinary study is exemplified by the work of Heath and Potter, Hebdige, Marcus, Melly, Mosse, and Theweleit. (As cited in the bibliography)

[31] Thompson "Ideology and Modern Culture" 2000. p.54.

[32] Dorst, p.98, from Schowalter, p.26.

[33] Schowalter is here referencing Raymond Williams' use of this term.

[34] Barthes from *The Rustle of Language*, p.52.

[35] Ibid.

[36] Such studies on the RAF include the work of Varon, Phillips, Peters and others.

[37] The rhetoric in this methodological framing is inspired by Clark, p.xv.

[38] See bibliography for the Foucault books referenced here.

[39] A wider discussion on these themes can be found in David Halperin, John J. Winkler, and Froma T. Zeitlin, *Before Sexuality: The Construction of the Erotic Experience in the Ancient World*, (Princeton: Princeton University Press, 1990) p.5. Cited in Conroy, p.2.

[40] This framing draws from Conroy, p.2.

[41] See Martin Jay's argument in his introduction to Teresa Brennan and Martin Jay, ed. *Vision in Context: Historical and Contemporary Perspectives on Sight*. P.1-12.

[42] In this regard, it can be argued that the visual is a high order of signification than verbal language because of its ability to speak a universal language and convey much greater detail.

[43] This framing draws from Murphy, p.23.

[44] Foucault, *Discipline and Punish*, p.217. Cited by Conroy, p.3.

[45] Cited from Murphy, p.2. A famous example of usage of the term "gaze" is John Berger's well-known art history study, *Ways of Seeing*. Penguin: London, 1972.

[46] As discussed in Martin Jay's *Downcast Eyes: The Denigration of Vision in Twentieth-Century French Thought*.

[47] Donna Haraway, "The Persistence of Vision" in *Writing on the Body: Female Embodiment and Feminist Theory*, ed. Katie Conroy, Nadia, Medina, and Sarah Stanbury (New York: Columbia University Press, 1997), p.283-295,

quotation at p.288. Cited in Conroy, p.3.

[48] See Foster's edited collection, *Vision and Visuality*.

[49] In a similar vein, Holly has remarked that "What those of us who study visual representations need right now—if we are going to continue to produce new and unsettling questions rather than just reproduce canonized knowledge." Holly, 1996, p.41, from Brown, p.86.

[50] But two pages later in his text, Feldman also writes that he opposes "the "postmodern" tendency of aestheticizing power, "As opposing to continuing the postmodern tendency of aestheticizing power, this analysis identifies acts of aestheticization as intrinsic to power." From Feldman, in J. David Slocum, p.286.

[51] Mirzoeff, *Watching Babylon*, p.12.

[52] From Buck-Morss, (from audio tape, 2004, minute 39) cited from Brown, p.91.

[53] From Schowalter, p.16.

[54] This framing draws from Brown, p.91.

[55] Bal, 2003, p.24. Cited in Brown, p.92.

[56] Schowalter, p.22.

[57] Sabine Hake, p.121. This framing draws from Schowalter, p.23.

[58] Roland Barthes, *Mythologies*, p.11. This framing draws from Schowalter, p. 22.

[59] Barthes, *Mythologies*, p.110.

[60] Barthes, *Camera Lucida*, p.59, this framing draws from Brown, p.99-100.

[61] *Camera Lucida*, p.59.

[62] Barthes, *Camera Lucida*, p.12.

INDEX

www.ingramcontent.com/pod-product-compliance
Lightning Source LLC
Chambersburg PA
CBHW072130170526
45158CB00004BA/1320